Representations of China in British Children's Fiction, 1851–1911

SHIH-WEN CHEN
The Australian National University

Routledge
Taylor & Francis Group

LONDON AND NEW YORK

First Published 2013 by Ashgate Publisher

Published 2016 by Routledge
2 Park Square, Milton Park, Abingdon, Oxfordshire OX14 4RN
711 Third Avenue, New York, NY 10017, USA

First issued in paperback 2016

Routledge is an imprint of the Taylor & Francis Group, an informa business

British Library Cataloguing in Publication Data
A catalogue record for this book is available from the British Library.

The Library of Congress has cataloged the printed edition as follows:
Chen, Shih-Wen.
  Representations of China in British Children's Fiction, 1851–1911 / By Shih-Wen Chen.
    pages cm.—(Ashgate Studies in Childhood, 1700 to the Present)
  Includes bibliographical references and index.
  ISBN 978-1-4094-4735-1 (hardcover: alk. paper)
  1. Children's stories, English—History and criticism. 2. Chinese in literature. 3. China—In literature. I. Title.

  PR830.C513C48 2013
  823.009'9282—dc23

                                                              2012041273

ISBN 13: 978-1-138-24900-4 (pbk)
ISBN 13: 978-1-4094-4735-1 (hbk)

For my parents

Contents

Contents

List of Figures

Acknowledgements

I am deeply indebted to Gillian Russell and Benjamin Penny for their mentorship and guidance throughout the course of my writing this book. Without their wide expertise, invaluable suggestions, and kind encouragement, this project would not have been completed. Research for this book was supported by a travel grant from the Australian National University to undertake research in the United Kingdom. My sincere thanks to the staff at the following libraries for their assistance: British Library, National Art Library, Bodleian Library, Cambridge University Library, London University School of Oriental and African Studies Library, the Australian National University Library, and the National Library of Australia. I am grateful to Ole and Jan Bay-Petersen for inviting me to stay with them when I was conducting research in the Cambridge University Library.

Sally Mitchell suggested that I contact Claudia Nelson about my manuscript, and I would like to thank them both for supporting the publication of the volume in the *Ashgate Studies in Childhood, 1700 to the Present* series. I am also grateful to T.H. Barrett and Helen Groth for their comments on earlier versions of the manuscript. I wish to thank Deakin University and Australasian Children's Literature Association for Research for permission to use excerpts from my article 'China in a Book: Victorian Representations of the "Celestial Kingdom" in William Dalton's *The Wolf Boy of China*', *Papers: Explorations into Children's Literature*, 21.1 (2011): 1–18, in Chapter 2.

I am thankful for my colleagues at the Australian Centre on China in the World, the Australian National University who encouraged me during the process of preparing the book manuscript. Many friends I met in Canberra have supported me through the years, in particular Shu-Ling Yeh, Sherry Hung, Crystal Tien, Lennon Chang, Sin Wen Lau, Fanny Huang, Dom Chien, Gloria Lai, Olivia Mo, Jimmy Cheng, Wing Wong, Nancy Chiu, Alison Mo, Robert and Margaret Brown, and Diana Williams. Thank you for the conversation and advice. Special thanks to Maple Lee and Amy Lin, who have always been there for me. Finally, I would like to dedicate this book to my beloved parents, Tung-jung Chen and Pi-fen Liu Chen, and to my sister, Hsiao-Wen Chen, for their continued love and support.

Note on Chinese Romanization

There are several systems of Chinese romanization, the earliest attributed to Matteo Ricci, the Italian Jesuit who travelled to China in 1583. Nicolas Trigault, another Jesuit missionary to China, later modified Ricci's system of representing Chinese in Roman script. In the nineteenth century, British diplomat Thomas F. Wade developed a system of transliteration based on British missionary Robert Morrison's work, which was then modified by Herbert A. Giles, who served in the British consular service. The Wade-Giles system, as it became known, was widely used until 1979, when *Hanyu Pinyin*, which was developed in the People's Republic of China in the 1950s, became the standard for Chinese romanization according to the International Organization for Standardization. I use the *Hanyu Pinyin* system for Chinese romanization in this book. For citations from sources where alternative systems of transcription are used, all Chinese names and terms, with the exception of Peking (Beijing) and Canton (Guangzhou) which are familiar historical place names, are given in their original form with *Pinyin* equivalent in square brackets where possible. For titles of books and articles, the original romanization is retained.

Chapter 1

A Kaleidoscope of Knowledge: Children, Knowledge, and China in Victorian and Edwardian Britain

My papa and I went up and made the proper ceremony. The Emperor gave my
papa a ruyi [a ritual gift], ... and took off a little yellow purse hanging by his side
and gave it to me. He wanted me to say a few words in Chinese, which I did, to
thank him for the present.

—from the diary of George Thomas Staunton (12 years old)[1]

In an illustration by English artist William Alexander, a member of Lord
Macartney's Embassy to China (1792–1794), 12-year-old George Thomas
Staunton (1781–1859), page of the Ambassador, receives a silk purse from the
Qianlong Emperor. The boy had been brought before the Emperor when he asked
if anyone in the group could speak Chinese.[2] In fact, young George was the only
member of the Embassy who had proficiency in the language, having learned
Chinese from two missionaries who were returning to China from Naples, where
he and his father Sir George Leonard Staunton (1737–1801) had travelled to hire
some interpreters for the Embassy. Some of Lord Macartney's objectives for going
to China include trying the negotiation of a reduction of export-import duties,
gaining additional trade ports, enticing China to import more British products,
and acquiring more information about the 'Celestial Kingdom'.[3] As Pamela Kyle
Crossley has said of young George Staunton's role in the Embassy:

It is hard to believe that the success of such a grand undertaking by the world's
most ambitious empire rested almost entirely on the shoulders of a well-behaved,
home-sick boy, and almost as difficult to imagine the pressures upon the child as
the complex and rigid ritual demands of the two empires came closer and closer
to collision.[4]

---

[1]   George Thomas Staunton, 'Staunton Diary 1792–1793: Journey to China, 1792–
1793', China: Trade, Politics & Culture, 1793–1980, 2007 <http://www.china.amdigital.
co.uk/collections/doc–search–results.aspx?documentid=188041&searchmode=true&previ
ous=0> [accessed 19 May 2012].

[2]   George Thomas Staunton, *Memoirs of the Chief Incidents of the Public Life of Sir
George Thomas Staunton, Bart* (London, 1856), p. 12.

[3]   David E. Mungello, *The Great Encounter of China and the West, 1500–1800*
(Lanham, MD, 1999), p. 96. For more information on the Embassy, see James Louis
Hevia, *Cherishing Men from Afar: Qing Guest Ritual and the Macartney Embassy of 1793*
(Durham, 1995).

[4]   Pamela Kyle Crossley, *The Manchus* (Oxford, 2002), p. 147.

Young George's meeting with the Emperor is a significant historical moment not only because it was a notable incident in the first Embassy to China, but more importantly, it suggests that children had the potential to play an important role in Sino-British relations.

Although Macartney's Embassy was regarded as a diplomatic failure, it succeeded in collecting a great deal of information about China, which was presented to the British public in a number of government reports widely circulated after the Embassy's return, such as Aeneas Anderson's *A Narrative of Lord Macartney's Embassy to China* (1795) and George Leonard Staunton's *An Authentic Account of an Embassy from the King of Great Britain to the Emperor of China* (1797).[5] These authors' books appeared in a list called 'Works upon China' that was published in August 1849 in the *Chinese Repository* (1832–1851), a monthly periodical started by the first American missionary to China E.C. Bridgman (1801–1861).[6] Comprising over 370 English and French texts, this list is an indicator of how books on China proliferated during the nineteenth century as British contact with the 'Celestial Kingdom' increased, particularly in the wake of the First Opium War (1839–1842), when Hong Kong became a colony of Britain and five treaty ports were opened to foreign residence and trade. Who was reading these books and what did they do with the information they obtained? Most of the books on the list were targeted at adult readers with an interest in China, in particular missionaries, diplomats, merchants, and travellers. However, the fact that Jane Austen depicted the heroine of *Mansfield Park* reading a book about Macartney's Embassy indicates that young nineteenth-century readers were also expected to read these books about China.[7]

This book is concerned with how children's fiction published from the mid-nineteenth to the early twentieth century disseminated and popularized 'knowledge' of China through various discourses about 'the Chinese'. It examines the role of children's writers in mediating between the leading China 'experts' of the time and young readers by drawing on and utilizing the wealth of material provided by travel writers, embassy officials, missionaries, and journalists to construct certain visions of China for children.

Engaging with China in the Nineteenth Century

The number of British travellers to China greatly increased after the Treaties of Tianjin were signed on 26 June 1858 towards the end of the Second Opium War (1856–1860), because foreigners were then given the right to travel in the interior of China, the Yangzi River was opened to foreign ships, and Christian missionaries

---

[5]   Aeneas Anderson, *A Narrative of the British Embassy to China, in the Years 1792, 1793, and 1794* (London, 1795); George Leonard Staunton, *An Authentic Account of an Embassy from the King of Great Britain to the Emperor of China* (3 vols, London, 1797).

[6]   'List of Works upon China', *Chinese Repository*, XVIII.VIII (1849): pp. 416–44.

[7]   Jane Austen, *Mansfield Park: A Novel*, ed. James Kinsley (Oxford, [1814] 1990), pp. 140–41.

were allowed to do mission work in the inner provinces.[8] After the Opium Wars interest in China reached new heights: Chinese products were highly sought after and China itself became 'a marketable commodity'.[9] Books providing information about the 'half-known' country became a valuable commodity because people wanted to become acquainted with this land which had previously been closed to foreign trade. As more British subjects came into contact with China, more writing about the country appeared. Numerous descriptions of firsthand experiences in China could be found in travel books, personal memoirs, embassy and missionary reports, speeches, and letters. By 1892, the amount of writing on China had multiplied exponentially. As Henri Cordier indicated in *Half a Decade of Chinese Studies (1886–1891)*:

> None but a bibliographer can have an exact idea of the enormous literary and scientific production having China as its object. In my *Bibliotheca Sinica*, published between the years 1878–1885, I have tried to give a complete survey of the immense field of researches on China. It is a little over five years since, and I have in print a supplement, a volume in itself, which shows more than any other fact the important place taken nowadays by studies not only of a scientific interest, but equally indispensable to commerce and politics.[10]

In 1901, a book review in *The Times* commented on the 'crowd of books on China'. By 1904, according to an article entitled 'The Flood of Books about China', the two Opium Wars, 'the trouble with France in the eighties [Sino-French War (1884–1885)], the war with Japan in 1894 [Sino-Japanese War (1894–1895)], and most of all the Boxer business of 1900 onwards, have been the source or fountain of a steady stream of booklets, volumes, and tomes in sets, running to a frightful aggregate'.[11] The words 'crowd', 'frightful', and 'flood' suggest a sense of being overwhelmed and inundated by this mass of information being published at such an unprecedented rate that the reading public felt threatened with 'information overload'.

The explosion of knowledge during the nineteenth century can be attributed to expanded sources of information and greater demand for knowledge from a society with higher income and more educational opportunities. Technological developments in printing, engraving, papermaking, and transport made mass production and

---

[8]   See the Appendix for a timeline of major events in Sino-British relations, 1839–1911.

[9]   Catherine Pagani, 'Chinese Material Culture and British Perceptions of China in the Mid-Nineteenth Century', in T.J. Barringer and Tom Flynn (eds), *Colonialism and the Object: Empire, Material Culture, and the Museum* (London, 1998), pp. 28–40 (pp. 29; 34).

[10] Henri Cordier, *Half a Decade of Chinese Studies (1886–1891)* (Leyden, 1892), p. 1.

[11] 'Reviews of Books', *The Times*, 20 August 1901, p. 5. All articles from *The Times* mentioned in this book were accessed online at *The Times* Digital Archive, 1785–1985 <http://www.gale.com/Times/>; 'The Flood of Books about China', *North China Herald and Supreme Court and Consular Gazette*, 29 July 1904, pp. 234–5 (p. 234).

4 Representations of China in British Children's Fiction, 1851–1911

distribution of information much easier. Ordering, archiving, and reproducing this mass of information became a central concern.[12] As Thomas Richards observes in his *The Imperial Archive: Knowledge and the Fantasy of Empire*, Victorians were obsessed with trying to control knowledge and order it in a systematic way because they believed that 'the control of Empire hinge[d] on a British monopoly over knowledge'.[13] He argues that the Victorian archive was 'a prototype for a global system of domination through circulation, an apparatus for controlling territory by producing, distributing, and consuming information about it'.[14] However, according to Richards, the imperial archive was a 'fantasy' because it was not located in a central vault but comprised of documents scattered across the globe, making it impossible to fully monitor, control, and manipulate the information.

In *Useful Knowledge: The Victorians, Morality, and the March of Intellect*, Alan Rauch argues persuasively that during the nineteenth century, 'knowledge was being produced and consumed at such an unprecedented rate that few could ignore its growing impact on the culture'.[15] He emphasizes the importance of considering 'the seemingly peripheral constructions and popularizations of knowledge, such as encyclopedias and children's books ... as both cultural signifiers and cultural forces' because 'knowledge has been – and continues to be – fetishized as something valuable for its own sake'.[16] In 1812, Joseph Guy stated in the preface to *Guy's Pocket Cyclopædia*: 'useful knowledge ... will give intelligence to youth, it will accustom them to habits of reflection and inquiry, and teach them to look on objects around them with the EYE OF REASON'.[17] Realizing that 'knowledge' was a valuable currency, publishers marketed their books in response to the Victorian thirst for 'useful knowledge'. For example, Thomas Nelson had a 'books of useful knowledge' category in its 1874 catalogue and C. Knight had 'The Library of Entertaining Knowledge' series.

Knowledge about China was not confined to print culture. Its presence in material culture in the form of willow pattern plates and other objects has been discussed by Catherine Pagani, Elizabeth Hope Chang, and Sarah Cheang.[18]

---

[12]   Martin Daunton, 'Introduction', in Martin Daunton (ed.), *The Organisation of Knowledge in Victorian Britain* (Oxford, 2005), pp. 1–27 (p. 16).

[13]   Thomas Richards, *The Imperial Archive: Knowledge and the Fantasy of Empire* (London, 1993), p. 7.

[14]   Ibid., p. 17.

[15]   Alan Rauch, *Useful Knowledge: The Victorians, Morality, and the March of Intellect* (Durham, 2001), p. 21.

[16]   Ibid., pp. 6; 3.

[17]   Joseph Guy, *Guy's Pocket Cyclopaedia: Or Miscellany of Useful Knowledge* (London, 1810), p. ix.

[18]   Catherine Pagani, 'Objects and the Press: Images of China in Nineteenth-Century Britain', in Julie F. Codell (ed.), *Imperial Co-Histories: National Identities and the British and Colonial Press* (Madison, NJ, 2003), pp. 147–66; Elizabeth Hope Chang, *Britain's Chinese Eye: Literature, Empire and Aesthetics in the Nineteenth Century* (Stanford, 2010); Sarah Cheang, 'The Ownership and Collection of Chinese Material Culture by Women in Britain, ca. 1890–1935' (unpublished doctoral dissertation, University of Sussex, 2003).

China was also very much a part of British visual culture from the mid-nineteenth century onwards. Victorians were invited to 'visualize' China by attending various exhibitions or shows, including the Chinese Collection at Hyde Park, the Great Exhibition of 1851, the Chinese junk *Keying*, Albert Smith's 'Mont Blanc to China', and numerous missionary exhibitions such as *The Orient in London* (1908).[19]

In 1842, American collector Nathan Dunn (1782–1844), who had lived in China for over a decade, introduced the British to his 'Ten Thousand Chinese Things', previously exhibited in the United States at the Philadelphia Museum before arriving in London's Hyde Park. Although the admission price (2s 6d) was higher than the entrance fee of most London shows (usually 1s), large crowds flocked to see the exhibition when it was opened to the general public on 23 June 1842 because they regarded it 'as one of the duties of the London season'.[20] *The Times* reported that the exhibit was 'amongst the most curious ever opened in London'.[21] Those outside the capital also had the opportunity to view the collection because it toured large towns and cities in Britain after 1846. The exhibition catalogue sold well despite a *Chinese Repository* article that addressed its inaccuracies: by 1844, sales of the pamphlet had accumulated to 54,000 and Catherine Pagani estimates that more than 300,000 copies of the London edition were sold.[22] As an illustration in the *Illustrated London News* reveals, children were among the visitors to the 'Ten Thousand Chinese Things' exhibition (see Figure 1.1).[23]

The article in the *Illustrated London News* praises the exhibit for teaching by 'things rather than words', claiming that as 'a means of education this enterprise is invaluable'.[24] Therefore it is not surprising that Old Humphrey (pseudonym of George Mogridge), the narrator of the well-received *The Celestial Empire; or, Points and Pickings of Information about China and the Chinese* (1844),

---

[19] For more information on the *Keying* see Pagani, 'Objects and the Press', pp. 154–8. For more information on the 'Mont Blanc to China' show, see J. Monroe Thorington, *Mont Blanc Sideshow: The Life and Times of Albert Smith* (Philadelphia, 1934). For information on missionary exhibitions, see Sarah Cheang, '"Our Missionary Wembley": China, Local Community and the British Missionary Empire, 1901–1924', *East Asian History*, 32/33 (2006/2007): pp. 177–98.

[20] Alan Cox, 'Pagoda and Celestial Palace: The Chinese Collection in Knightsbridge', *Westminster History Review*, 3 (1999): pp. 19–24 (p. 19).

[21] 'The Chinese Collection', *The Times*, 5 November 1844, p. 1. For more information on the exhibit, see Elizabeth Phillips, 'A Pagoda in Knightsbridge', *The Journal of Pre-Raphaelite Studies*, IV.2 (1984): pp. 37–42.

[22] See 'Ten Thousand Chinese Things Relating to China and the Chinese', *Chinese Repository*, XII.11 (1843): pp. 561–82; Cox, 'Pagoda and Celestial Palace', p. 21; Pagani, 'Chinese Material Culture', p. 35.

[23] 'The Chinese Collection, Hyde Park Corner', *Illustrated London News*, 6 August 1842, pp. 204–5 (p. 205).

[24] Ibid., p. 204.

Fig. 1.1   'The Chinese Collection, Hyde Park Corner' from the *Illustrated London News*, 6 August 1842 (Mary Evans Picture Library).

informs his young readers that he has been to the exhibit many times and urges them to visit as well, because it is 'the best Collection of Chinese Curiosities in the whole world'.[25] He also notes that the collection will correct some misguided views of China:

> Should it be that you happen to think, as hundreds do, that the Chinese are a race of sleek-headed simpletons, incapable of works of art, the Exhibition will at once reprove and correct you. The proprietor of it has three good things in his possession, good sense, good taste, and a good knowledge of China.[26]

This statement suggests that China should not be underestimated and that children who thought dismissively of the Chinese must be corrected.

---

[25]   Old Humphrey, *The Celestial Empire; or, Points and Pickings of Information About China and the Chinese* (London, 1844), p. 9. George Mogridge (1787–1854) first used the pseudonym 'Old Humphrey' in 1833 when he began writing for the Religious Tract Society's periodical *The Weekly Visitor*.

[26]   Ibid., pp. 8–9.

Why did British children need to have 'good knowledge' of China? Old Humphrey explains that 'late events have rendered it [China] of increasing importance to Great Britain. Some knowledge of it, then, becomes interesting, if not necessary to all; and you would hardly like to be found ignorant of that which other young people know'.[27] Because his book was published in 1844, 'the late events' Old Humphrey referred to must have been China's defeat in the First Opium War (1839–1842) and the signing of the Treaty of Nanjing on 29 August 1842 which allowed the British, whose previous activities were restricted to an area called the Factories near the Canton River, to step outside the boundaries to conduct trade in five treaty ports. Old Humphrey notes that people may have different views of the Opium War but 'true philanthropists will unite in the desire that it may lead to the prosperity of both Great Britain and China'.[28]

The narrator identifies China as an important country to know about not only because of Britain's interest in it, but more significantly, because one does not want to be found 'ignorant', like the 'hundreds' that think 'the Chinese are a race of sleek-headed simpletons'. He implies that it would be shameful to be found 'ignorant' compared to other young people. Considering that *The Celestial Empire* was priced at 3s 6d, it was clearly meant for middle- and upper-class households headed by parents who wanted their children to succeed in a society where 'cultural capital' (to borrow Pierre Bourdieu's term) was becoming an important thing to possess.[29] Just as a visit to a museum or an exhibit such as the Chinese Collection at Hyde Park was an indicator of 'good taste', being knowledgeable about China distinguished one from the 'hundreds' of uninformed people who held a simplistic view of the Chinese. As Dennis Denisoff points out, during the nineteenth century, 'the young did function as possessions with currency within a system of cultural exchange'.[30] Therefore it could also be argued that knowledgeable children could also be seen as part of their parents' 'symbolic capital' (also Bourdieu's term). Being a parent of well-educated sons and daughters would help elevate one's status and prestige in a society where most bourgeois households had an encyclopædia.[31] In the context of this cultural climate, parents who wished the best for their children were not only encouraged to purchase encyclopædias by salesmen who suggested that 'a family deprived of an encyclopedia is a family that is willing to limit its children', but also

---

[27] Ibid., p. 5.

[28] Ibid., p. 88.

[29] Pierre Bourdieu and Jean Claude Passeron, *Reproduction in Education, Society and Culture*, 2nd edn (London, 1990); Pierre Bourdieu, 'The Market of Symbolic Goods', *Poetics*, 14.1–2 (1985): pp. 13–44. For discussion on the importance of cultural capital to Victorians, see Lara Kriegel, *Grand Designs: Labor, Empire, and the Museum in Victorian Culture* (Durham, 2008).

[30] Dennis Denisoff, 'Small Change: The Consumerist Designs of the Nineteenth-Century Child', in Dennis Denisoff (ed.), *The Nineteenth-Century Child and Consumer Culture* (Aldershot, 2008), pp. 1–26 (p. 8).

[31] Daniel R. Headrick, *When Information Came of Age: Technologies of Knowledge in the Age of Reason and Revolution, 1700–1850* (New York, 2000), p. 172.

books such as Old Humphrey's which provided specific knowledge about China.[32] As the motto of the weekly *Poor Man's Guardian* (1831–1835) proclaimed: 'Knowledge is Power.'

For Victorians, knowledge about China was worth acquiring. However, according to Old Humphrey, because 'China is too long, too wide, too crowded with people, too strange, too full of curiosities, too everything to be brought into a small compass', he will *'point out*, and to *pick out*, for your advantage, what will most amuse you, and what is best deserving of your attention'.[33] The repetition of the word 'too' also anticipates the 'frightful' flood of books on China that would inundate the book market 60 years later. China is presented as a country filled with too much complex information for young readers to be able to navigate on their own. Just as children needed adults to guide them when visiting Nathan Dunn's exhibit, which may have been very overwhelming with numerous Chinese objects, child readers needed someone like the avuncular Old Humphrey to 'pick out' and 'point out' the 'knowledge' that would be most advantageous for them to have.

Old Humphrey informs readers that he aims to provide a 'careful, correct, and sprightly selection of such things as well afford young people the most pleasure and the most profit'.[34] In using the word 'profit', he hints that by consuming this information about China, young readers' cultural capital could potentially be converted into economic capital. At the end of the book, he states, 'I have now given you "points and pickings" of China enough to occupy your thoughts. See, then, that you turn your knowledge to advantage'.[35] His imperative tone suggests that children were expected to take action and not simply treat these facts as entertaining information.

How could young British readers turn their knowledge to their advantage? As an article in the influential magazine *Boy's Own Paper* (1879–1967) entitled 'How to Become a Student Interpreter in China, Japan, and Siam' (1893–1894) reveals, towards the end of the nineteenth century, it was advantageous to have knowledge of Asian languages such as Chinese because this could potentially lead to a promising career. The *Boy's Own Paper* author points out the benefits of serving as a student interpreter for the British Consul: he 'has an important future before him, for the consul is in those busy Eastern ports a guardian of English commercial interests, a dispense of law, justice, and hospitality, and above all, he is a representative of that sovereign lady on whose "empire the sun never sets"'.[36] As this article reveals, knowledge of China and the Chinese no longer functioned simply as cultural capital but could be turned into economic capital because those possessing this linguistic capability could become 'guardians' of British interests,

---

32   Rauch, *Useful Knowledge*, p. 3.
33   Old Humphrey, *The Celestial Empire*, pp. 1–2 (emphasis in the original).
34   Ibid., p. 2.
35   Ibid., p. 316.
36   F.R.R., 'How to Become a Student Interpreter in China, Japan, and Siam', *Boy's Own Paper*, 16 (1893–1894): p. 207.

bring law and order to the East, and represent the glorious British Empire. One of the aims of this book is to identify what other 'knowledge' about China was considered advantageous for Victorian and Edwardian children to acquire. If we adopt Michael Bentley's definition of knowledge ('paradigms of what was and what was not to count as worth knowing'), the question then becomes: What did authors think was worth knowing about China and the Chinese?[37]

The Celestial Empire is just one of the numerous texts on China for children published in Great Britain in the nineteenth century, many of which were reprinted in the United States. Another author who sought to capitalize on Britain's growing fascination with China was William Dalton, who wrote *The Wolf Boy of China; or Incidents and Adventures in the Life of Lyu-Payo*. Published in 1857, a time when the passion for 'facts' dominated the education sector and children's book market, *The Wolf Boy of China* guides readers through China as if it was a large museum exhibition, filled with information about the customs and manners of the Chinese. A contemporary reviewer claimed that 'the odd customs of the Celestial people are represented with rigid truthfulness' in this book.[38] Having never travelled to China, Dalton relied on various sources to create an 'encyclopaedic' picture of the place. One of his main sources was Jean-Baptiste Du Halde's *The General History of China* (1735), which was considered the most authoritative source on China until well into the nineteenth century.

Fifty years after Dalton was commended for his extensive knowledge of foreign lands, popular children's writer Charles Gilson was praised for his 'wide knowledge of the world'.[39] This emphasis on 'accurate knowledge' and 'rigid truthfulness' suggests an urgent need to demystify and understand the Chinese, who were often presented as 'inscrutable' and hence unpredictable and dangerous.[40] Authors such as Dalton and Gilson tried to mediate a complex textual discourse on China that had been developing in Europe for hundreds of years, seeking to make these erudite texts more accessible for the child reader by combining 'instruction' with 'amusement' in their stories. While scholars have discussed the role international exhibits, museums, libraries, and other sites played in making knowledge of China accessible to the British public, few have considered the part children's books played in this process. Despite the wealth of material related to

---

[37] Michael Bentley, 'The Evolution and Dissemination of Historical Knowledge', in Martin Daunton (ed.), *The Organisation of Knowledge in Victorian Britain* (Oxford, 2005), pp. 173–98 (p. 175).

[38] 'Reviews: Christmas Books for Children', *Baptist Magazine*, L (1858): pp. 31–4 (p. 33).

[39] The Old Fag, 'Editorial (Captain Charles Gilson)', *The Captain*, XVII (1907): pp. 568–9 (p. 568).

[40] The phrase 'inscrutable Chinese' was in use since the 1880s. For example, E.F. Knight wrote in his 1884 novel, 'the inscrutable Chinese have their own quarter'. E.F. Knight, *The Cruise of the "Falcon": A Voyage to South America in a 30-ton Yacht* [London, 1886], p. 355.

China in Victorian and Edwardian children's literature, relatively few scholarly works have been published on the subject.[41]

Scholarly discussions of the image of foreigners in Victorian and Edwardian children's literature have tended to focus on Africa or India. Images of China, however, have been examined in only a few books and articles, such as in Câecile Parrish's *The Image of Asia in Children's Literature, 1814–1964*, Laurence Kitzan's *Victorian Writers and the Image of Empire: The Rose-Colored Vision*, and Kathryn Castle's *Britannia's Children: Reading Colonialism through Children's Books and Magazines*, which discusses the representation of Africa, India, and China in late nineteenth-century children's textbooks and periodicals. According to Castle, '[w]hile the Chinese character might have in reality remained less controlled, and less "knowable", than either the Indian or the African, this did not deter the annuals from creating an image of the country which reflected national concerns and abiding stereotypes'.[42]

Many scholars have emphasized the negative discourse and stereotypical images of the Chinese in late nineteenth-century children's literature, concentrating on the portrayal of Chinese villains and the establishment of an 'Us' versus 'Them' mentality. While acknowledging the imperialist rhetoric and stereotypes evident in many texts, I present in this book some children's texts that challenge the conclusions made by critics that read Victorian and Edwardian children's literature through their interpretation of Edward Said's concept of Orientalism, which argues that the West, because of a dominating desire to govern the Orient, tame its hostility, and claim authority over it, constructed it as uniform, backward, inferior, fixed, and unchanging.[43] I argue that the uniformity of negative stereotypes in children's writing of the Victorian and Edwardian period has been exaggerated. For example, Castle's claim that 'the young would arguably have looked with fear and suspicion on Chinese encountered within the boundaries of their own country' is repudiated by A. Harcourt Burrage's 'Ching-Ching Memoirs', which reveals that children in the late nineteenth century enthusiastically greeted a Chinese man who lingered around Fleet Street because they thought he was Ching-Ching, the popular character created by E. Harcourt Burrage, which will be discussed in Chapter 3.[44] Comparing stories set in China with those about Africa, Castle states, '[t]here was no parallel to the "adoption" of the English into African tribes, or stories of brother turning against his own to

---

[41]   While the works of Julia Ching and Willard Gurdon Oxtoby, Jonathan Spence, Raymond Dawson, Adrian Hsia, Colin Mackerras, Jerome Ch'en, Thomas Lee, Eric Reinders, David Porter, Jeng-Guo S. Chen, Longxi Zhang, Tao Zhijian and others provide insight into how different European nations perceived China throughout history, their texts focus mostly on the writings of travellers, missionaries and embassy officials.

[42]   Kathryn Castle, *Britannia's Children: Reading Colonialism through Children's Books and Magazines* (Manchester, 1996), p. 157.

[43]   Edward W. Said, *Orientalism* (New York, 1978), p. 96.

[44]   Castle, *Britannia's Children*, pp. 141–2.

save an English life'.[45] However, as Chapters 4 and 5 will show, stories set during the Taiping Rebellion (1850–1864) and Boxer Uprising (1899–1901) feature Chinese characters risking their lives to save their English and American friends.

Just as some scholars criticize children's texts for racist misrepresentations of the Chinese, they often misrepresent the texts by choosing passages selectively to support their argument or by only discussing books of a particular genre. Because the rise of the adventure story genre in the late 1860s coincided with the confidence in the expanding British Empire and the need to encourage British youth to become patriotic empire builders dedicated to sustaining the glory and power of Great Britain, these texts tend to reflect more stereotypical images of foreigners. It is therefore not surprising that critics have mostly examined Victorian adventure stories, a popular topic among researchers of children's literature and postcolonial scholars.[46]

In recent years, a number of scholars have pointed out the limitations and inadequacies of the postcolonial approach. For example, Lynn Festa and Daniel Carey contend that employing postcolonial theory may 'allow elements of material analysis ... to be subsumed under a postcolonial rationale, as scholars fall into the trap of writing to the theory, rather than to the history or to the text'.[47] When writing about the Victorian period, postcolonial critics have tended, in the words of Douglas A. Lorimer, to represent the Victorians as 'the racist Other in binary opposition to our implicit nonracist Self. This reconstruction often relies on a limited selection of sources wherein extreme racist views are presented as representative opinion'.[48] Christopher Herbert warns that our judgement can be distorted if 'we implicitly

---

[45] Ibid., p. 156.

[46] Much research on Victorian children's literature has focused on the genre of 'boy's adventure story' with regard to the ideology of imperialism, discourses on masculinity, and tropes such as the 'faithful' servant, the 'evil' natives, and the 'noble savage'. See Joseph Bristow, *Empire Boys: Adventures in a Man's World* (London, 1991); Joseph Campbell, *The Hero with a Thousand Faces* (Princeton, 1968); Martin Burgess Green, *Dreams of Adventure, Deeds of Empire* (New York, 1979); John M. MacKenzie (ed.), *Imperialism and Popular Culture* (Manchester, 1986); Richard Phillips, *Mapping Men and Empire: A Geography of Adventure* (London, 1997); Robert H. MacDonald, *The Language of Empire: Myths and Metaphors of Popular Imperialism, 1880–1918* (Manchester, 1994); Kelly Boyd, *Manliness and the Boys' Story Paper in Britain: A Cultural History, 1855–1940* (New York, 2003); Patrick Howarth, *Play up and Play the Game: The Heroes of Popular Fiction* (London, 1973).

[47] Lynn Festa and Daniel Carey, 'Introduction: Some Answers to the Question: "What Is the Postcolonial Enlightenment?"' in Daniel Carey and Lynn Festa (eds), *The Postcolonial Enlightenment: Eighteenth-Century Colonialism and Postcolonial Theory* (Oxford, 2009), pp. 1–33 (p. 24).

[48] Douglas A. Lorimer, 'Reconstructing Victorian Racial Discourse: Images of Race, the Language of Race Relations, and the Context of Black Resistance', in Gretchen Holbrook Gerzina (ed.), *Black Victorians/Black Victoriana* (New Brunswick, 2003), pp. 187–207 (p. 187).

and uncritically take as our standard of historical comparison a utopian imaginary nation whose popular opinion would be free of xenophobia and such vices, if only it existed'.[49] From his close reading of Victorian Mutiny literature, he concludes that this body of texts do not monolithically express confidence in the British right to rule.

Similarly, it is important not to treat Victorian and Edwardian children's fiction related to China as a homogeneous group of texts that adhere to 'abiding stereotypes'. The representation of the Chinese was not stable during this time. If one wanted to support the idea that Victorian children's literature presented the Chinese according to 'stereotyped patterns', one could quote the following passage from *The Lands of the Rising Sun* (1895):

> People in China think the left the place of honour, begin a book at the end, read down a page instead of across; they do not say Mr. John Smith, but Smith John Mr.; their men wear petticoats and their women wear trousers; they put white on for a funeral ... It is just like a land behind the looking-glass where left and right get all twisted round.[50]

At first glance this statement seems to be another example that supports the claim that all British authors presented China as a topsy-turvy nation where 'everything goes by opposites'.[51] However, the narrator warns several pages later, 'It is not fair to think that everything is bad in China; the people ... love their homes and are exceedingly dutiful and obedient to their parents; they are good to the destitute, and they are, on the whole, hard-working, temperate, and honest'.[52] If we only read the first part, we might come to the conclusion that child readers were being taught to define themselves as everything the Chinese were not through the use of binary oppositions. However, a closer reading reveals that positive qualities of diligence, honesty, and filial piety were also attributed to the Chinese character.

The aim of this book is not to argue that stereotypes about topsy-turvydom and images of the Chinese as rat-eating people with long fingernails who administered cruel punishments did not exist, but to present from the rich repository of children's texts co-existing representations that were more complex and ambiguous. It is easy to read selectively and argue that children were consuming material that, according to Castle, secured 'the youth into the imperial ethos' through 'both positive identification with Britishness and a distancing from the undesirable "other"'.[53] However, to approach these texts from a postcolonial perspective and conclude that they simply performed the function of reaffirming British superiority over Chinese inferiority is to miss the rich textures evident in many of them.

---

[49]   Christopher Herbert, *War of No Pity: The Indian Mutiny and Victorian Trauma* (Princeton, 2008), p. 16.

[50]   W.T.A. Barber, *The Lands of the Rising Sun: A Talk with English Boys and Girls about China, Corea and Japan* (London, 1895), p. 5.

[51]   Ibid.

[52]   Ibid., p. 26.

[53]   Castle, *Britannia's Children*, p. 8.

This book aims to provide a more expansive look at representations of China and the Chinese in Victorian and Edwardian children's fiction. An intensive close reading of these texts reveals contradictions and ambivalences. The plurality of viewpoints about China and the Chinese that are present in these stories should not be dismissed as insignificant exceptions. As Lee Sterrenburg has pointed out, 'there is a tendency to acknowledge possible exceptions to hegemonic metropolitan discourse, only to discount those exceptions as infrequent or nonsignificant'.[54] However, he continues, these 'exceptions can be diverse and significant. And they have been there in the archive all along'.[55] The texts I examine provide examples of the diversity of images of China and a broad spectrum of views on the Chinese, illustrate the complexity evident in children's texts, and demonstrate the historically complex relationships between Britain and China. This study adds to the current scholarship on nineteenth-century representations of the Chinese by identifying and further elucidating a range of texts that have thus far mostly received little critical discussion.

In this study, I trace the way different discourses on China were developed in children's fiction from the mid-nineteenth century to the early twentieth century, specifically between the years 1851 and 1911. I choose to examine children's fiction starting in the mid-nineteenth century for two reasons. First, according to Jürgen Osterhammel, it was during the 1850s that 'China formed an integral part of the military, economic, and mental history of European and, in particular, of British imperialism'.[56] Though never a formal colony of Britain (with the exception of Hong Kong), China was part of its 'informal' Empire. British relations with the Chinese during the second half of the nineteenth century was marked by several conflicts, from the two Opium Wars (1839–1842, 1856–1860) to the Taiping Rebellion (1850–1864) to the Boxer Uprising (1899–1901). It was also during the 1850s that China 'experts' objected to what they perceived to be misrepresentations of China. For example, in 1854, the Inspector General in China's Imperial Maritime Customs Service Sir Robert Hart (1835–1911) complained that

> [w]riters in treating of China and the Chinese have in most instances fallen into the error of generalization unsupported by premises. *Exo uno disce omnes* is applicable in many matters: but given one particular Chinese – one particular spot of Chinese ground, from neither of these can one say what ought to be the character and customs in another part of the Empire, or what ought to be the habits of individuals in another Province.[57]

---

[54]   Lee Sterrenburg, 'Significant Evidences and the Imperial Archive: Response', *Victorian Studies*, 46.2 (2004): pp. 275–83 (p. 275).

[55]   Ibid., p. 283.

[56]   Jürgen Osterhammel, 'Britain and China, 1842–1914', in Andrew Porter (ed.), *The Oxford History of the British Empire III: The Nineteenth Century* (Oxford, 1998), pp. 146–69 (p. 146).

[57]   Robert Hart, *Entering China's Service: Robert Hart's Journals, 1854–1863* (Cambridge, MA, 1986), p. 143.

A few years later, Rev. William Milne (1815–1863), who was sent to China in 1839 by the London Missionary Society, condemned the 'revolting' trend in children's textbooks and magazines to 'pamper to this greed for stories of the cruel and heartless features in heathen nations' which fill children's minds with 'monstrous and hideous notions of their fellow-men'.[58] He attempted to present a more accurate and balanced portrait of China and the Chinese in *Life in China*. Milne's comment links to the second reason why my study begins in the mid-nineteenth century: it was during this period that British children's texts, which were regularly reviewed in prominent literary journals, became an important and influential literary genre. Publishers, observing the rising literacy rate among the youth of Britain, were eager to cater to this section of the reading public because they formed a significant part of the total population. Edward Salmon observes that before 1850, books specifically published for boys and girls 'from ten or twelve to eighteen or twenty years of age ... were few and far between'.[59] While there were articles on China published in missionary magazines for children before 1851, it was after the Great Exhibition of 1851 that a great deal of information about China began to appear on the children's book market. I conclude the study at 1911 because it marks the end of the Qing dynasty (1644–1911). To consider the literature on China published after the overthrow of the Manchu government would be going beyond the scope of this book, because China was then cast into a state of political turmoil with revolutionaries, warlords, and other parties wreaking havoc on the country over a prolonged period of time. More importantly, after the revolution of 1911 the British viewed China differently because it was no longer a monarchy like Britain. As Lilian E. Cox informed her child readers, '[u]ntil that time China had been an empire; New China dates from then'.[60] Because the 'New China' of 1912 marked the end of an epoch, it is therefore a pertinent place to end this study.

To illustrate the importance of the role British children's literature plays in revealing national concerns and attitudes, many historians of children's literature quote French academic Paul Hazard's assertion that 'England could be reconstructed entirely from its children's books'.[61] This statement suggests that by examining children's books published in England, one can gain a clear understanding of English culture and society because these books can be seen as a repository of the values that adults hoped to pass on to the young.[62] While one can

---

[58] William Milne, *Life in China* (London, 1857), p. 47.

[59] Edward Salmon, 'Books for Boys [1888]', repr. in Lance Salway (ed.), *A Peculiar Gift: Nineteenth Century Writings on Books for Children* (Harmondsworth, 1976), pp. 371–86 (p. 371).

[60] Lilian Edith Cox, *If I Lived in China* (London, 1933), p. 35.

[61] Paul Hazard, *Books, Children & Men*, trans. Marguerite Mitchell (Boston, 1944), p. 128.

[62] See Peter Hollindale, 'Ideology and the Children's Book', in Peter Hunt (ed.), *Literature for Children: Contemporary Criticism* (London, 1992), pp. 19–40 (p. 30); John Stephens, *Language and Ideology in Children's Fiction* (Harlow, UK, 1992), p. 238.

identify the images of China and the Chinese that the authors wished to transmit to their readers, one cannot claim that the readers accepted these impressions without questioning. Differences in socio-economic status, educational level, and gender make it difficult to make conclusions about the reading practices of children at any given historical moment. Attempts at generalizations are also hindered by the fact that the number of unrecorded acts of reading far surpasses the amount of available records. Accessing children's reading experiences is particularly difficult because, as Peter Hunt points out, 'children can only rarely usefully articulate their reactions' and recent empirical studies reveal that 'children tend to mediate their ideas to suit the researcher'.[63] Other critics argue that children's reactions to a text are often more unpredictable because of their limited range of reading experiences.[64] Therefore, this book does not equate the desire of the authors to inculcate certain images of China and the Chinese with the effect the stories had on young readers, for to do so would be committing what Jonathan Rose has termed the 'receptive fallacy' where it is assumed that readers receive the message intended by the author or interpreted by the critic.[65] In other words, this book is not a study of reader reception of the texts, although I will discuss how a few readers remember some of the stories. Even though the message that child readers receive may not be the one intended by the author, childhood reading materials are still worth investigating because, according to Joyce Carol Oates, books we read as children 'seem to soak into the very marrow of our bones and to condition our interpretation of the universe thereafter'.[66]

Children's Literature and New Historicism

In 'Missed Opportunities and Critical Malpractice: New Historicism and Children's Literature', Mitzi Myers advocates a New Historicist approach to children's literature which is worth quoting at some length:

> [it would] *integrate* text and socio-historic context, demonstrating on the one hand how extraliterary cultural formations shape literary discourse and on the other how literary practices are actions that make things happen – by shaping the psychic and moral consciousness of young readers but also by performing more diverse kinds of cultural work, from satisfying authorial fantasies to legitimating or subverting dominant class and gender ideologies ... from popularizing new knowledges and discoveries to addressing live issues like slavery and the condition of the working class. It would want to know how and why a tale

---

63   Peter Hunt, 'Necessary Misreadings: Directions in Narrative Theory for Children's Literature', *Studies in the Literary Imagination*, 18.2 (1985): pp. 107–21 (p. 108).

64   Yulisa Amadu Maddy and Donnarae MacCann, *African Images in Juvenile Literature: Commentaries on Neocolonialist Fiction* (Jefferson, NC, 1996), p. 9.

65   Jonathan Rose, 'Rereading the English Common Reader: A Preface to a History of Audiences', *Journal of the History of Ideas*, 53.1 (1992): pp. 47–70 (p. 49).

66   Joyce Carol Oates, *The Faith of a Writer: Life, Craft, Art* (New York, 2004), p. 13.

or poem came to say what it does, what the environing circumstances were (including the uses a particular sort of children's literature served for this author, its child and adult readers, and its culture), and what kinds of cultural statements and questions the work was responding to. It would pay particular attention to the conceptual and symbolic fault lines denoting a text's time-, place-, gender-, and class-specific ideological mechanisms, being aware that the most seemingly artless and orthodox work may conceal an oppositional or contestatory subtext. It would examine a book's material production, its publishing history, its audiences and their reading practices, its initial reception, and its critical history including how it got inscribed in or deleted from the canon.[67]

Using Myers's framework, I address questions such as: What function do the stories have in popularizing knowledge of China? What knowledge about China was considered 'useful'? What did the authors assume the child audience already knew about China? What changes in representations of the Chinese, if any, occurred during this time period? What were the dominant discourses used in the stories? Do certain visions of China become 'fixed' and rearticulated in the texts? If so, what are they? How are significant historical events such as the Taiping Rebellion and the Boxer Uprising portrayed in the texts? As more information about China became available towards the end of the century, how did the children's authors respond to this ever increasing supply of new knowledge?

As Martin Daunton has pointed out, although there were different mechanisms in place for validating knowledge in the Victorian era, it was becoming more and more challenging to prevent outdated information from being continuously transmitted. Because efficient mechanisms for dispelling pre-existing misconceptions were not necessarily widely available, the danger of transmitting inaccurate information always existed.[68] Was 'outdated' information about China being transmitted to children via these children's texts? To answer this question, I will identify the sources of information on China that were available at the time of the author's writing and which ones he or she used. By identifying the materials these authors drew from the 'imperial archive', to use Thomas Richards's term, one is able partially to reconstruct the authors' reading and provide an answer to the question posed at the beginning of this book: Who was reading the texts on China and what did they do with this information? Because the authors consulted various sources on China and pulled bits and pieces from these books into their own works, these texts were polyphonic; identifying the sources they used will also explain why these stories were often a site of conflicting or contradictory views on China, thus demonstrating that the generalizations that previous critics have made about children's texts about the Chinese are overly simplistic. Another issue related to identification of sources is the question of what authorial voice is speaking.

---

[67]   Mitzi Myers, 'Missed Opportunities and Critical Malpractice: New Historicism and Children's Literature', *Children's Literature Association Quarterly*, 13.1 (1988): pp. 41–3 (p. 42) (emphasis in the original).

[68]   Daunton, 'Introduction', p. 5.

The line between literature for adults and literature for children is blurred when we take into account the fact that certain passages from adult books on China were frequently copied almost verbatim into these children's texts. The production of knowledge of China for children was a complex one influenced by many factors. Therefore, I will also consider how market trends, generic conventions, gender, and class influenced and shaped these texts.

This book looks at the representation of China and the Chinese across a range of different genres and types of publication prepared for children of this period – travelogue storybooks, historical novels, adventures stories, and periodicals. These texts are hybrid commodities because not only are they generically a mixture of fact and fiction, but they often combine conventions of the adventure story genre, travel writing, evangelical writing, and historical fiction. Many of these stories also deal with hybrid (mixed-race) identities. Common themes and issues addressed include miscegenation, the relationship between language and identity, the notion of 'passing', and the use of disguise in relation to performing 'Chineseness'. The texts discussed were chosen because their authors were popular prolific writers of children's literature and most were positively received by contemporary critics.

This body of texts on China is worth examining for three reasons. First, they provide examples of how Sino-British relations were influential in the representation of China in children's literature and they also illustrate how Britain's relationship with China was interpreted for children. Second, they complicate the notion that nineteenth-century children's literature simply parroted the dominant ideologies of the age. In fact, I suggest that children's literature was a less restrictive genre that allowed authors to explore contentious issues such as mixed-race identity and miscegenation. Third, these texts exemplify how authors responded to the nineteenth-century 'knowledge explosion' and offer insights into how attitudes towards children's relationships with knowledge changed over the course of the century.

Recently Kimberley Reynolds's *Radical Children's Literature: Future Visions and Aesthetic Transformations in Juvenile Fiction*, Julia L. Mickenberg's *Learning from the Left: Children's Literature, the Cold War, and Radical Politics in the United States*, and Marah Gubar's *Artful Dodgers: Reconceiving the Golden Age of Children's Literature* have challenged notions of children's literature as a conservative genre that invariably parrots the dominant ideologies of the time. Reynolds posits that 'children's literature provides a curious and paradoxical cultural space: a space that is simultaneously highly regulated and overlooked, orthodox and radical, didactic and subversive'.[69] Reynolds argues for a closer attention to the complexity evident in children's texts which often reflect ambivalent or radical ideas. My reading of these texts on China takes up Reynolds's challenge to reconsider interpretations of Victorian children's texts that read them as always only reinforcing the ideologies of Empire. The texts will

---

[69] Kimberley Reynolds, *Radical Children's Literature: Future Visions and Aesthetic Transformations in Juvenile Fiction* (Basingstoke, 2007), p. 3.

be considered chronologically to trace the changes in attitudes toward China and consider the historical context out of which such images emerged.

As Old Humphrey informed readers in 1844, after the 'opening of China' as a result of the Opium War, there was hope that 'useful knowledge may spread through the Celestial Empire'.[70] For the characters in Anne Bowman's *The Travels of Rolando*, which will be discussed in the next chapter, spreading 'useful' knowledge in China was one of their objectives, but more importantly, they wished to acquire new knowledge of China itself, ultimately disseminating this knowledge to eager child readers.

---

[70]   Old Humphrey, *The Celestial Empire*, p. 88.

Chapter 2
Exploring the Celestial Kingdom: William Dalton and Anne Bowman's Vision of China

> We hazard nothing in asserting, that there are at this moment, in our own incomparable island, thousands and tens of thousands of boys – ay, and of girls, too – who are in possession of more available knowledge than ever were any of their grandparents ...
>
> —Cecil Hartley, Preface to *The Travels of Rolando* (1852)[1]

In 1852, Cecil Hartley, editor of the 'corrected and improved' edition of *The Travels of Rolando* (first translated from the French in 1804), declared the adage 'there is no royal road to the acquisition of knowledge' was no longer accurate.[1] The Victorian child was in a very different position from his or her parents and grandparents because of the nineteenth-century 'knowledge explosion'. Hartley explains that due to 'improved' methods of instruction adopted 'within the last twenty or thirty years', 'every art and every science may now be acquired in less than half the time, and with less than half the labour, that were formerly exacted ...'.[2] One of the 'improved methods of instruction' he referred to was the use of fictional *'personal adventure'* to introduce readers to different countries.[3] As the subtitle of *The Travels of Rolando: Containing, in a Supposed Tour around the World, Authentic Descriptions of the Geography, Natural History, Manners, and Antiquities of Various Countries* emphasizes, although the tour itself is 'supposed', the descriptions of the world are 'authentic'. This kind of fictional travel narrative, also known as the travelogue storybook, was a popular genre utilized by nineteenth-century authors to facilitate the 'acquisition of knowledge' among children.[4]

Travelogues for children were popular in both the United States and England in the 1840s and 50s. Two of the most successful travelogue series, Jacob Abbott's *Rollo Holiday* series (1832–1879) and Samuel Griswold Goodrich's *Tales of Peter Parley* (1827–1860), featured many journeys to distant places, including China. These fictional travel narratives offered authors a convenient way to introduce

---

[1]   Cecil Hartley (ed.), *The Travels of Rolando; or, a Tour Round the World*, trans. Lucy Aikin, rev. edn (New York, 1852), p. iv.

[2]   Ibid., p. iii.

[3]   Ibid., p. iv (emphasis in the original).

[4]   See Virginia Haviland, *The Travelogue Storybook of the Nineteenth Century* (Boston, 1950), pp. 7–8.

information about various countries to children because plot twists could be utilized to expatiate on the history, geography, and customs of each place visited by the protagonist. Cecil Hartley's revised edition of *The Travels of Rolando* was published a year after the Great Exhibition of 1851, and in that respect, his confidence in the methods of acquiring knowledge can be said to be influenced by the 'spirit of encyclopaedism', which, according to the German newspaper *Allgemeine Zeitung* was felt during the Great Exhibition.[5] Alan Rauch has characterized the 'encyclopaedic spirit' as being grounded in

> some common ideas: first, that it is indeed possible to classify the world, at least in discrete parts; second, that an adequate re-creation of that world can be contained within a book or a series of books; and, third, that it is possible to present all facets of the world in a way that is accessible to the public. And, while these criteria cannot be taken as absolutes, they reflect the sense of orderliness that remains an implicit justification for the organized accumulation of knowledge into texts.[6]

To coincide with the Great Exhibition of 1851, John Betts released a board game consisting of 35 squares called 'The Royal Game of the Gathering Nations: Exhibition of the Industry of All Nations'. The game is a good example of the encyclopaedic spirit because it attempted to classify and contain the world on a board and make information about countries such as China accessible to the public. The first player to land on the last square, 'The Crystal Palace', would win the game. Each square had an accompanying description and one of the players was to read it aloud when someone landed on that particular square. Square 13, China, was described thus:

> China is an empire on the east of Asia, possessing a soil of more than common fertility, producing the choicest of fruits, flowering shrubs, medicinal plants, and trees peculiar to itself. Amongst the first-named, may be mentioned, the orange, lemon, citron, and pomegranate; and amongst the last, the tea tree, the leaves of which form so important an article of commerce with, this and many other countries. The birds of China are also very beautiful. Its magnificent rivers are crowded with small boats and vessels, employed for all manner of purposes, and many of them forming the only habitation of their owners; and the banks crowned with pagodas and temples, give a very picturesque effect to the landscape. China contributed a variety of elaborate ivory and wood carvings to the Great Exhibition; it also sent samples of tea, revolving lanterns, gongs, & c & c.[7]

---

[5]   Raymond Corbey, 'Ethnographic Showcases, 1870–1930', *Cultural Anthropology*, 8.3 (1993): pp. 338–69 (p. 340).

[6]   Alan Rauch, *Useful Knowledge: The Victorians, Morality, and the March of Intellect* (Durham, 2001), p. 34.

[7]   *The Royal Game of the Assembling of the Nations: Exhibition of the Industry of All Nations* (London, [1851]).

In reality, China did not send in an official contribution to the Exhibition; the Chinese section of the exhibit was comprised of objects contributed by English and American collectors. This game combined instruction with amusement, just as Anne Bowman and William Dalton attempted to do in their novels.

Scholars have argued that in the late eighteenth century and throughout the nineteenth century, many British and American writers, such as George Anson, John Barrow, and Charles Dickens, presented negative views of the Chinese as child-like, cruel, corrupt, conceited, dirty, dishonest, ignorant, xenophobic, and afraid to lose face.[8] China was frequently characterized as a 'peculiar' nation that had become unprogressive and stagnant.[9] For example, in 'The Great Exhibition and the Little One', Charles Dickens and R.H. Horne state that if readers compare China's section of the Great Exhibition to that of Britain's, they will see the contrast 'between Stoppage and Progress'.[10] Doloni, one of Anne Bowman's characters in *The Travels of Rolando; or, A Tour Round the World. Second Series, Containing a Journey through Mesopotamia, Persia, Kamschatka, China, and Thibet* (1853), echoes this view, commenting that in China '[n]othing progresses; nothing degenerates; all is eternal sameness'.[11] Throughout 'The Great Exhibition and the Little One', readers are asked to consider 'the greatness of the English results, and extraordinary littleness of the Chinese'.[12] In the first few pages of *The Wolf Boy of China; or Incidents and Adventures in the Life of Lyu-Payo* (1857), William Dalton compares the Chinese to a mouse content to live inside a 'little box', even though it is aware that a big world exists outside. He claims that the Chinese were shocked when they realized that China is actually 'very little' after some missionaries showed them a map of the world.[13] Dalton's use of the word 'little' echoes Dickens and Horne's article. Both Bowman and Dalton's books include

---

[8]   See Stuart Creighton Miller, *The Unwelcome Immigrant: The American Image of the Chinese, 1785–1882* (Berkeley, 1969); Jerome Ch'en, *China and the West: Society and Culture, 1815–1937* (London, 1979).

[9]   David Porter, 'A Peculiar but Uninteresting Nation: China and the Discourse of Commerce in Eighteenth-Century England', *Eighteenth-Century Studies*, 33.2 (2000): pp. 181–99 (p. 191); James M. McCutcheon, '"Tremblingly Obey": British and Other Western Responses to China and the Chinese Kotow', *The Historian*, XXXIII.4 (1970): pp. 557–77; Raymond Stanley Dawson, *The Chinese Chameleon: An Analysis of European Conceptions of Chinese Civilization* (London, 1967); Colin Mackerras, *Western Images of China* (Oxford, 1989).

[10]   Charles Dickens and R.H. Horne, 'The Great Exhibition and the Little One', *Household Words*, 3 (1851): pp. 356–60 (p. 360).

[11]   Anne Bowman, *The Travels of Rolando; or, a Tour Round the World. Second Series, Containing a Journey through Mesopotamia, Persia, Kamschatka, China, and Thibet*, 2nd edn (London, [1853] 1854), p. 252.

[12]   Dickens and Horne, 'The Great Exhibition and the Little One', p. 358.

[13]   William Dalton, *The Wolf Boy of China; or, Incidents and Adventures in the Life of Lyu-Payo* (Philadelphia, [1857] 1884), p. 12. Further references to this book are given after quotations in the text.

statements that may tempt one to dismiss them as providing negative stereotypical views of China, but a close reading of the texts reveals distinctive ideas about race, miscegenation, and mixed-race children.

Anne Bowman and William Dalton: Mediators of Knowledge

Neither Anne Bowman nor William Dalton travelled to China. Before devoting her time to writing full-length novels, Bowman (c.1795–1886) ran a printing and booksellers business with her brother in Richmond, Yorkshire where they published books of local interest such as *Bowman's Guide to Richmond and the Neighbourhood*. Like Bowman, William Dalton (1821–1875) belonged to 'an old Yorkshire family', but was born in London, where he worked as a journalist and was sometime editor of the *Daily Telegraph* and sub-editor of the *Morning Advertiser*.[14] Without firsthand experience of China, both authors had to rely on secondary sources for their information on China, and as the previous chapter has demonstrated, there were hundreds of books and articles for them to choose from. In fact, as early as 1830, W.W. Wood felt the need to justify why another work on China was needed when respected historians and diplomats had already published lengthy volumes dedicated to the country:

> Some reasonable excuse will in all probability be expected for the perpetration of a work on China, when we have already the ponderous volumes of Du Halde, De Guignes, Grosier, Staunton, Barrow, and several minor works by other authors. ... To the historian or the antiquary, these folios of Jesuitical labours are invaluable, but to one who is anxious to be made acquainted with the prominent traits of Chinese manners and customs, they are by no means calculated to afford a speedy gratification.[15]

He suggested that these works were not likely to be perused by the average reader because in order to gain information on 'the leading features of the country and its inhabitants', one must 'wade through such a mass of comparatively uninteresting matter, and tediousness of detail'. Therefore, 'few choose to purchase their knowledge of China at the price of so much patient research'.[16] For Victorians experiencing the 'knowledge explosion' for the first time, 'speedy gratification' became a central concern for those seeking information. Wood's comment that not many people were patient enough to read the multi-volumed works on China makes the texts examined in this book more significant because they reveal how adults like Bowman and Dalton, who, unlike Wood, did not have personal

---

[14] See Thompson Cooper, *Men of the Time: A Dictionary of Contemporaries, Containing Biographical Notices of Eminent Characters of Both Sexes*, 8th edn (London, 1872), p. 277.

[15] W.W. Wood, *Sketches of China, with Illustrations from Original Drawings* (Philadelphia, 1830), p. vii.

[16] Ibid.

experience of the country, mediated the 'ponderous volumes' of books on China from the 'imperial archive' for a mass audience, including not only child readers but potential consumers such as parents, teachers, and relatives. During the researching and writing process, the authors attempted to harness knowledge, wading through and filtering the mass of information about China for those wishing 'to be made acquainted with the prominent traits of Chinese manners and customs'.

Dalton quotes extensively from his two acknowledged sources, French Lazarist missionary M. Huc's *Travels in Tartary, Thibet and China, 1844–1846* and Marco Polo's *The Travels of Marco Polo*. His unacknowledged sources include famous eighteenth-century texts such as Jean-Baptiste Du Halde's *The General History of China* and George L. Staunton's *An Authentic Account of an Embassy from the King of Great Britain to the Emperor of China*, as well as nineteenth-century books such as Charles Gutzlaff's *A Sketch of Chinese History*, John Francis Davis's *The Chinese: a General Description of the Empire of China and its Inhabitants*, and articles in newspapers and journals such as *The Times* and the *Canton Miscellany*. Although Bowman does not specify her sources, she, like Dalton, consulted M. Huc's *Travels in Tartary, Thibet and China, 1844–1846* for information on Tibet. Her main sources of information on China were the works of Robert Fortune, such as *Three Years' Wanderings in the Northern Provinces of China* (1847) and *A Journey to the Tea Countries of China* (1852). Fortune the Scottish horticulturalist, Huc the French missionary, Davis the British diplomat, and Gutzlaff the German missionary were regarded as some of the leading authorities on China at the time. A reviewer of *The Wolf Boy of China* felt the need to test 'the truthfulness of many of the descriptions by comparing them with the statements of Davis, Gutzlaff, Huc, and Fortune' before concluding that the 'Celestial people are represented with rigid truthfulness' in Dalton's novel.[17] Despite sharing similar sources by famous China 'experts', Bowman and Dalton's representations of China and the Chinese differ in many ways.

Anne Bowman's China

The protagonists in two of Bowman's adventure stories, *The Boy Voyagers* (1859) and *The Travels of Rolando* (1853), travel to China. The latter book was the sequel to *The Travels of Rolando* (1799), originally written in French by Louis François Jauffret (1770–1840), translated into English by Lucy Aikin in 1804, and edited by Cecil Hartley in 1852.[18] Bowman explains in her preface that she wrote the sequel

---

[17] 'Reviews: Christmas Books for Children', *Baptist Magazine*, L (1858): pp. 31–4 (p. 33).

[18] Louis François Jauffret's *Voyages de Rolando et de ses compagnons de fortune autour du monde* was published in 1799. Throughout the 1790s, Jauffret published numerous children's texts and works on the subject of childhood. He was also interested in the 'science of man' and formed the Society of Observers of Man in 1800. They believed that 'the study of the child was the foundation of the knowledge of man' and that those interested in anthropology

because she had enjoyed reading *The Travels of Rolando* as a child and 'pin[ed]' to know the conclusion to the adventures of the hero and his friends.[19] In her preface to *The Travels of Rolando; or, A Tour Round the World. Second Series* (*TR*), which was mostly likely read by potential adult buyers, Bowman professes not to have 'the fertile imagination of Jauffret, or the polished style of Miss Aikin', but hopes to provide 'sketches which may excite inquiry' and 'suggestions which may encourage research'.[20] According to many of her books' prefaces, her primary purpose for writing is for children to gain a deeper appreciation of God by discovering more about nature. For example, in her preface to *The Castaways* she states:

> it is desirable to implant in the minds of the young a taste for natural objects, to encourage them to look, with a microscopic eye, on the faultless works of creation, and thus to foster love and veneration for the Mighty Creator ... To forward this end, the author has successfully given former works to the public, and again ventures to offer such a tale of adventure as may captivate the fancy, while lessons of useful knowledge and examples of piety and morality may improve the understanding ...[21]

In asserting that a child's observations in nature would lead to 'veneration for the Mighty Creator', Bowman reflected the belief in natural theology as espoused by William Paley in his popular *Natural Theology: or, Evidences of the Existence and Attributes of the Deity* (1802). Bowman's emphasis on developing a taste for 'natural objects' among the young echoes the view expressed by influential educator Maria Edgeworth (1767–1849) who claimed in *Practical Education* (1798) that '[n]atural history is a study particularly suited to children: it cultivates their talents for observation, applies to objects within their reach, and to objects which are every day interesting to them'.[22] Bowman's statement also reflects the attitude of many nineteenth-century children's authors, who, according to Alan Rauch, believed that 'knowledge was not only a powerful tool used to instill young minds with a sense of the power and wonder of God but also the means of inculcating patterns of moral conduct'.[23] Female authors such as Bowman were heavily involved in popularizing knowledge of natural history for the young during the nineteenth century.[24]

---

should take up this 'useful' task. See Adriana S. Benzaquen, 'Childhood, Identity and Human Science in the Enlightenment', *History Workshop Journal*, 57 (2004): pp. 35–57 (pp. 46–8).

[19]   Bowman, *Rolando*, p. v.

[20]   Ibid., pp. v–vi. Further references to this book are given after quotations in the text.

[21]   Anne Bowman, *The Castaways; or, the Adventures of a Family in the Wilds of Africa* (London, 1857), n. pag.

[22]   Maria Edgeworth and Richard Lovell Edgeworth, *Practical Education* (New York, 1855), p. 253.

[23]   Rauch, *Useful Knowledge*, p. 47.

[24]   Priscilla Wakefield, who believed that 'to behold God in His works is the true end of all our knowledge, and of natural history in particular', was another writer who popularized natural history for children. Quoted in Rauch, *Useful Knowledge*, p. 47.

Many scientific trends swept through nineteenth-century Britain, including botany, geology, entomology, archaeology, and palaeontology. Amateurs, many of them women, not content to be passive consumers of knowledge, enthusiastically gathered ferns, collected rocks, and searched for insects.[25] In the 1830s and '40s, women displayed their passion for natural history by becoming popularizers of science through contributions to generalist magazines such as the *Penny Magazine*. Print culture offered these women who were not given the chance to become professional scientists an outlet for their scientific interests. According to Ann B. Shteir, women writers working between 1830 and 1860 performed 'important work as cultural mediators of botanical knowledge, and their expositions often served as "first steps" to botany'.[26] These writers earned praise from the historian and philosopher of science William Whewell (1794–1866), who commented that Victorian women were effective popularizers of science.[27] However, women were not merely transmitters of scientific knowledge; they also assumed the role of 'moral teacher'. As Barbara T. Gates puts it, '[m]ost of the early women popularizers preferred to imagine their audience as receptive but uninformed women and children who would function as virtual tabulae rasae, querying and then waiting to receive the scientific word'.[28] In the 1850s, science became increasingly professionalized, making it more difficult for women to publish their observations in serious journals.[29] They could, however, still demonstrate knowledge of natural history through fiction.

In *The Travels of Rolando*, Bowman utilizes familiar characters created by Jauffret, namely, Abbe Doloni (historian), Montval (naturalist), Martin de la Bastide (geographer), St Kassian (philanthropist), Louis Segnier (student of natural history), Dr Codonel (surgeon), and Ingardin (farmer and merchant) to provide information about natural history as well as many other topics. At the beginning of the novel, Rolando's friends decide to travel with him as he embarks on a voyage in search of his parents and brother. Before arriving in China, they stop in Bombay, Bagdad, Bokhara [Bukhara], and many other localities which had not been introduced in Jauffret's *The Travels of Rolando*. Using the 'conversation' or 'dialogue' style exemplified in works such as *Conversations on Natural Philosophy* (1821) and *China: A Dialogue, for the Use of School* (1824), Bowman is able to convey large amounts of facts about China to her readers.[30]

[25] Barbara T. Gates, *Kindred Nature: Victorian and Edwardian Women Embrace the Living World* (Chicago, 1998), p. 36.

[26] Ann B. Shteir, *Cultivating Women, Cultivating Science: Flora's Daughters and Botany in England, 1760 to 1860* (Baltimore, 1996), p. 197.

[27] Gates, *Kindred Nature*, p. 37.

[28] Ibid., p. 38.

[29] Ibid., p. 3.

[30] Jane Marcet, *Conversations on Natural Philosophy: In which the Elements of that Science are Familiarly Explained and Adapted to the Comprehension of Young Pupils* (Hartford, 1821); [Robert Morrison], *China: A Dialogue, for the Use of School: Being Ten Conversations, between a Father and his Two Children, Concerning the History and*

For example, when Rolando and his friends reach the Great Wall, Doloni asks his Chinese friend Ki-chan, 'what is the actual length of this amazing structure? … I have heard that it is 2,000 miles in length. I look to you for the truth'. Ki-chan replies, 'we must limit the extent of it to about 1,500' (*TR* 247).

Rolando and his friends initially regard China as highly romantic and dream-like: they 'felt as if transported to some land of enchantment, and never perceived the distance [they] went, till [they] entered the walls of Pekin, as if in a dream' (*TR* 248). When Rolando informs readers that the rice-fields, fertile plains, country houses, and tiny lakes that they travel past seem to be 'the very China depicted on the porcelain cups we had admired so much in our childhood', he is defining China in domestic terms (*TR* 248). Blue willow pattern plates, typically featuring pagodas, bridges, pigtailed men, and foot-bound women, were the most ubiquitous household item during the *Chinoiserie* craze of the eighteenth century. By the 1780s, mass production of 'Chinese' porcelain had become common in Britain, making it possible for people like Bowman to own porcelain teacups and willow pattern plates. By alluding to familiar household items to help her young readers visualize China, Bowman was employing a technique previously utilized by Samuel Goodrich (Peter Parley) in *Manners and Customs of the Principal Nations of the Globe* (1849), where he assumes that '[e]very one is familiar with their dress, personal appearance, and aspect of their houses, from the drawings in their porcelain'.[31] Similarly, in *The Boy Voyagers* (*BV*), when Walter Thornville comments that '[i]t would be very pleasant to have a peep into that land of wonders, to see the pagodas, the mandarins with the pigtails and the yellow buttons, and the women with the tiny little feet that they cannot walk with', he is also evoking willow pattern plates and porcelain cups from home.[32] As expected, in China, the 'scenery depicted on the old China tea-cups … delighted the boys [Walter and Frank Freeman] with the picturesque effect' (*BV* 376).

Rolando and his friends are able to enter the 'most impenetrable' China as 'scientific travellers' who will 'examine its natural productions, its antiquities, and its progress in arts and sciences' because they had helped Ki-chan, the son of an important mandarin in Peking (*TR* 191; 207).[33] It is significant that they are neither merchants nor soldiers, roles that would have been more contentious

---

Present State of that Country (London, 1824). For discussion on this style, see Rauch, *Useful Knowledge*, p. 52.

[31]   Samuel Griswold Goodrich, *Manners and Customs of the Principal Nations of the Globe* (Boston, 1849), pp. 342–3.

[32]   Bowman, *The Boy Voyagers; or, the Pirates of the East* (London, 1859), p. 177. Further references to this book are given after quotations in the text.

[33]   Bowman probably named this character Ki-chan after reading Huc's book because the text mentions Ki-chan, the imperial commissioner who engaged in negotiations in 1839 with Mr Elliott, the English plenipotentiary at Canton. Huc explains that Ki-chan was accused of betraying the Chinese and was banished to Tartary by the Emperor. Evariste Régis Huc, *Travels in Tartary, Thibet and China, During the Years 1844–1846*, trans. William Carew Hazlitt, 2nd reprint edn (2 vols, Chicago, 1900), p. 173.

and possibly threatening to the Chinese. Because their mission is to investigate China's arts and sciences, it was considered more neutral and 'safe', reflecting Bowman's stance as a female popularizer of science. However, though nominally scientific travellers, they also function as imperial agents because they survey the land and gather intelligence about China. As Sara Mills, Mary Louise Pratt, and others have demonstrated, female travel writers often represented the colonized country as a place abundant in flora and fauna which could be categorized by Western science.[34] Similarly, China is constructed as a treasure chest of flora and fauna waiting for Rolando and his friends to explore. The group takes the route from Canton to the Bohea Mountains in northern Fujian [now known as the Wuyi Mountains] that Scottish horticulturalist Robert Fortune (1812–1880) describes in *A Journey to the Tea Countries of China* (1852), and *Three Years' Wanderings in the Northern Provinces of China* (1847).[35] Bowman would probably have been familiar with Fortune's work because his books, which describe his experiences in China collecting plants for the Royal Horticultural Society and the East India Company, were reviewed in prominent newspapers and journals such as the *Edinburgh Review*. To enhance the element of danger in his books, Fortune allocates many pages to descriptions of his disguises, explaining to readers how he metamorphosed into a 'Chinaman' after shaving his head and wearing a pigtail. He emphasizes the threat of being exposed as a foreigner whereas Bowman's characters can travel safely throughout China undisguised. Even Rolando is surprised that 'none turned aside to notice [them]' (*TR* 250).

Unlike Fortune, who faced many difficulties travelling through China, the explorers travel with ease because they have the blessing of Ki-chan and the Emperor. Because the Emperor had given 'written orders to his people to aid all [their] wishes, and take no reward', Rolando and his friends are free to take what they desire (*TR* 258). Therefore they obtain, among other things, 'beautiful specimens' of many 'gorgeous flowers, yet unnamed by European botanists' (*TR* 309). Like Fortune, who introduced approximately 200 species of plants to England after his trips to China, Rolando's friends collect many specimens which will be shipped back to Europe to be categorized and classified. By engaging in these tasks, they are following in the footsteps of numerous voyagers who had, since the eighteenth century, travelled to distant lands to conduct trade as well as to discover and survey natural resources.[36] In describing the group's travels, the narrator invites young readers to also participate in the discovery process, gathering knowledge about the resources available in China.

---

[34] Sara Mills, 'Knowledge, Gender, and Empire', in Gillian Rose and Alison Blunt (eds), *Writing Women and Space: Colonial and Postcolonial Geographies* (New York, 1994), pp. 29–50 (p. 41).

[35] For more information about Fortune's life and travels to China, see Mary Gribbin and John Gribbin, *Flower Hunters* (Oxford, 2008), pp. 189–214.

[36] Mary Louise Pratt, *Imperial Eyes: Travel Writing and Transculturation* (London, 1992), p. 38.

During their travels, Rolando's friends learn about Chinese plants such as *Nelumbium* (lotus), *Cronton sebiferum* (tallow tree), *Gossypium religiosum* (shrubby cotton), and *Bambusa* (bamboo). According to Mary Ellen Bellanca, some critics believed that the use of scientific nomenclature in natural history writing 'connoted appropriate authority and credibility' while others found it was a sign of 'distasteful pomposity'.[37] In including the Latin names of the plants, Bowman may have been trying to boost her credibility as a popularizer of science. She may also have expected children to remember scientific plant names because nineteenth-century educators such as Alphonso Wood believed that memorizing scientific labels was an appropriate way to train children's minds in logic.[38] Perhaps this scientific nomenclature was included for the benefit of parents, because, according to Arthur Kenyon's *Letters from Spain, to his Nephews at Home* (1853), mothers read *The Travels of Rolando* to their children.[39]

The narrator seems to suggest that because Rolando and his friends are on a mission to 'diffuse, as well as to obtain knowledge' they can legitimately explore China, uncover all its secrets, and plunder all its riches (*TR* 207). China has remained closed for too long and would benefit greatly if it had contact with the outside world, especially Europeans. Ki-chan, who had 'learned something of that profound knowledge of science which distinguishes those great nations', extols the value of science and promotes the opening of China, remarking: 'were I absolute in China, I would throw open the gates of her capital to the world. I would barter her riches for the inventions of science, the treasures of art, the hoards of learning possessed by other nations' (*TR* 160; 191). Ki-chan's use of the word 'barter' hints at increased trade relations with Britain and an 'open door' policy which would make China's 'riches' available to the rest of the world. Although five treaty ports along the coast of China had recently been opened after the end of the First Opium War, the text suggests that China was still too insular and would benefit greatly if the 'guarded gate of the jealous empire' was flung wide open for travellers and merchants to enter at their will (*TR* 248). However, Bowman also adheres to her role as 'moral teacher' by criticizing 'the excessive love of gain of the foreign merchants' at Canton which has 'increased the natural antipathy the Chinese feel towards all strangers' (*TR* 318–19).

---

[37]   Mary Ellen Bellanca, *Daybooks of Discovery: Nature Diaries in Britain, 1770–1870* (Charlottesville, VA, 2007), p. 149.

[38]   Alphonso Wood was the author of *First Lessons in Botany: Designed for Common Schools in the United States* (1849). See Kaye Adkins, '"Foundation-Stones": Natural History for Children in *St. Nicholas Magazine*', in Sidney I. Dobrin and Kenneth B. Kidd (eds), *Wild Things: Children's Culture and Ecocriticism* (Detroit, 2004), pp. 31–47 (p. 40).

[39]   Arthur Kenyon, *Letters from Spain, to His Nephews at Home* (London, 1853), p. v.

The Pursuit of Knowledge

Aware of 'the charm of fiction to youthful readers', Bowman chose the adventure story genre to 'blend lessons of useful knowledge and Christian truth with a narrative of adventure'.[40] Throughout *The Travels of Rolando*, heavy emphasis is placed on the pursuit of knowledge and characters are commended for their efforts in obtaining it. For example, Rolando and his friends have a 'love of knowledge' and Ki-chan possesses an 'ardent desire for knowledge' (*TR* 121; 288). Rolando and his friends wish to travel 'in order to acquire knowledge' and believe that 'God sent [them] to be active and inquiring in the world, that [they] may improve [them] selves and all mankind, till the whole world has equal knowledge' (*TR* 28; 71). Rolando's statement echoes John F.W. Herschel's view that those 'who admire and love knowledge for its own sake ought to wish to see its elements made accessible to all ...'.[41] St Kassian highlights the importance of making knowledge accessible to everyone when he criticizes the fact that in ancient Egypt, 'knowledge was limited to the few, exclusively and jealously preserved by the priests and princes, and the people were but machines in their hands' (*TR* 3). He contrasts this with the current situation: 'education is spreading abroad, and will one day be diffused among all ranks, overthrowing the bulwarks of pride, and sweeping away the labyrinths of ignorance in its resistless course' (*TR* 3). For St Kassian, the ultimate goal of diffusing knowledge was to make all men brethren, which can only be achieved when the 'moral and intellectual progress of the age' is combined with the 'blessed light of Christianity' to 'raise the condition of humanity' (*TR* 3–4). These statements reflect the Enlightenment ideal of progress and the belief that knowledge should be made public and distributed equally, not hoarded by the select few.[42] Therefore the legacy of Jauffret's Enlightenment spirit can be felt throughout Bowman's sequel.

Bowman and Chinese Women

Considering Bowman's emphasis on achieving 'equal' knowledge and her vocation as a female writer, it is not surprising that she would be concerned about the education of Chinese women. In *The Boy Voyagers*, Bowman uses Miss Griffin, Minna's governess, to 'protest' against the 'despotism' over women in 'most eastern countries' (*BV* 372). Minna and Miss Griffin meet the 'tame and drowsy' wife and daughters of a Chinese merchant who seem to have 'no aim beyond that of dressing themselves to the greatest advantage' (*BV* 373). Readers are warned about the dangers of cultural insularity when they find 'the placid

---

[40]   Anne Bowman, *Esperanza; or, the Home of the Wanderers* (London, 1855), n. pag.

[41]   John F.W. Herschel, *A Preliminary Discourse on the Study of Natural Philosophy*, new edn (London, 1840), p. 69.

[42]   See Jeremy D. Popkin, 'Periodical Publication and the Nature of Knowledge in Eighteenth-Century Europe', in Donald R. Kelley and Richard H. Popkin (eds), *The Shapes of Knowledge from the Renaissance to the Enlightenment* (Dordrecht, 1991), pp. 203–13 (p. 211).

women of China rejoicing in their luxurious indolence' (*BV* 374). After conversing with the women, who demonstrate 'total absence of intellectual cultivation', Miss Griffin concludes that if the Chinese do not educate their women, there is no hope for 'the improvement and elevation of the character of the Chinese' (*BV* 373). Like Lucy Aikin who advocated female education and rights for women, Bowman emphasizes the importance of education for China's improvement process.

According to Kathyrn Ready, some Enlightenment historians 'saw a direct correlation between the status of women and the state of society as a whole'.[43] For example, William Alexander asserts in *The History of Women* (1779) that 'the rank and condition, in which we find women in any country, mark out to us with the greatest precision, the exact point in the scale of civil society, to which the people of such country have arrived'.[44] The condition of Chinese women in Bowman's books cannot compare with that of the British not only because they lack education, but also because of their bound feet, which Minna describes as 'odd-looking' and 'useless' (*BV* 374). After meeting the Chinese women Minna and Miss Griffin feel 'grateful that they had the freedom of thought, mental employment, and the perfect use of their limbs' (*BV* 374). Minna sympathizes with the foot-bound women, imagining that their feet must ache terribly. Bowman provides a detailed description of the process of foot-binding for readers who may be unfamiliar with it: 'in infancy the toes are bent over and bandaged, the pressure increasing from year to year, till at last the ball of the foot fits into the hollow of the sole, and forms that shapeless mass' (*BV* 374). Frank, who refers to the bound feet as 'hoofs', hopes that 'one of the first reforms the English introduce' will be 'the suppression of cruelty to the foot' (*BV* 374). However, the first English anti-footbinding society was only established in 1874 by John Macgowan (d. 1922) of the London Missionary Society and such societies only became more active almost 40 years after Bowman's book was published, when Alicia Little (1845–1926) founded the Society for the Suppression of Foot-Binding (Natural Foot Society) in 1895.[45] In criticizing the Chinese custom of foot-binding and raising awareness of the Chinese women's need for education, the narrator reiterates the idea of British superiority over the 'less-civilized' societies and the assumption that the British are morally obligated to help.

---

[43]   Kathryn Ready, 'The Enlightenment Feminist Project of Lucy Aikin's *Epistles on Women* (1810)', *History of European Ideas*, 31.4 (2005): pp. 435–50 (p. 440).

[44]   William Alexander, *The History of Women: From Their Earliest Antiquity, to the Present Time; Giving an Account of Almost Every Interesting Particular Concerning That Sex, Among All Nations, Ancient and Modern*, 3rd edn (2 vols, London, 1782), vol. 1, p. 151. A 'Ladies' Society for the Promotion of Female Education in China, India, and the East' was established in the first half of the nineteenth century.

[45]   For the history of foot-binding, see Hong Fan, *Footbinding, Feminism, and Freedom: The Liberation of Women's Bodies in Modern China* (Portland, OR, 1997) and Dorothy Ko, *Cinderella's Sisters: A Revisionist History of Footbinding* (Berkeley, 2005). For more information about the role missionaries played in anti-footbinding, see Alison R. Drucker, 'The Influence of Western Women on the Anti-Footbinding Movement 1840–1911', *Historical Reflections*, 8.3 (1981): pp. 179–99.

Returning Home

The characters in *The Boy Voyagers* leave China 'with little regret' because 'though the Chinese appeared to be a quiet people, and the land a fruitful land, none of them would choose to live amidst such perils and treacheries' (*BV* 382; 380). However, before sailing off, they manage to buy 'such Chinese curiosities as their purses could afford' (*BV* 381). Again, as in *The Travels of Rolando*, China is depicted as a treasure chest or a curiosity cabinet filled with wonderful objects available for the taking. Like the characters in *The Boy Voyagers*, Rolando and his friends also leave China 'without regret' having 'all enjoyed, in different degrees, [their] residence in this remarkable country ...' (*TR* 319). When Rolando prepares to leave China, Ki-chan seeks permission from the Emperor to travel to Europe to 'perfect himself in the knowledge of the languages, the useful arts and sciences, and the modes of government in the nations of Europe'. It is important to note, however, that he could only achieve this 'under [Rolando and his friends'] direction' (*TR* 288). Readers may have assumed that he would return to China to conduct reforms after 'perfecting' himself on the modes of government gleaned from European nations. However, according to Rolando, after Ki-chan arrives in England, he proposes to return to China 'occasionally, and enlighten with his experience his native land, but his habits and tastes are becoming every day more assimilated to those of the country we have adopted, and I trust we shall never lose him' (*TR* 399). There is little chance that Ki-chan would settle back in China after experiencing life in England.

Although Rolando is originally from France, Bowman's explorers ultimately settle down on a noble estate in one of England's most beautiful counties. Rolando confesses that though 'the spirit of adventure is not yet quenched', his friends 'unanimously declare they are satisfied to remain in a country where Art brings her wonders, and Nature her beauties, to your very feet; where a gentle sovereign rules lovingly a free people ...' (*TR* 399–400). This statement echoes Rolando's father's commands at the beginning of the story, when he tells Rolando to 'go forth into the world, study the wonders of creation, mark the good and evil of life. If you be spared, return home, to contrast the comforts of that home with the miseries you will have seen, and to thank God for his mercy in placing you in a land of civilization, plenty, and peace' (*TR* 44). These statements reveal Bowman's second purpose in disseminating knowledge of the world to children: she wishes to instill a greater appreciation and love for Britain, which is depicted as the ideal country. In other words, Bowman could expand Old Humphrey's assertion that 'The more I tell you of the great empire of China, the more, I trust, you will like Great Britain' to: 'the more I tell you about the world, the more, I trust, you will like Great Britain'.[46] The more Bowman's readers knew of other lands, the more they were able to use this knowledge to reflect back on Britain's position in the world and be grateful for their blessed homeland.

---

[46] Old Humphrey, *The Celestial Empire; or, Points and Pickings of Information About China and the Chinese* (London, 1844), p. 3.

Bowman was exceptional for being one of the first female authors to have established a reputation for boy's adventure fiction. However, she was still operating within accepted gender norms, because her stories set in China reflect feminine concerns such as natural history and foot-binding. Her representation of China is worth examining for the way she envisioned the country based on domestic willow pattern plates and highlighted the natural resources of a newly opened territory richly abundant with unfamiliar plants awaiting discovery. China is presented as a land ready for British intervention both in terms of religion and commerce because Ki-chan converts to Christianity and the Emperor gives Rolando and his friends permission to inspect China's industries. More importantly, the adventures that these characters experience ultimately lead them to a greater appreciation of God, for at the end of *The Boy Voyagers*, Bowman writes, 'their adventures would prove a confirmation of the truth that no people can be enlightened and happy who are not blessed with the knowledge of Christianity – the freedom of the children of God' (*BV* 406).

Although Bowman received mixed reviews from contemporary critics, most reviewers would probably have agreed on one thing: her stories 'never lose sight of [their] didactic aim'.[47] Another writer with a didactic goal was William Dalton, who won approbation from contemporary critics for penning book-length novels set in China which 'entwined the roses and lilies of romance around the sturdy tree of knowledge'.[48]

William Dalton's China

William Dalton wrote children's fiction set in places such as China, Japan, Africa, Ceylon, and the Indian Archipelago.[49] Little is known about his life, except that financial difficulties compelled him to apply three times to the Royal Literary Fund for assistance. In a letter of support addressed to the Fund, which had been established in 1790 to assist published authors with financial difficulties, Dalton's friend William Brough states that Dalton's 'unique' books demonstrate 'immense research' and that he was 'the first romance writer to open the rich mines of legendary and historic lore in the gigantic empires of the far East'.[50] Published in 1857, *The Wolf Boy of China; or Incidents and Adventures in the Life of Lyu-Payo* was Dalton's first children's book. On the inscription page, Dalton identifies

---

[47]   Horace Stebbing Roscoe St John, 'Our Library Table: The Kangaroo Hunters; or, Adventures in the Bush', *Athenaeum*, 1628 (1859): p. 48.

[48]   'The Wolf Boy of China', *Morning Post*, 10 December 1857, p. 3.

[49]   See *The English Boy in Japan; or, The Perils and Adventures of Mark Raffles among Princes, Priests, and People, of that Singular Empire* (London, 1858), *Lost in Ceylon: in the Woods and the Wilds of the Lion King of Kandy* (London, 1861), and *The Nest Hunters; or, Adventures in the Indian Archipelago* (London, 1863).

[50]   William Brough, 'Letter to the General Committee of the Royal Literary Fund', in *Archives of the Royal Literary Fund, 1790–1918* (London, 1982). For more information on the Fund, see Janet Adam Smith, *The Royal Literary Fund, 1790–1990* (London, [1990]).

the novel as a 'book for boys' and dedicates it to his son. Perhaps in an attempt to broaden the potential readership, publishers reprinted the book under the title *John Chinaman; or, Adventures in Flowery Land* in 1858. Besides *The Wolf Boy of China*, Dalton published two other books on China: *The War Tiger; or, Adventures and Wonderful Fortunes of the Young Sea Chief and His Lad Chow: A Tale of the Conquest of China* (1858) and *The Wasps of the Ocean; or, Little Waif and the Pirate of the Eastern Seas: A Romance of Travel and Adventure in China and Siam* (1864), the sequel to *The Wolf Boy of China*.

In contrast to *The Travels of Rolando* and *The Boy Voyagers*, *The Wolf Boy of China* received many reviews, almost all of them positive. Reviewers showered accolades on the book and recommended it for adults as well as children. For example, the *Morning Herald* stated that 'though designed for boys, we can testify that it has charms for old as well as young'.[51] By 1860 the book had already gone into its third edition.[52] In a letter written to the Royal Literary Fund on 3 November 1863, Dalton himself declares that his works 'attained a considerable popularity among all ages'. He attributes his books' mass-market appeal to 'the simple fact that each, in addition to its story, contains a mass of information historical, religious, legendary and otherwise connected with the hitherto but little known and less understood Empire of the East, not easily to be found elsewhere'.[53] His statement suggests that although there may have already been many volumes written about China by Jesuits and other specialists, these books were too erudite for the general public to appreciate.

Most of the contemporary reviews assert that the book is worth reading for its facts about China. A reviewer of *The Wolf Boy of China* in *The Observer* claimed, 'A more interesting and more complete collection, *in petto*, of all that has been known of China and the Chinese does not exist in the English language'.[54] In labelling the work as a 'complete' collection of 'all' that has been known of China, the reviewer is assessing the book based the standards set by the 'spirit of encyclopaedism'. As one critic observes, the Great Exhibition of 1851 'inspired and compelled the production of numerous narrative and cataloguing texts' that 'ordered the event' and 'gave meanings to its displays ...'.[55] Dalton may have been inspired by the Great Exhibition and the 'Ten Thousand Chinese Things' exhibition

---

[51] This quote comes from an advertisement for *The Wolf Boy of China* in 'Books Published by E. Marlborough and Co' (1866) found in Annie Ward, *My Mother, or Home Scenes in Yorkshire* (London, 1866).

[52] The second edition published by E. Marlborough lists the title as *The Wolf Boy of China. A Chinese Story: Being the Adventures of Lyu-Payo among Merchants, Mandarins, Soldiers, Sailors, and People both Wild and Civilized.*

[53] William Dalton, 'Letter to the General Committee of the Royal Literary Fund', in *Archives of the Royal Literary Fund, 1790–1918* (London, 1982).

[54] 'A "Wonder Book" on China', *The Times*, 11 September 1858, p. 9.

[55] Lara Kriegel, 'Narrating the Subcontinent in 1851: India at the Crystal Palace', in Louise Purbrick (ed.), *The Great Exhibition of 1851: New Interdisciplinary Essays* (Manchester, 2001), pp. 147–9.

to create his own 'exhibition catalogue' of China. In fact, some of the information included about China in the novel is lifted from William B. Langdon's *Descriptive Catalogue of the Chinese Collection*, suggesting that Dalton probably visited the exhibition.[56]

In *The Wolf Boy of China*, Dalton guides readers through China as if it was a large museum exhibition, filled with 'a mass of information' about the 'strange' customs and manners of the Chinese. Dalton's novel serves as a vehicle for 'displaying' an exotic China: festivals such as the moon festival, Feast of Flowers, and Feast of Lanterns are described in detail; as well as activities that range from cricket baiting to coal burning. Dalton deliberately allows his characters to travel all over China so that he can introduce various Chinese cities, landscapes, and landmarks such as the Great Wall, the Imperial Canal, Canton, and Peking. He transfers the 'spirit of encyclopaedism' into China when he describes the 'fresh butter exhibition' at the Feast of Flowers where 'there were historical and ethnographical portraits of all the different races ...' (184). In disseminating staggering amounts of 'facts' about China, Dalton presents himself as an expert on 'the Celestial Kingdom' who is able to lead children on a comprehensive tour of the country.

The Wolf Boy of China, set during the years after the First Opium War (1839–1842), possibly during the Miao Rebellion (1854–1873), which was a series of serious revolts that raged for almost 20 years in the province of Guizhou, features a half-British, half-Miao hero named Herbert Richardson, better known as Lyu Payo.[57] His father, Captain Richardson, is an English officer-turned-merchant, and his mother, Sang, is a Miao princess. Lyu is known as the 'wolf-boy' because his mother's family is 'a brave race, who live among the mountains, in the province of Kwei-chou, and are called by themselves the Miao-tse, but by the rest of the Chinese people, wolf-men and women' (15).[58] Richardson and his family live in Canton, where he runs a business with a Chinese Christian named Tchin, who had been saved by the Captain during the war. One day Tartar child-stealers attempt to kidnap Lyu.[59] While Captain Richardson and Tchin try to rescue the

---

[56]   For example, the reference to 'ya-yuh' (police) on page 173 can be found in the catalogue on page 32. Information about the Tan-hoo people on page 21 comes from page 70 of the catalogue. See William B. Langdon, *Ten Thousand Chinese Things*, 19th English edn (London, 1842).

[57]   The Miao are an ethnic minority in south China. For more information on the Miao Rebellion, see Robert D. Jenks, *Insurgency and Social Disorder in Guizhou: The 'Miao' Rebellion, 1854–1873* (Honolulu, 1994).

[58]   Miao actually means 'sprout' and tse [zi] means 'son' or 'child'. Since Dalton was basing most of his knowledge of the Miao and the Chinese on eighteenth-century sources, it is not that surprising that he wrote about the interracial marriage between Captain Richardson and Sang because *The Citizen of the World* (1762) ends with a letter from Oliver Goldsmith's fictional Chinese narrator Lien Chi Altangi writing that his son marries a European woman.

[59]   In Dalton's time, the word Tartar referred to the Manchus, rulers of the Qing dynasty.

boy, one of the thieves stabs the Captain. He falls into the river and disappears. After searching futilely for Richardson, Tchin assumes that his business partner is dead and offers to adopt Lyu and Sang as his children. He takes them to Peking to live with his brother Hieul and sister-in-law Chang, who secretly plot to get rid of the newcomers. Hieul's hopes for monetary gain are realized during the Feast of Lanterns, when he seizes the opportunity to take Lyu out alone after Tchin falls ill. Hieul sells Lyu to a bonze (Buddhist priest) who takes him to Kounboum [Kumbum, in historic Tibet, near Xining]. Lyu manages to escape from the city and overcomes many difficulties to be reunited with his family. They sail to the Portuguese colony of Macao. However, Lyu's grandfather dies before he can return to 'his beloved hills' and Sang and Lyu decide to stay in Macao because there is no reason for them to return to 'the mountains of *Koei-cheou*' now.[60] Therefore, Richardson and Tchin start another business in Macao and the family settles into their new life there.

The novel is significant for several reasons. First, it is one of the earliest full-length Victorian children's novels set in China that investigates the complexity and fluidity of mixed-race identity and identity formation through reading. Not only is it rare to find a mixed-race hero in nineteenth-century children's fiction, but few Victorian texts, not to mention children's books, deal with the complicated issues addressed in *The Wolf Boy of China*, such as the role of women, issues of religion, and, most notably that of racial tensions between the Han Chinese and other ethnic minorities such as the Miao, Tartars, and Si-fan [Xifan].[61] Secondly, one is able to reconstruct the author's reading about China from his novel, shedding light on the question of who was reading the numerous Victorian texts on China and what they did with the information. Third, although initially priced at five shillings, making it unaffordable for most British working-class families, and thus limiting its potential audience, the book was published in the United States and went into many editions, including a German translation, indicating its readership expanded to encompass Germans and Americans.[62]

---

[60] Dalton uses *Kwei-chou* at the beginning but *Koei-cheou* at the end of the book, suggesting that he consulted different sources. The fact that he did not use a uniform spelling for Guizhou could either be seen as an indicator of how he rushed to finish a manuscript without ensuring consistency or his uncertainty about how to reconcile different renderings of Chinese words.

[61] According to Robert H.G. Lee, 'Si-fan is the name applied to the nomadic Tibetans who occupied the large expanse of grassland situated at the headwaters of the Yellow River, the Min River, and the Chin-ch'uan River (the present Ahpa Tibetan Autonomous Chou)': Robert H.G. Lee, 'Frontier Politics in the Southwestern Sino-Tibetan Borderlands During the Ch'ing Dynasty', in Joshua A. Fogel and William T. Rowe (eds), *Perspectives on a Changing China: Essays in Honor of Professor C. Martin Wilbur on the Occasion of His Retirement* (Boulder, CO, 1979), pp. 35–68 (p. 36).

[62] William Dalton, *Lyu-Payo, Der Wolfssohn: Abenteuer, Natur–U. Sittenschilderungen, Kriegs– Und Friedensbilder Aus Dem Reiche Der Mitte*, trans. Johannes Ziethen (Leipzig, 1859).

It is clear that readers were expected to learn something from *The Wolf Boy of China*, because when they opened the 1884 edition of the book, they would have noticed a Chinese proverb on its title page: 'something is learned every time a book is opened'.[63] In addition to this proverb, each of the chapter titles is adorned by a Chinese adage and many others are interspersed throughout the text. Although Dalton does not specify his source, all of these proverbs are taken from Sir John Francis Davis's *The Chinese* (1836) and *Sketches of China* (1841), two critically acclaimed works that became popular among the general population because, according to the *Saturday Review*, they were 'readable' and 'easily accessible to the English public'.[64] Therefore, it is not surprising that Dalton read Davis's books while writing his novel.

Dalton and the French Sinologists

Dalton's main unacknowledged source of information on China was the English translation of the four-volume *Description geographique, historique, chronologique, politique, et physique de l'Empire de la Chine et de la Tartarie chinoise* (1735) by French Jesuit historian Jean-Baptiste Du Halde (1674–1734), who was responsible for editing missionary reports for *Lettres edifiantes et curieuses* (34 volumes, 1702–1776). Considered the most authoritative source on China until well into the nineteenth century, this work was translated into English not long after its publication. As critics have pointed out, eighteenth- and nineteenth-century writers who wished to delve into the topic of China could borrow from the works of Du Halde and did not have to worry about being accused of plagiarism if they quoted passages from the books without acknowledgement.[65] British writers could consult two English translations of Du Halde's work, Richard Brookes's *The General History of China* (1736) and Green and Guthrie's *A Description of the Empire of China* (1738–1741).

The most direct evidence of Dalton having read both translations lies in the names Lyu Payo, Hieul, and Tchin, which appear in a Chinese story entitled 'The Practice of Virtue Renders a Family Illustrious' that is included in volume 3

---

[63]   This aphorism is a translation of the Chinese proverb *kaijuan youyi* which could also be more literally translated as 'there are always advantages in opening a book'. Although Dalton does not specify his source, he most likely came across this saying in volume 2 of John Francis Davis's *The Chinese* because it is number 58 on Davis's list of Chinese 'Aphorisms'; See John Francis Davis, *The Chinese: A General Description of the Empire of China and Its Inhabitants* (2 vols, London, 1836), vol. 2, p. 161.

[64]   'The Chinese', *Saturday Review*, 25 July 1857, p. 87. See Davis, *The Chinese*, vol. 2, pp. 158–63; John Francis Davis, *Sketches of China: Partly during an Inland Journey of Four Months, between Peking, Nanking, and Canton; with Notices and Observations Relative to the Present War* (2 vols, London, 1841), vol. 2, pp. 94–100.

[65]   Qian Zhongshu, 'China in the English Literature of the Eighteenth Century', in Adrian Hsia (ed.), *The Vision of China in the English Literature of the Seventeenth and Eighteenth Centuries* (Hong Kong, 1998), pp. 117–213 (p. 120).

of *The General History of China* and in volume 2 of *A Description of the Empire of China*.[66] There are slight differences in the romanization of some of the characters' names in the two translations. Lyu Payo is probably a combination of Green and Guthrie's 'Lyu pau' ('Lyu, the Treasure') and Brookes's 'Liu pao' ('Liu the Treasure') because Dalton explains it means '*Lyu the Treasurer*', for Sang 'had resolved that her boy should be the treasurer of all her happiness' (16). Dalton also borrows from the plot line, making Tchin a kind merchant like the Tchin in the Chinese story, while basing Hieul's wicked behaviour on Lyu pau/Liu pao's dubious conduct. Instead of passively copying the entire plot of 'The Practice of Virtue Renders a Family Illustrious', however, Dalton transforms it into his own by making Lyu a young half-Miao, half-British hero who undergoes many trials and adventures throughout various parts of China.

Like Dalton, Du Halde, who lived in Paris all his life, did not have firsthand experience of China and relied on various sources for information on the country. He gathered information mostly from corresponding with Jesuit missionaries in China, reading their memoirs, conversing with them when they returned, or editing their reports. For example, Du Halde notes that he derived 'The Practice of Virtue Renders a Family Illustrious' from the work of Père D'Entrecolles (1664–1741), who travelled to China as a Jesuit missionary in the late 1600s.[67] Du Halde also consulted the works of Père Le Comte (1655–1728) in describing a 'young brisk Bonze', which Dalton used in his narrative of Lyu's first meeting with the bonze during the Feast of Lanterns.[68] Jesuit mathematician Louis Le Comte, who arrived in China in the 1680s and worked in Shanxi and Shaanxi, probably could not have anticipated that his observations on China would eventually be transmitted to readers centuries later in the form of a children's novel.[69]

The Wasps of the Ocean

Readers of the first edition of *The Wolf Boy of China* who were eager to find out what happened to Lyu in Macao would have had to wait seven years to read about his further adventures. In 1864, Dalton's publisher released his sequel to *The Wolf*

---

[66] See Jean-Baptiste Du Halde, *The General History of China: Containing a Geographical, Historical, Chronological, Political and Physical Description of the Empire of China, Chinese-Tartary, Corea and Thibet*, trans. Richard Brookes, 3rd edn (4 vols, London, [1736] 1741), vol. III, pp. 114–34 and Jean-Baptiste Du Halde, *A Description of the Empire of China and Chinese-Tartary, Together with the Kingdoms of Korea and Tibet: Containing the Geography and History (Natural as well as Civil) of those Countries*, trans. Green and Guthrie (2 vols, London, 1741), vol. 2, pp. 147–67.

[67] Du Halde, *The General History of China*, vol. III, pp. 44–5.

[68] Ibid., p. 44.

[69] Le Comte wrote a memoir called *Nouveaux memories sur l'etat present de la Chine*. For a biography of Le Comte, see John W. Witek, 'Louis Le Comte', in Gerald H. Anderson (ed.), *Biographical Dictionary of Christian Missions* (Grand Rapids, MI, 1999), p. 390.

Boy of China, entitled *The Wasps of the Ocean; or, Little Waif and the Pirate of the Eastern Seas: A Romance of Travel and Adventure in China and Siam*. Unlike the first book, which is narrated in the third person, the sequel is narrated by Lyu Payo/Herbert, now 20 years old. Herbert informs readers that his father would have 'ended his days in peace and prosperity' in Macao had it not been for two personal tragedies that occurred within the space of a week: the death of both his wife Sang and his business partner Ching (spelled Tchin in the first book). After this devastating loss, Captain Richardson does not wish remain in Macao and desires to return to England. However, some business affairs must be attended to in Siam before they can depart. Herbert, delighted at the prospect of returning to England, journeys to Bangkok to investigate the mysterious disappearance of their business contact Mi.

Herbert travels with Dick Orme, a 25-year-old Anglo-American who has been falsely accused of stealing from the San Francisco company that the Richardsons conduct business with. Dick heads for Siam because he believes the real thief, a man named Captain Crafty, is residing there. The 'Little Waif' in the book's title is a Caucasian girl dressed as a 'slim boy in a tattered dress, with a large slouch hat' who travels with Dick and Herbert because her adoptive aunt was killed by pirates, or as the Chinese call them, 'Wasps or Rats of the Ocean'.[70] Orphaned Little Waif, who has never known her real name or any relatives, is left with nobody to take care of her except Dick. After a series of plot twists, they eventually find Crafty and discover his relationship to Mi. Most surprisingly, readers are told that Crafty is Little Waif's father and Dick is her half-brother. In the end, Herbert and Little Waif marry in San Francisco and six months later they travel back to England with Captain Richardson. Herbert notes that they settle in a house in London – 'the very house, in fact, beneath the roof-tree of which I have so many months been penning the story of my travels and adventures in the lands and waters of the Golden Dragon and the White Elephant'.[71] Although Herbert was born in India and raised in China, this conventional ending represents his return to his 'real' home – metropolitan London, from which his experiences abroad could be narrated. Herbert's mixed-race background raises interesting questions about nineteenth-century notions of race.

The Mixed-Race Hero

The Wolf Boy of China and *The Wasps of the Ocean* are significant because very few mid-nineteenth-century children's texts feature mixed-race characters. In 1859, another Dalton novel featuring a mixed-race character was published: *The White Elephant; or, The Hunters of Ava and the King of the Golden Foot*. Câecile Parrish claims that the half-English, half-Laotian hero of *The White Elephant*

---

[70]   William Dalton, *The Wasps of the Ocean: or, Little Waif and the Pirate of the Eastern Seas: A Romance of Travel and Adventure in China and Siam* (London, 1869), pp. 36; 6.

[71]   Ibid., p. 412.

makes 'repeated derogatory generalisations about his fellow half-castes, such as "A rogue he may be, most half-castes are" or "all half-castes are treacherous"'.[72] However, she wrongly attributes these remarks to him because both of these statements are spoken by another character named Mr Johnson. In fact, the hero believes that the assertion 'all half-castes are treacherous' is 'ungenerous'.[73] While Parrish's argument that the Eurasian in nineteenth-century children's literature is a 'figure of fun: servile, ingratiating, pompous, longwinded ...' may be true in some cases, it does not apply in Dalton's novels.[74] Dalton treats his mixed-race characters favourably and does not represent them as 'marginal, tragically flawed' or 'deeply conflicted', which is often the case in mixed-race literature.[75]

Although Lyu is the hero of *The Wolf Boy of China*, he differs dramatically from the typical Caucasian adventure-story hero. Instead of being regarded with disgust for being a mixed-race child, Lyu navigates between the Miao, Si-fan, and Han communities with ease. Perhaps the reason Dalton chooses to make Lyu half-Miao instead of half-Han Chinese is because his audience knew relatively little about the Miao, but may have already had negative stereotypical ideas of the Chinese entrenched in their minds. Lyu's Miao background also heightens his marginal status as well as the 'romantic' or 'exotic' nature of *The Wolf Boy of China*. In addition, because the Miao were enemies of not only the ruling Manchu government, but also of the Han Chinese and Si-fan, the element of danger and excitement is increased.

In 1854, Swiss scientist Louis Agassiz stated that 'nobody can deny that the offspring of different races is always a half-breed, as between animals of a different species, and not a child like either its mother or its father'.[76] 'Half-breeds' were believed to be sterile and degenerate. Therefore, Victorians anxious about 'the survival of the superior "race"' felt strongly about maintaining racial purity.[77] In discussing the representation of Eurasians in late nineteenth- and early twentieth-century British Indian literature, Loretta M. Mijares comments that as a standard trope, the half-caste is 'granted a strange agency' where he has the power 'to choose the inherent qualities of his own make-up' and 'is generally perverse enough to pick the worst qualities of the two races'.[78] Mijares posits that

---

[72] Câecile Parrish, *The Image of Asia in Children's Literature, 1814–1964* (Clayton, Vic., 1977), p. 25.

[73] William Dalton, *The White Elephant; or, the Hunters of Ava and the King of the Golden Foot* (New York, 1860), p. 54.

[74] Parrish, *The Image of Asia*, p. 25.

[75] For analysis of tragic mixed-race characters see Jonathan Brennan, 'Introduction', in Jonathan Brennan (ed.), *Mixed Race Literature* (Stanford, 2002), pp. 1–56; Isabelle Thuy Pelaud, '"Mettise Blanche": Kim Lefvre and Transnational Space', in Jonathan Brennan (ed.), *Mixed Race Literature* (Stanford, 2002), pp. 122–36.

[76] 'Agassiz and the Edinburgh Chair of Natural History', *The Monthly Journal of Medicine*, XX (1855): pp. 363–73 (p. 368).

[77] Ibid.

[78] Loretta M. Mijares, 'Distancing the Proximate Other: Hybridity and Maud Diver's *Candles in the Wind*', *Twentieth Century Literature*, 50.2 (2004): pp. 107–41 (p. 120).

'[t]his convoluted rhetoric of relocated agency and blame enables a disavowal not only of responsibility to the entity fathered by the colonizer but also of similitude between father and bastard child'.[79]

Dalton's presentation of a mixed-race character does not reinforce the widely held stereotypes about 'worst qualities' and instead emphasizes positive qualities and strengths. Not only is Captain Richardson a responsible father who loves his son, there is also a striking similarity between the two. Contrary to possessing the worst qualities of the Miao 'race' and the British 'race', Lyu seems to have inherited the positive traits of both – courage, compassion, filial piety, intelligence, nobility, physical strength, and Christian morality. In 1854, Josiah C. Nott (1804–1874) expressed the view that '[t]he infusion of even a minute proportion of the blood of one race into another, produces a decided modification of moral and physical character'.[80] Most Victorians believed this 'modification' resulted in weakened offspring, but in the case of Lyu, the modification that occurs is a positive one.

On the racial hierarchy, Dalton places the minority 'races' in China (Miao and Si-fan) high above the majority (Han). According to Dalton's description, the Miao are a 'simple people', 'uniformly good-tempered, pleasing, and industrious' (248; 247). Considering that he consulted the works of Charles Gutzlaff, who describes Guizhou as the 'Switzerland of China', it is not surprising that Dalton informs readers that Lyu found 'freedom and hospitality' everywhere in Guizhou (246).[81] Gutzlaff also compares the Miao to the Scottish Highlanders.[82] In the novel, Dalton draws a parallel between the Miao and the Scottish when he compares Lyu's perseverance to that of Scottish hero Robert the Bruce (1274–1329), 'who, after many failures in his attempt to beat King Edward, happening to see a spider after many failures succeed in reaching its web, made another effort, beat Edward, and became king of Scotland' (262). The story of Robert the Bruce and the spider was popularized by Sir Walter Scott (1771–1832) in his children's history of Scotland *Tales of a Grandfather* (1828–1830). Like Scott, Dalton presents a nostalgic yearning for the romantic past as reflected in the Miao, who are independent, brave, and proud. In creating a romantic adventure in the tradition of Scott, Dalton is encouraging readers to approach *The Wolf Boy of China* as they would a novel by the popular writer, providing them with a familiar framework to receive the book.

---

[79]   Ibid.

[80]   Lola Young, 'Hybridity's Discontents: Rereading Science and "Race"', in Avtar Brah and Annie E. Coombes (eds), *Hybridity and Its Discontents: Politics, Science, Culture* (London, 2000), pp. 154–70 (p. 157).

[81]   Charles Gutzlaff, *China Opened: or, a Display of the Topography, History, Customs, Manners, Arts, Manufactures, Commerce, Literature, Religion, Jurisprudence, etc. of the Chinese Empire* (2 vols, London, 1838), vol. 1, p. 163.

[82]   The British have admired the strong martial qualities of 'highlanders' such as Nepal's Gurkhas. For more detailed discussion, see Lionel Caplan, '"Bravest of the Brave": Representations of "The Gurkha" in British Military Writings', *Modern Asian Studies*, 25.3 (1991): pp. 571–97.

Dalton describes Lyu's personality traits in much more detail than his physical appearance. In fact, not much is known about Lyu's physical features except that he wears a queue and has a fair complexion. With the exception of the bonze, nobody else in the novel seems to recognize him as a Eurasian child. Unlike half-castes in colonial fiction, Lyu does not pose a 'threat' because he never attempts to 'pass' as British and does not possess the 'dangerous invisibility' that colonial writers were often anxious about.[83] In choosing not to emphasize physical features, Dalton is implying that 'knowledge' of a culture is possibly more important for survival. For example, it is not enough for Captain Richardson to go undetected disguised as a boatman while searching for Lyu. In order to obtain vital information about where his kidnapped son might be held, he must use his knowledge of Chinese customs. When he spots a sympathetic-looking Chinese man, Richardson laments that he had lost his only son and 'would have no child behind him to perform the customary ceremonies at his funeral or sweep his tomb', knowing that the Chinese man would consider this a serious misfortune and offer to help (21).

In choosing to refer to his hero as 'Lyu' rather than 'Herbert' in *The Wolf Boy of China* Dalton seems to focus on Lyu's 'Miao-ness' more than his 'British-ness'. Although Lyu's 'wolf' side is emphasized, most of the time he passes off as a Han Chinese and his ability to do so ensures his survival. In fact, although both of his parents are not Han Chinese, he is educated as one. Lyu speaks Mandarin Chinese and the Miao dialect, but the novel does not mention him speaking English, although it may be assumed that he uses this language when conversing with his father. In the sequel, however, although Herbert states that he 'may fairly claim to be considered worthy' of both [English and Chinese] nations, 'or at least no disgrace to either', he does not exhibit any 'Chinese' characteristics in the book.[84] Furthermore, he does not mention that his mother is Miao and not Han Chinese, which was so crucial in the first book.

As a mixed-race character who can shift between British and Chinese identities with ease, Herbert spends the first half of his youth 'under the tutelage of Chinese scholars' and the latter 'under that of an English missionary'.[85] Because of his racial ambiguity, he can shed the markers of his 'Chinese' identity like a chameleon when it suits him. Dalton's characters are able to make the most of the fluidity of their racial identity. As Robert Young points out, Anthony Trollope argued for the advantages of racial 'amalgamation' in *The West Indies* (1859) because he believed it would be beneficial for colonization to have 'different attributes of black and white'.[86] However, because Dalton's characters do not stay in China, his reasons for supporting racial amalgamation seem to have little to do with colonization.

---

[83] Mijares, 'Distancing the Proximate Other', p. 115.

[84] Dalton, *Wasps*, p. 1.

[85] Ibid.

[86] Robert Young, *Colonial Desire: Hybridity in Theory, Culture and Race* (London, 1995), p. 141.

Jonathan Brennan observes that in mixed-race texts, there is a tradition of 'successive naming' (the adoption of new names at a critical juncture in life) and 'multiple naming' (the acquisition and use of multiple names).[87] The critical juncture in Lyu Payo/Herbert's life occurs when he is 20. In adopting the name Herbert after his mother's death and preparing to return to England, he casts off his Chinese name and takes on his English one to mark his affiliation with the British. Not only does Herbert have a new name, he has also constructed a new identity through his European clothing. This change could also be an outward symbol of the transition from childhood to adulthood. The difference between the 'old' Herbert and the 'new' Herbert is particularly evident when comparing illustrations in *The Wolf Boy of China* and *The Wasps of the Ocean*. Because image and text work together to affect reader reception, it is important to consider how the mixed-race Lyu/Herbert is visually depicted in both novels.

Dalton does not provide many details of Lyu/Herbert's physical features. Therefore the illustrators of *The Wolf Boy of China* and *The Wasps of the Ocean* could utilize the ambiguity of his physical appearance for their own purposes. As can be seen in Figure 2.1 and Figure 2.2, the younger Lyu/Herbert bears no similarity to his older self. In Figure 2.1, an illustration in *The Wolf Boy of China* by M'Connell, he wears Chinese style dress and has a pigtail. His embroidered clothes suggest that he comes from a wealthy family. In Figure 2.2, an illustration by C.F. Nicholls from *The Wasps of the Ocean*, Lyu/Herbert has grown up (signified by his moustache). He has completely morphed into a Caucasian-looking man for his pigtail has been replaced by short curly hair; instead of dressing in loose-fitting Chinese clothes, he wears a tailored European suit and hat. In Macao, which he describes as a 'half Portuguese, half Chinese city', he does not have to pass for a Han Chinese, and therefore no longer needs a pigtail. Because Herbert is a businessman in Macao, perhaps the illustrator felt a suit was the most proper attire for someone conducting international business, but Herbert's physical features are distinctly different: he has thick eyebrows and his eyes look much larger.

Readership

In recent years, scholars have highlighted the importance of examining marginalia to illuminate reading practices and provide insights into how readers responded to a text. For example, H.J. Jackson has demonstrated that children's marginalia can reveal readers' attitudes in 'a particularly raw state'.[88] Marginalia in my personal copy of a 1884 American edition of *The Wolf Boy of China* reveals that although Dalton identified the novel as a 'book for boys' and dedicated it to his son, at least one girl owned and read the novel. Her name can be found in several places in the

---

[87]   Brennan, 'Introduction', p. 24.
[88]   H.J. Jackson, *Marginalia: Readers Writing in Books* (New Haven, 2001), p. 19.

LYU'S ADVICE TO THE BONZE.

Page 67.

Fig. 2.1   'Lyu's advice to the bonze', from *The Wolf Boy of China* (1884 edition).

book: 'Elizabeth Lin' and 'Lizzie' are written in cursive at the top and right-hand side of the illustration to page 67 and on page 217, her full name is written out: 'Elizabeth Linster'. The name 'Elizabeth' was once imprinted on the title page but has since been erased. This repetition of names coincides with Jackson's observation that children frequently wrote their names 'over and over again in one book'.[89]

---

[89]   Ibid.

THE HAPPY RESULT.

Fig. 2.2   'The happy result', from *The Wasps of the Ocean* (1864) (The
                Bodleian Libraries, The University of Oxford. Shelfmark 250
                m.227, image between pages 406 and 407).

It also may indicate how much Elizabeth valued 'ownership' of a book: by inscribing her name on the book, she is asserting that it is her possession. Elizabeth engaged with the text by copying the title on top of pages 15 and 218 – 'The "Wolf-People"' and 'Lyu sails to the West', but what is most interesting is her opinion written at the end of the first chapter – 'pretty good' (16) (see Figure 2.3). Although nothing is known about Elizabeth's age and family background or when and where she read the book, her positive assessment indicates that at least one female reader enjoyed the first chapter of the story.

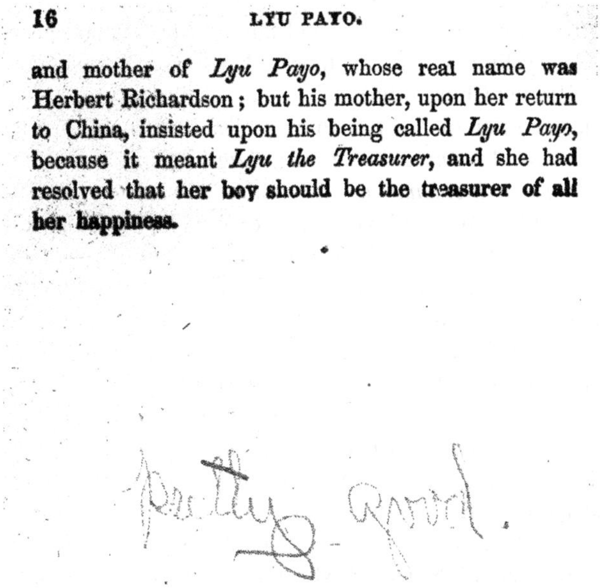

16   **LYU PAYO.**

and mother of *Lyu Payo*, whose real name was Herbert Richardson; but his mother, upon her return to China, insisted upon his being called *Lyu Payo*, because it meant *Lyu the Treasurer*, and she had resolved that her boy should be the treasurer of all her happiness.

Fig. 2.3   Marginalia in *The Wolf Boy of China* (1884 edition).

In 'Reading as Poaching', Michel de Certeau argues that the reader 'invents in texts something different from what they "intended." He detaches them from their (lost or accessory) origin. He combines their fragments and creates something un-known in the space organized by their capacity for allowing an indefinite plurality of meanings'.[90] As de Certeau suggests, the process of reading itself is a creative one that can lead to a variety of meanings. The idea of readers as poachers

---

[90] Michel de Certeau, 'Reading as Poaching', in *The Practice of Everyday Life*, trans. Steven Rendall (Berkeley, 2002), pp. 165–76 (p. 169).

can be seen in a further example of a childhood experience of engaging with *The Wolf Boy of China* from the late American politician John E. McDonough's *Idyls of the Old South Ward* (1932). McDonough's memoir about growing up in Chester, Pennsylvania calls into question simplistic assumptions about the child reader.

Although the evidence of reading provided in McDonough's memoir may not represent a typical reader's experience, it elucidates how readers can assert their individualism and refuse to be controlled by a text. In addition, it shows that reading is influenced by a range of contexts. McDonough (d. 1944) recalls that when he was a child, he often went to visit his eccentric friend Frederick J. Hinkson, Jr., a former active Republican who had retired from politics to sell shoe supplies. Before the Fourth of July celebrations of 1882, Hinkson had given the young McDonough money to buy books for his library. Given the freedom to choose books based on his 'whim and fancy', McDonough purchased '"The Phantom Wife," by Emma Garrison Jones; "Kit Carson's Revenge," by Beadle, and "The Wolf Boy in China"' (95).

An American edition of *The Wolf Boy of China* was published under the title *John Chinaman; or, Adventures in Flowery Land* in Boston in 1858 and as *The Wolf Boy of China; or Incidents and Adventures in the Life of Lyu-Payo* in 1859. Because the title of McDonough's volume, 'The Wolf Boy in China' differs slightly from *The Wolf Boy of China* and the name of the author is not specified, it is possible that he had bought a pirated copy of Dalton's work. Furthermore, because it cost less than 20 cents, making it significantly cheaper than the 5-shilling first British edition and the 75-cent first American edition, we can see that the book was later marketed as popular literature along with Beadle's dime novels.

It is worth noting that McDonough purchased books based on personal preferences, which supports Jan Fergus's argument that children have agency – not only do they decide what they want to read, sometimes their tastes differ from people's expectations.[91] For example, Fergus discovered in the borrowing records of Rugby students that boys aged 8 to 14 read *Goody Two-Shoes*, traditionally considered a 'girl's book'. Similarly, McDonough made an unexpected choice in 'The Phantom Wife' because Emma Garrison Jones was noted for writing women's romance fiction such as *Will She Win?* (1888), *Lady Ryhope's Lover* (1890), and *Wedded in a Hour* (1891).

Perhaps taking McDonough's interests into consideration, Hinkson discarded the other two books and 'plunged into' 'The Wolf Boy in China', the story of 'a boy of a wolf clan who was journeying through the Celestial Kingdom, as it was then known'. In this 'interesting book for male juvenile readers', one of the most notable characters 'was a philosophic old soul who after the manner of Confucius expressed himself in cryptic parable, adage and proverb, one of which seemed to roll off his lips for all of the situations in the book' (95). Festivals seem to be the

---

[91] Jan Fergus, 'Solace in Books: Reading Trifling Adventures at Rugby School', in Andrea Immel (ed.), *Childhood and Children's Books in Early Modern Europe, 1550–1800* (New York, 2006), pp. 243–59 (p. 245).

least likely of times for reading, but during the reading process, children such as McDonough seem to be able to enter a space where noises are temporarily blocked out, because he describes engaging with the text of 'The Wolf Boy in China' as a 'quiet dissipation', suggesting that he became oblivious to the 'incessant discharge of fireworks' outside (95). As de Certeau describes of reading, 'to read is to be elsewhere, where *they* are not, in another world'.[92] Instead of merely reading the book aloud, Hinkson translated the text into Latin and before the evening passed, a 'considerable' portion of the work had 'become clothed in Latin, in which translation the subtle humor of the old philosopher was developed in a delightfully amusing way' (95). A knock at the door interrupted the process of translation, forcing them to leave the 'merry sheets of the Latinized "Wolf Boy"' aside (96). The unexpected callers, a woman and her uncle, were descendents of the Salkelds, the original owners of the house, who had come seeking a memorandum of the family. On the eve of Independence Day celebrations, Hinkson shared some 'interesting gossip of pre-independence days' with his visitors and rummaged through his documents, producing a letter penned by a previous Salkeld (97). Because he was unwilling to part with the letter, the woman copied its contents on the 'back of a sheet of Latinized "Wolf Boy in China"', making her yet another potential reader or user of the Hinkson version of Dalton's text (99).

After the pair departed, Hinkson and McDonough returned to the story. McDonough's experience with the text became even more interesting when Hinkson, finding Lyu's 'journey through the Gobi desert ... so drab', asked the boy 'to provide an appropriate melody with which to cheer him on his perilous way' (99). Before the fireworks ushered in the first minutes of the Fourth of July, McDonough, choosing the melody of the latest popular ballad 'Oh Dem Golden Slippers', pretended to be Lyu singing in the Gobi desert. Rather than regarding Lyu as the undesirable 'Other' and wishing to distance himself from this mixed-race character, McDonough channels Lyu in his performance.

Considering that African-American Philadelphian James A. Bland's song 'Oh Dem Golden Slippers' (1879) was itself is a parody of the spiritual song 'Golden Slippers', McDonough's ability to transform a 'serious' text such as *The Wolf Boy of China* into something light and comical becomes even more noteworthy. Reading this book and translating it into Latin during America's celebration of Independence Day, Hinkson and McDonough asserted their own independence from any message the author may have been trying to convey. Instead of being manipulated by the text, they literally 'poached' it (to borrow de Certeau's term) and invested it with new meaning in the act of translation and performance.

De Certeau, employing the image of readers as travellers, argues that they are 'like nomads poaching their way across fields they did not write, despoiling the wealth of Egypt to enjoy it themselves'.[93] McDonough and his friend took 'a trip into China' along with Lyu, but instead of being submissive recipients of

---

[92]   de Certeau, 'Reading as Poaching', p. 173 (emphasis in the original).

[93]   Ibid., p. 174.

'knowledge' of China transmitted from the thirteenth century onwards, they were active playful readers who worked collaboratively to find amusement in the text and creatively appropriated it for their own purposes. Regardless of the accuracy of the information presented about China in this novel, they enjoyed engaging with the text, interpreting it, and giving it new meaning.

The inherent unpredictability and creativity of reading is demonstrated both in Dalton's writing of *The Wolf Boy of China* and the reactions of child readers to the text. Dalton's 'Celestial Kingdom' came into being through the process of reading and poaching, modifying and transforming, imagining and creating. Rather than merely writing a colonialist text set on securing the child reader into the imperial ethos, Dalton produced a cultural space from which a plurality of meanings could proliferate in unexpected ways. The novel illustrates children's literature's 'paradoxical' nature because it contains both didactic and subversive elements that simultaneously resist and reinforce orientalizing tendencies and positions. On one hand, Dalton was continuing in the long tradition of writers who replicated textual knowledge in their confidence that the world could be recreated and contained in a book. On the other, he created a vision of China that was far from simplistic.

Conclusion

Robert Knox, the influential British lecturer on anatomy wrote of the Chinese in 1850:

> China appears to have been completely stationary; she neither invented nor discovered; their arts must have belonged to some other race, from whom she borrowed without rightly comprehending them. Their religion is a puzzle; their morals of the lowest; of science they can have none, nor is it clear that they comprehend the meaning of the term. A love for science implies a love of truth: now truth they despise and abhor. I do not believe there is an individual Chinaman who could be made to comprehend a single fact in physical geography. So profound was their ignorance, their want of foresight and of common sense, that they could not send a single person to Europe so as to give any information about the armament which ultimately overthrew and plundered them. An English or French engineer possesses more practical knowledge than the united *savans* of their empire.[94]

Compared to Knox's evaluation of the Chinese, Anne Bowman and William Dalton provided a more complex vision of China in their novels for children. One cannot come to a simple conclusion about Victorian children's texts on China because there are complicated views expressed in many of them. Even within the 1850s timeframe, the representation of China and the Chinese differed dramatically in the works of two authors who imparted and popularized 'knowledge' on China by incorporating 'facts' about China from leading China 'experts' of the time into

---

[94]   Robert Knox, *The Races of Men: A Fragment* (Philadelphia, 1850), p. 188.

their fiction. Moreover, even the depiction of the Chinese in their earlier novels (*The Travels of Rolando* and *The Wolf Boy of China*) compared with the portrayal of the Chinese in their later books (*The Boy Voyagers* and *The Wasps of the Ocean*) differs, because in the later novels we find more negative or conservative views of the Chinese. Bowman's Chinese are admired for their industrious character in *The Travels of Rolando* while the 'Celestials' are condemned for being scoundrels in *The Boy Voyagers*. Similarly, Lyu's 'Miao-ness' is celebrated in *The Wolf Boy of China* but he is 'whitened' and settles down to a typical English gentleman's life in London at the end of *The Wasps of the Ocean*. This conventional conclusion to the sequel of *The Wolf Boy of China* suggests that as a grown man, Lyu/Herbert loses the freedom to be radically different. Although Dalton reverts to a less radical image of the mixed-race hero, he seems to have gained more knowledge of the Chinese language over the years because his decision to change Tchin's name to 'Ching' in *The Wasps of the Ocean* indicates he may have noticed the difference between the French and British system of romanizing Chinese and chose to use the British method in his sequel.

Although a considerable amount of knowledge about China had already been published in the mid-nineteenth century, available sources for information on its interior provinces were more limited because Bowman and Dalton were preparing their novels before the signing of the Treaties of Tianjin (which allowed foreigners to traverse beyond the 30-mile boundary surrounding the treaty ports) in 1858. Therefore, many of their sources were published in the eighteenth century and both novelists reveal the effects of reading these Enlightenment texts in their writings for the Victorian junior reader. For Bowman, nature pointed to the existence of a Creator and therefore the more knowledge children gained of the natural world, the greater their reverence would be for God and the divine order. In addition to reflecting Enlightenment belief in natural theology, Bowman increased awareness of China's natural resources via borrowed passages from Robert Fortune's books, while Dalton contributed to raising awareness of the different ethnic groups in China, particularly the Miao, via Du Halde's voluminous works. Bowman presents a more conventional view of China and the Chinese, painting the land as a rich emporium and imagining the landscape through the romanticized vision of the 'China' depicted on willow pattern plates and porcelain cups. Dalton also refers to these familiar household items but conveys an entirely different interpretation of the Chinese painted on them. The narrator of *The Wolf Boy of China* claims that the Chinese people, who look 'so ridiculous on our plates and dishes, for the simple reason that, having paid very little attention to the art of drawing, they have caricatured themselves … have really some reason to be proud of their race' because they invented and discovered many things such as gunpowder, paper money, and printing.[95] Readers are informed that in reality the Chinese are *not* caricatures but highly creative, pragmatic people who contributed many useful inventions.

---

[95] Dalton, *The Wolf Boy*, pp. 10–11.

One of Bowman's main purposes for disseminating knowledge about China and the rest of the world was to instill greater appreciation for Great Britain, 'a country ... where amidst the glorious vestiges of the past blossoms the promise of a still more glorious future' (*TR* 400). She exhibited confidence in the benefits of opening China up for religious and commercial purposes. Because she was writing after Britain's victories in the First Opium War and the signing of the Treaty of Nanjing (1842) while Dalton was penning his story during the Arrow Incident (1856) which sparked the Second Opium War, it is not surprising that Bowman was more hopeful about 'free trade' in China and the positive influence this would have on Britain.

Compared to Bowman, Dalton presents a much bleaker view of England's future, because a description of the Tower of the Thundering Winds in *The Wolf Boy of China*, which 'was built in the time of the philosopher Confucius, 2,500 years since' and 'now only partly in ruins', causes the narrator to ask,

> Where shall we all be in 2,500 years hence? Whole empires will have arisen, decayed, and become lost; nay, perhaps, the civilized inhabitants of some yet undiscovered country, may be sending out vessels of discovery to dig from the bowels of the earth monuments of that mighty England, that they will only know as we know Pompeii, Xanthus, and other cities – from books.[96]

Dalton's rumination on the rise and fall of empires reflects eighteenth-century and early nineteenth-century ambivalences about the pursuit of Empire. The image of 'ruins' in *The Wolf Boy of China* point to the Romantic poets' works and C.F. Volney's *The Ruins, or Meditations on the Revolutions of Empires and the Law of Nature* (1791), which highlights the transience of empire. While writing about China, Dalton is meditating on Britain: he is not confident that 'mighty England' will still reign supreme in 2,500 years. The disturbing fact is that England's status as a powerful empire would not be everlasting because empires inevitably decline. Ultimately the light emanating from Britain's glorious monuments will be extinguished. However, the narrator emphasizes that books containing knowledge about England will survive, just as texts about Xanthus and Pompeii did.

While Bowman and Dalton were writers who provided a great deal of information on China based on extensive research, the next chapter will focus on Edwin Harcourt Burrage, an author who approached China and the Chinese from an entirely different perspective.

---

[96]   Ibid., p. 300.

Chapter 3
From Comic Trickster to Brilliant Detective: E. Harcourt Burrage's 'Immortal' Ching-Ching

A description of Canton would not fail to be interesting, for it is one of the most densely-populated places in the world. Its teeming life, its narrow streets, its gates, and the wall that surrounds it, the population on its river, and all the quaintness that distinguishes it throughout, have been written of again and again, and every schoolboy ought to know something of its wonders.

—E. Harcourt Burrage, *Daring Ching Ching* (1886)[1]

Fig. 3.1   'The stern dipped under the water and put them all in peril', from *Cheerful-Daring-Wonderful Ching-Ching* (n.d.).[2]

---

[1]   E. Harcourt Burrage, *Cheerful-Daring-Wonderful Ching-Ching* (London, [n.d.]), p. 233.

[2]   Ibid.

Sir John Francis Davis, Robert Fortune, and other authors consulted by Anne Bowman and William Dalton in the 1850s all wrote about Canton. By the 1880s, this important treaty port had become so familiar to the British that Edwin Harcourt Burrage (1839–1916), author of *Daring Ching Ching, or, the Mysterious Cruise of the Swallow*, felt justified in not providing a 'full description' of it because 'all the quaintness that distinguishes it throughout, have been *written of again and again*' [my emphasis].[3] He urged ignorant readers to 'rush to his geography' for information regarding this 'famous Chinese port' because they would not find many details about it in his story.[4] Although Burrage wrote 'every schoolboy ought to know something of its wonders', he chose not to mediate this growing knowledge about Canton and China for his young readers, encouraging them to consult the vast resources available to them on their own. He was confident they would be able to find the information themselves, a sentiment shared by an author for the children's periodical *Chatterbox* (1886–1953) who claimed in 1881: 'It is simply impossible to describe China in two columns or so of Chatterbox. Nor is it necessary. The knowledge of young people is so increased, that, as Lord Macaulay was called "A Book in Breeches," so every schoolboy may be termed "A Geography in Trowsers [*sic*]."'[5] The *Chatterbox* author and Burrage were optimistic about the amount of knowledge children were receiving in school and their ability to gather information on their own without guidance from adults.

Burrage's approach to dealing with China and the Chinese thus differed dramatically from Bowman and Dalton: he was more interested in amusing his readers than imparting knowledge of China to them. This is indicative of the trend in children's literature in the latter part of the nineteenth century which saw a departure from an emphasis on instruction to an emphasis on amusement. In addition, the fact that Burrage was a hack writer who was pressured to produce several serials each week also suggests he probably would not have had time to research the places he was writing about. Burrage does not seem to have consulted any secondary texts for his descriptions of China for this brief episode in *Daring Ching Ching* and probably based them on his limited knowledge and impressions of the country. For example, the scenes in China are compared to 'a willow-pattern plate multiplied by ten thousand, with hundreds of additional specimens of quaintness in it' such as 'uncouth idols, representations of monsters, odd-looking, unnatural shrubs, and a variety of Chinese eccentricities queer enough in appearance to take one's breath away'.[6] As can be seen in Figure 3.1,

---

3   Ibid., p. 224.

4   Ibid. Geography books that mention Canton include John Guy, *Geography for Children*, 21st edn (London, 1848), p. 78; Nicolas Lenglet Dufresnoy, *Geography for Children, or, a Short and Easy Method of Teaching and Learning Geography: Designed Principally for the Use of Schools*, 22nd edn (London, 1806), pp. 99–100; *Geography, by a Lady; for the Use of Children* (London, 1849), p. 83.

5   'A Tour around the World: 16. China', *Chatterbox*, XXII (1881): p. 174.

6   Burrage, *Cheerful-Daring-Wonderful Ching-Ching*, pp. 230–31.

the prominent pagoda in the background and the Chinese man on the right-hand side of the illustration suggest that China is visualized through familiar household items like the willow pattern plate. Although Bowman also envisaged China based on her idea of porcelain, she presented the country as charming and picturesque while Burrage depicted it as an odd curiosity.

The characters in *Daring Ching Ching*, led by Handsome Harry, sojourn in Canton as they attempt to stop a villain named Adrian. Ira Staines, a young American who has joined Handsome Harry's crew, regards China as a 'barbarian country' and emphasizes the importance of being acquainted with 'the language and manners and customs of the people' so that one is not misunderstood or 'taken up, hanged, or shot, or goodness knows what'.[7] However, unlike Ki-chan in Bowman's *The Travels of Rolando* who introduces the language, manners and customs of the Chinese to Rolando, Ching-Ching, who is supposedly from Peking, is unable to function as a cultural informant for his non-Chinese friends because he cannot communicate with the Chinese people he encounters in Canton, where he feels he is 'among barbarians who knew not his tongue'.[8] In using the word 'barbarians' to describe the Southern Chinese, the narrator distances Ching-Ching from them.

Attempts at conversation with the Governor of Canton fail because neither had 'the least notion what the other said'.[9] There are two possible reasons for this difficulty in communication. First, Burrage may have been accurately representing the dialect differences between the Northerners and the Southerners of China. However, when confronted with the question of where he is from, Ching-Ching merely replies that he lives in England but evades the question of whether he is a 'native of England'. His initial response to the question is 'I arsk [*sic*] dem, I say, if dey see any reasoners for axing ob a queshion?' When asked again, he answers 'Dat am de queshion ob an ass!'[10] Therefore the scene may be hinting that Ching-Ching is perhaps not really from China, because the narrator describes him as being 'wonderfully overcome' by the Governor's garden, which 'are to be found in every part of China'. If Ching-Ching was really from Peking, the text suggests, he would not have expressed 'astonishment' at the Governor's garden because 'there must have been similar gardens' in China's capital.[11]

Ching-Ching, who first appeared as a supporting comic relief character in 'Handsome Harry of the Fighting Belvedere' (1876), a story serialized in *The Boy's Standard* (1875–1892), and later featured in his own magazine called *Ching Ching's Own* (1888–1893), is a distinctive character previously unimagined

---

7   Ibid., p. 233.
8   Ibid., p. 229.
9   Ibid., p. 231.
10 Ibid., p. 230.
11 Ibid., p. 231.

in children's fiction.[12] Contrary to being a stereotypical Chinese villain, he is an entertaining comic personality who later becomes a heroic detective. The emergence of Ching-Ching marks a transition from the pedagogical tendencies of authors such Bowman and Dalton, concerned to impart 'facts' about far-off China, to a more playful close encounter with 'the Chinese'. It is worth examining Ching-Ching in more detail as his popularity came to surpass that of Handsome Harry, the 'young, handsome, tall, lithe, and muscular' typical adventure-story hero.[13] In addition, the readership of the Ching-Ching adventures most likely exceeded that of *The Travels of Rolando* or *The Wolf Boy of China* because the stories were serialized in cheap penny papers known as 'penny dreadfuls', making them more affordable than Bowman and Dalton's novels, which cost between 3 and 5 shillings.

The texts examined in this book are hybrid commodities, and this is particularly evident in relation to Ching-Ching because the character was also a commodity that was used as a 'brand' to boost magazine sales. The 'Ching-Ching' name became profitable because like the popular fictional characters Curious George and Harry Potter, Ching-Ching spawned related merchandise, ranging from posters to watches to medals, all coveted by young readers.[14] In 1889, there was even a 'Ching Ching and Chums Marrionettes' show that toured around England and in 1910 a film based on his exploits called *Ching-Ching's Revenge* was released.

Although Burrage initially operated within formulaic penny dreadful plotlines involving evil pirates and brave sailors, he produced a subversive Chinese character which has thus far received little scholarly attention compared to (in)famous characters associated with the penny dreadful press such as Sweeney Todd, Dick Turpin, and Jack Sheppard.[15] The few twentieth-century critics who have written about Ching-Ching describe him as a popular 'Chinese teenage detective in England' or 'a sort of juvenile Charlie Chan'.[16] None of these critics discuss Ching-Ching in detail however.

---

[12]   Ching-Ching's name is later rendered as 'Ching Ching'. In this book, I refer to the character as 'Ching-Ching' throughout.

[13]   E. Harcourt Burrage, *Handsome Harry of the Fighting Belvedere. Vols 1–3; &, Its Sequel Cheerful Ching-Ching* (London, [1876?]), p. 32. 'Cheerful Ching-Ching' is paginated separately.

[14]   Daniel Hade, 'Curious George Gets Branded: Reading as Consuming', *Theory into Practice*, 40.3 (2001): pp. 158–65. Posters were given away in the first four issues of *Ching Ching's Own* and on 9 November 1889 it was announced that 20 watches would be given away. See 'Announcement', *Ching Ching's Own*, VI.73 (1889): p. 127.

[15]   See for example, John Bush Jones, 'From Melodrama to Tragedy: The Transformation of Sweeney Todd', *New England Theatre Journal*, 2.1 (1991): pp. 85–97; Matthew Buckley, 'Sensations of Celebrity: Jack Sheppard and the Mass Audience', *Victorian Studies*, 44.3 (2002): pp. 423–63; James Sharpe, *Dick Turpin: The Myth of the English Highway* (London, 2004).

[16]   E.S. Turner, *Boys Will Be Boys: The Story of Sweeney Todd, Deadwood Dick, Sexton Blake, Billy Bunter, Dick Barton, Et Al* (London, 1957), p. 75; Jess Nevins, *The Encyclopedia*

E. Harcourt Burrage and the Penny Dreadful Press

Improvements in printing technology and the abolition of tax on paper greatly increased the number of cheap publications in circulation during the second half of the nineteenth century. Writing in 1880, Francis Hitchman estimated that 'between five and six millions of penny papers' circulated in London every week.[17] The majority of these papers, he asserted, were characterized by 'a senile imbecility on the one hand, or an irrational sensationalism on the other ...'. People who read these papers, he continued, are 'not those who want to think, but those who wish to escape from thought ...'.[18] The sensational papers that Hitchman referred to, whose origins can be traced back to the gothic novel, were often known as 'penny dreadfuls'. According to John Springhall, there are at least six different meanings for the term:

> First, it is used as a general term of abuse for cheap papers or fiction of any description written throughout the nineteenth and early twentieth centuries. Second, it is used to describe highly coloured, criminal, or Gothic penny-issue novels of the 1830s and '40s, such as those issued by publisher Edward Lloyd (1815–1890) from Salisbury Square in weekly or monthly parts. Third, a more appropriate application of the term is to the successors of these novels – directed, from the 1850s onwards, toward a more specifically juvenile market – culminating in the publications of the NPC [Newsagent's Publishing Company] of the 1860s. Fourth, 'penny dreadful' is just as often used as a label for penny magazines or the cheap weekly boys' papers appearing from the mid-1860s onwards, mostly associated with Edwin Brett or the Emmett brothers. And a fifth usage applies the term not only to the boys' journals themselves, but also to the long-running weekly serials they contained. These serials, if successful, were then published in separate weekly parts and later in collected shilling volumes, the latter of which provides us with a sixth definition.[19]

The Boy's Standard, the boys' paper that Ching-Ching first appeared in, fits into the fourth definition provided by Springhall. Because of the gory details and lurid woodcuts included in the stories, penny dreadfuls, usually 8 or 16 pages long, were described as 'blood-and-thunders' (or 'bloods') and 'gallows literature'.[20]

of Fantastic Victoriana (Austin, TX, 2005), pp. 161–2; John Springhall, 'Disreputable Adolescent Reading: Low-Life, Women-in-Peril and School Sport "Penny Dreadfuls" from the 1860s to the 1890s', in Mike Huggins and J.A. Mangan (eds), *Disreputable Pleasures: Less Virtuous Victorians at Play* (Abingdon, Oxon, 2004), pp. 103–23 (p. 117).

[17] Francis Hitchman, 'The Penny Press', *Macmillan's Magazine*, 43 (1881): pp. 385–98 (p. 385). Hitchman was known mostly for his biographical studies.

[18] Ibid.

[19] John Springhall, '"A Life Story for the People?": Edwin J. Brett and the London "Low Life" Penny Dreadfuls of the 1860s', *Victorian Studies*, 33.2 (1990): pp. 223–46 (pp. 226–7).

[20] Sheila A. Egoff, *Children's Periodicals of the Nineteenth Century: A Survey and Bibliography* (London, 1951), p. 19; Elizabeth James and Helen R. Smith, *Penny Dreadfuls*

Authors of these formulaic melodramatic tales, often writing under alliterative pseudonyms such as 'Ralph Rollington' or 'Brenchley Beaumont', depicted criminal heroes who defied the law, killed without mercy, escaped unscathed, and triumphantly succeeded in whatever they did.

According to the author of an article in the *Edinburgh Review*, approximately five million children were enrolled in schools in England in 1887.[21] This number reflects the effect of the Forster's Education Act (1870) on children's school attendance because after the Act was passed, children aged 5 to 12 were provided with the opportunity for elementary education. The author of the article states that these 'happy millions are being diligently crammed day by day ... with every kind of so-called useful knowledge'.[22] However, because the schools were unable to satisfy students' 'passionate desire for fiction', these newly literate children had to search elsewhere for entertaining reading. The author found that 'penny dreadfuls' were in abundant supply and worried about the 'veritable mountain of pernicious trash' that 'millions of poor children' bought and 'devoured' with 'intense relish'.[23] Also writing in the 1880s, Hitchman claimed that 'There are some fourteen or fifteen papers published for their amusement every week, with a total circulation of at least a million and a half ... with few exceptions, these papers are silly and vulgar in the extreme ...'.[24] The fervour for penny dreadfuls among British youth has been regarded as the first kind of mass reading.[25] Teachers, clergymen, and journalists abhorred the fact that this 'garbage' was so popular among the young people, because in their view, the implicit message of these 'dreadfuls' was that the use of aggression was the most effective way to become rich. Critics objected to the coarse language, the glorification of crime, and disrespect towards authority exemplified in these stories.[26]

As Patrick A. Dunae points out, the critics were not as worried about the degradation of middle-class boys as they were about the plight of their working-class peers.[27] They assumed that middle-class boys only read the penny dreadfuls occasionally, while susceptible working-class boys, who, like women, were unable

---

and Boys' Adventures: The Barry Ono Collection of Victorian Popular Literature in the British Library (London, 1998), p. xii.

[21]   'The Literature of the Streets', *Edinburgh Review*, 165.337 (1887): pp. 40–64 (p. 40).

[22]   Ibid.

[23]   Ibid., p. 43.

[24]   Hitchman, 'The Penny Press', p. 396.

[25]   For more detailed discussion see Kevin Carpenter, *Penny Dreadfuls and Comics: English Periodicals for Children from Victorian Times to the Present Day* (London, 1983).

[26]   However, Jonathan Rose argues that while the middle-class critics viewed these texts as 'dangerous trash', working-class readers revealed in their memoirs that they thought of them as 'harmless trash' – knowing they were unedifying but still enjoying reading them for entertainment purposes. For more detailed discussion, see Jonathan Rose, 'Rereading the English Common Reader: A Preface to a History of Audiences', *Journal of the History of Ideas*, 53.1 (1992): pp. 47–70 (p. 59).

[27]   Patrick A. Dunae, 'Penny Dreadfuls: Late Nineteenth-Century Boys' Literature and Crime', *Victorian Studies*, 22.2 (1979): pp. 133–50 (p. 135).

to distinguish between fiction and reality, immersed themselves in these titillating stories. Some claimed that the penny dreadfuls were directly responsible for the rise in juvenile delinquencies.[28] Critics believed that the working-class boys' misdemeanours might evolve into serious crime if they were fed tales completely lacking in reason or morality. For example, in 1888, the journalist Edward Salmon condemned the 'poisonous sheets' for polluting young readers' minds, claiming that the 'young mind is a virgin soil, and whether weeds or rare flowers and beautiful trees are to spring up in it will, of course, depend upon the character of the seeds sown'.[29] In order for 'beautiful trees' to grow in the minds of the youth, critics argued, they should digest adventure stories by respectable authors such as Sir Walter Scott and Captain Marryat.

The perceived increase in crime rates was not the only concern. The continuing rise of the working-class population was seen as potentially politically dangerous.[30] The middle-class minority worried that their power would be threatened if literate working-class youth grew up to favour radical journalism and 'misused' their electoral power when voting.[31] Others, such as Thomas Wright, deplored the penny dreadfuls not because they incited boys to criminality but because they

> usurped the place of the only reading by which, practically speaking, the foundations of a cultured taste could be laid, and the means to the end of a new happiness created … He who as a boy is found as a reader of the dreadfuls, will, in the vast majority of cases, be found as a man in the ranks of the non-reading or uncultured classes.[32]

Victorian boys were particularly attracted to the penny dreadfuls produced by the publishing houses of Edwin J. Brett and the Emmett brothers, representatives of the so-called 'gutter press'. In 1860, Edwin John Brett (1828–1895), a former engraver, became the manager of the infamous Newsagent's Publishing Company, known for producing violent penny serials such as *The Wild Boys of London; or the Children of the Night*. Eight years later, Brett left the company to open a new publishing house. Among the papers produced by his company, *Boys of England: A Young Gentleman's Journal of Sport, Travel, Fun and Instruction* (1866–1899) was the most successful, initially selling around 150,000 copies per week, four times more than the sales of his earlier papers. By the early 1870s, the weekly circulation of *Boys of England* had reached 250,000.[33] Although Brett claimed

---

[28]   However, Dunae points out that there was actually a decrease in juvenile crime in the last quarter of the nineteenth century. Ibid., p. 150.

[29]   Edward Salmon, *Juvenile Literature as It Is* (London, 1888), p. 233.

[30]   Joseph Bristow, *Empire Boys: Adventures in a Man's World* (London, 1991), p. 19.

[31]   Troy Boone, *Youth of Darkest England: Working-Class Children at the Heart of Victorian Empire* (New York, 2005), pp. 66–8.

[32]   Thomas Wright, 'On a Possible Popular Culture', *Contemporary Review*, 40 (1881): pp. 25–44 (p. 36).

[33]   Bristow, *Empire Boys*, p. 37.

his 'wild and wonderful' papers were 'healthy', 'honest', and 'pure', critics could see nothing positive about stories that glorified highwaymen, pirates, robbers, and other outlaws. Of these stories, the Jack Harkaway series, which began in 1871 and continued for over 30 years (eventually featuring Harkaway's son and grandson), became one of the most popular serials in Britain.[34] Created by an unsuccessful lawyer named Samuel Bracebridge Hemyng (1841–1901), this character, who has been characterized as 'a likeable, fearless and full-blooded' boy 'who took the whole world for his oyster and remained aggressively English', was so popular that eventually most people referred to these the penny dreadfuls as the 'Jack Harkaway' type of publication.[35]

Brett's fiercest rivals were the Emmett brothers, whose publication titles bore striking resemblance to Brett's magazines: *The Young Englishman, The Young Briton, Young Gentlemen of Britain*, and *Sons of Britannia*. In the end, Brett won this publication battle, for the Emmett brothers were forced out of business in 1875.[36] Other popular publishers include Charles Fox (editor of *The Boy's Standard*), Samuel Clark, and Albert John Allingham ('Ralph Rollington'). One of the Emmett brothers' former employees was Edwin Harcourt Burrage, creator of the Ching-Ching stories, who served as editor of Emmett's *Young Gentlemen of Britain* from 1868 to 1870.[37] Born in Norwich, Norfolk in 1839, Burrage, known as 'the boys' Charles Dickens', initially aspired to be an artist.[38] He began working on Fleet Street in the 1860s, where he rented a room in Wine Office Court and was briefly employed as an illustrator for the *Penny Mechanic*. However, after the magazine folded, Burrage could not find work due to his lack of artistic talent, causing him to reflect that his 'career as a draughtsman was simply two years of struggling with disappointment, waning hope, humiliation and despair'.[39] When he complained he could not find a job, his friend Charles Stevens, the first editor of *Boys of England* and one of the leading penny dreadful authors at the time, encouraged him to try writing. Burrage decided to submit a manuscript of a short love story to a 'publishing office of cheap journalism' near his home.[40] A fortnight

[34]   The first Harkaway dies in *Jack Harkaway and His Son's Adventures Round the World* (1875) and his grandson appears in *Jack Harkaway's Journal for Boys* (1893).

[35]   For discussion of the Jack Harkaway stories see James and Smith, *Penny Dreadfuls and Boys' Adventures*, pp. 93–6 and Percy H. Muir, *English Children's Books: 1600 to 1900*, 3rd rev. impression edn (London, 1979), pp. 111–12.

[36]   For further discussion on the rivalry between Brett and the Emmetts, see Carpenter, *Penny Dreadfuls and Comics*, pp. 21–9.

[37]   John Springhall, '"Boys of Bircham School": The Penny Dreadful Origins of the Popular English School Story, 1867–1900', in Roy Lowe (ed.), *History of Education: Major Themes* (London, 2000), pp. 386–408 (p. 394).

[38]   John Springhall, 'E.H. Burrage's "Carbineer and Scout": Another Henty Clone?', *Henty Society Bulletin*, IX.71 (1995): pp. 3–9 (p. 3).

[39]   E. Harcourt Burrage, *The Ruin of Fleet Street* (London, 1885), p. 10. This is a temperance tract that provides some insight into his early career.

[40]   Ibid., p. 17.

later, it was accepted and not long after, Burrage 'secured regular engagement' and became 'a full-blown Bohemian', earning 4 pounds a week.[41]

As a hack writer, Burrage often felt pressured to produce prodigious amounts of text in a short period of time, leading another boy's writer R.A.H. Goodyear to admit that his writing was 'sometimes slipshod ... but always his stuff pulsed with animation and vivid incident, conceived by one of the most fertile imaginations that ever devoted itself to the entertainment of boyhood'.[42] Likewise, Burrage's obituary in the *Surrey Mirror and County Post* (1916) hailed him as 'a brilliant writer of boys' stories, which achieved great popularity in their time', who 'possessed a facile pen, a vivid imagination, and a prodigious capacity for work'.[43] Burrage wrote prolifically, contributing hundreds of stories to papers such as *Young Briton, The Boy's Standard, The Boy's Weekly Novelette, The Boy's World, Our Boy's Paper, British Boys*, and *Boy's Stories of Adventure and Daring*. Ching-Ching, a recurring favourite in stories published over a period of 16 years, was undoubtedly his most famous and long-lasting character.

Ching-Ching and the Chinese in Victorian England

In 'Ching-Ching Memoirs' (1926), A. Harcourt Burrage, also a boy's writer, reveals that his father modelled Ching-Ching on a Chinese man who lingered near Fleet Street, 'whose sole occupation was to occasionally distribute bills for a tradesman in the near vicinity'.[44] It is unclear where this Chinese man lived, but most likely he would have come from Limehouse Causeway and Pennyfields, which had been considered London's 'Chinatown' since the 1880s.[45] After 1865, when Liverpool shipping companies such as Alfred and Philip Holt's Blue Funnel Line began trading with China, the number of Chinese in Britain increased.

---

[41]   Ibid., p. 24. It is possible that William Dalton and Burrage may have crossed paths because Dalton worked for the *Morning Advertiser* and *Daily Telegraph*.

[42]   R.A.H. Goodyear, 'Stories I Liked the Most–and Least', *Collector's Miscellany*, 3 (1933): pp. 44–6 (p. 46).

[43]   'The Death of Mr. E.H. Burrage', *Surrey Mirror and County Post*, 10 March 1916, p. 5. After his career on Fleet Street, Burrage lived in Reigate, Surrey for many years, and was elected a councillor of that borough in 1899. In 1916, he passed away at the age of 77 and was buried in Reigate Cemetery.

[44]   A. Harcourt Burrage, 'Ching-Ching Memoirs', *Vanity Fair*, II.22–4 (1926): pp. 135–6, 149–50, 165–6 (p. 149).

[45]   Limehouse Causeway and Pennyfields were two narrow streets near the West India Docks. The Chinese mostly lived in cities such as London, Liverpool, Cardiff, Bristol, and Glasgow. One of the earliest records of Chinese sailors appeared in a *Morning Chronicle* article dated 27 July 1782. By 1851, there were 78 Chinese people in Britain. Ten years later, the number increased to 147. See Lynn Pan, *Sons of the Yellow Emperor: The Story of the Overseas Chinese* (London, 1990), pp. 84–5; Anthony Shang, *The Chinese in Britain* (London, 1984), p. 9; Sascha Auerbach, *Race, Law and 'The Chinese Puzzle' in Imperial Britain* (Basingstoke, 2009).

Not all of them arrived directly from China however. Some moved to Britain from the United States, fleeing American persecution. Because there were only 202 Chinese people (mostly sailors) living in Britain in 1871, the racial landscape of 1870s and 1880s Britain was very different from the situation in the United States and Australia, where fears of the invasion of 'Asiatic hordes' had already exploded into several anti-Chinese campaigns, most notably during 1885–1886 in California and 1887–1888 in Australia.[46] In 1881, the population of Chinese in Britain was 665, and the number rose to 1,319 by 1911. While most were seamen, others worked in laundries, shops, grocery stores, restaurants, and lodging-houses.[47] According to Anthony Shang, nineteenth-century Chinese seamen frequently jumped ship hoping to find better-paid work. Afterwards, they might have registered again as sailors in a British port so that they would be entitled to the same rates of pay as British seamen.[48] Gregor Benton and Edmund Terence Gomez point out that Chinese seafarers were reputed to be anarchic and impossible to control.[49] This may have been a possible reason Burrage made Ching-Ching an anarchic comic seafarer in *Handsome Harry*.

According to G.R. Searle, most Victorians in the 1880s 'would never have set eyes on a "coloured" person – except in such exotic settings as London theatres, fairs, and showgrounds, or during the Queen's two Jubilees of 1887 and 1897 … "Coloured immigration" was on so small a scale that it hardly featured as a serious social or political problem'.[50] Ching-Ching's initial comic personality may have been based on the Chinese characters in British pantomimes, as Câecile Parrish suggests.[51] Chinese characters in pantomime appeared on stage in the mid-eighteenth century and Anne Veronica Whitchard notes that the 'Chinaman with his pendulous moustache had become as essential a part of pantomime as Pierrot or Harlequin'.[52] David Garrick's *Harlequin in China* was first performed at Drury Lane in 1754 and others such as *Pong Wong* (1820), *Chinese Sorcerer* (1823), and *The Conquest of the Golden Pagodas* (1827) followed.[53] Noted pantomime actor Joseph Grimaldi performed the title character in *Whang*

[46]   Luke Trainor, *British Imperialism and Australian Nationalism: Manipulation, Conflict, and Compromise in the Late Nineteenth Century* (Cambridge, 1994), p. 85.

[47]   In 1901 it was estimated that 61 percent of the Chinese were involved in this type of work, in 1911 there were 1,136 Chinese seafarers. See Colin Holmes, *John Bull's Island: Immigration and British Society, 1871–1971* (Basingstoke, 1988), p. 52; Pan, *Sons of the Yellow Emperor*, pp. 84–5.

[48]   Shang, *The Chinese in Britain*, p. 9.

[49]   Gregor Benton and Edmund Terence Gomez, *The Chinese in Britain, 1800–Present: Economy, Transnationalism and Identity* (Basingstoke, 2008), p. 310.

[50]   G.R. Searle, *A New England?: Peace and War 1886–1918* (Oxford, 2005), p. 20.

[51]   Câecile Parrish, *The Image of Asia in Children's Literature, 1814–1964* (Clayton, Vic., 1977), p. 16.

[52]   Anne Veronica Witchard, *Thomas Burke's Dark Chinoiserie: Limehouse Nights and the Queer Spell of Chinatown* (Aldershot, 2009), p. 30.

[53]   Ibid., p. 38. See also John O'Brien, *Harlequin Britain: Pantomime and Entertainment, 1690–1760* (Baltimore, 2004).

Fong, the Clown of China at Sadler's Wells in 1812, a show that included scenes of Chinese ladies quarrelling and throwing tea and crockery.[54] A few years later, a pantomime called *Harlequin and Fortunio; or, Shing-Moo and Thun-Ton* (1815) was staged at Covent Garden featuring many Chinese scenes and characters such as the Chinese Emperor and some Mandarins.[55] In 1865, a scene set in Canton could be seen during the Royal English Opera's 'Aladdin and his Wonderful Lamp' pantomime performance, which the *Illustrated London News* described as an 'elaborate scene' featuring 'various phases of the businesses carried on by Chinese tradesmen'.[56] In one of Ching-Ching's stories about his family, he claims his father was the Emperor's tailor, a detail Burrage may have borrowed from Aladdin because according to a poster for a performance of Aladdin at the Theatre Royal, Dunlop Street in 1866, the boy is the son of a Chinese tailor and his mother is named Ching-Ching.[57] In the 1890s, Aladdin was depicted as a boy from Peking.[58] The plot of *Handsome Harry* is similar to eighteenth-century Harlequin pantomimes which, according to John O'Brien, consisted of 'a "serious" part, usually drawn from classical mythology, alternating with a "comic" or "grotesque" part, which focused on the escapades of Harlequin, who used all the resources of stage trickery, most crucially the ability to disguise himself and to transform objects and persons …'.[59] Handsome Harry's desire to seek revenge echoes plots from classical mythology and Ching-Ching is like Harlequin who provides comic exploits.

Because the number of Chinese residents in Britain was quite small in the late nineteenth century, Burrage could imagine a character like Ching-Ching living in England after his adventures around the world. In the later stories, Ching-Ching intermingles with various multi-national residents of metropolitan London as well as English residents of townships such as Saxondale and Carlham without causing alarm or fears of the invasion of 'Asiatic hordes'. According to J.P. May, before 1906, the British attitude towards the Chinese presence in Britain was mostly one of indifference and even acceptance.[60] Benton and Gomez also report that

---

[54] David Mayer, *Harlequin in His Element: The English Pantomime, 1806–1836* (Cambridge, MA, 1969), pp. 140–41. For more information on Grimaldi, see Andrew McConnell Stott, *The Pantomime Life of Joseph Grimaldi: Laughter, Madness and the Story of Britain's Greatest Comedian* (Edinburgh, 2009).

[55] Mayer, *Harlequin in His Element*, pp. 143–5.

[56] 'The Theatres', *Illustrated London News*, 30 December 1865, p. 655.

[57] For the story of Ching-Ching's father as a tailor, see E. Harcourt Burrage, 'Cheerful Ching-Ching', in *Handsome Harry of the Fighting Belvedere. Vols 1–3; &, Its Sequel Cheerful Ching-Ching* (London, [1876?]), pp. 1–180 (p. 2). The pagination of Cheerful Ching-Ching starts again from p. 1.

[58] Raymond Mander and Joe Mitchenson, *Pantomime: A Story in Pictures* (London, 1973), n. pag.

[59] John O'Brien, 'Harlequin Britain: Eighteenth-Century Pantomime and the Cultural Location of Entertainment(s)', *Theatre Journal*, 50.4 (1998): pp. 489–510 (pp. 491–3).

[60] J.P. May, 'The Chinese in Britain, 1860–1914', in C. Holmes (ed.), *Immigrants and Minorities in British Society* (London, 1978), pp. 111–24 (p. 111).

the Chinese who settled in London 'had a good reputation, particularly in prewar days'.[61] The situation in the United States and Australia was very different because of the large influx of Chinese immigrants in the latter part of the nineteenth century. The perceived threat from the Chinese was expressed in yellow peril invasion stories such as the Australian journalist William Lane's 'White or Yellow?: A Story of the Race-War of A.D. 1908' (1888).[62] Ching-Ching was a distinct product of the 1870s to 1890s because the yellow peril ('Gelbe Gefahr'), a phrase coined by the German Kaiser in 1895, was not 'perceived as a realistic threat' in Britain until the last years of the nineteenth century and into the early twentieth century.[63] He was therefore a uniquely British phenomenon.

The Ching-Ching Phenomenon

Ching-Ching first appeared in the story 'Handsome Harry of the Fighting Belvedere' (1876), which was serialized in *The Boy's Standard* (1875–1892), a periodical criticized for 'sensationalism and silliness'.[64] The story begins on board the Belvedere, of which Handsome Harry is the captain. The crew is multi-national: the first-mate Tom True is 'noble, brave and upright' and described as 'a true British sailor – nimble, muscular, sunburnt, and good looking'.[65] Bill Grunt, the tall powerful boatswain of African descent, is good friends with Eddard Cutten, a white man with a wooden leg, and with 'good-natured, easy, and simple' Samson, a giant African American who used to be a slave on a cotton plantation.[66] Ching-Ching, who has all the physical features of a typical 'Chinaman'– a 'sallow face', 'almond-shaped eyes', and his head 'topped by a pigtail of great length', is

---

[61]   Benton and Gomez, *The Chinese in Britain*, p. 108.

[62]   This story was published as a 12-part serial in the Queensland Labour movement paper *Boomerang*. According to David Walker, early invasion fiction published through the 1880s reflected British anxieties about Russia, France, Germany, and other more immediate European threats. One of the earliest invasion stories was Sir George Tomkyns Chesney's 'The Battle of Dorking' (1871). See David Walker, *Anxious Nation: Australia and the Rise of Asia 1850–1939* (St Lucia, Qld., 1999), p. 100.

[63]   Ariane Knüsel, '"Western Civilization" against "Hordes of Yellow Savages": British Perceptions of the Boxer Rebellion', *Asiatische Studien/Etudes Asiatiques*, LXII.I (2008): pp. 43–84 (p. 46). For an early example of the yellow peril story, see Matthew Phipps Shiel, *The Yellow Danger* (London, 1898).

[64]   Hitchman, 'The Penny Press', p. 397. 'Handsome Harry' was well received in the United States, where it was reprinted four times in 'The Boys of New York', 'Happy Days', 'Golden Hours', and in weekly numbers. In 1899, Frank Tousey of New York published *Handsome Harry: Stories of Land and Sea*, a 32-page weekly journal, which lasted for only five months, from 27 January to 12 May 1899.

[65]   Burrage, *Handsome Harry*, p. 3.

[66]   Ibid., p. 162. Samson might be based on Captain Marryat's character Mesty – Jack Easy's friend who was formerly a slave but later worked as a corporal on a ship in *Mr. Midshipman Easy* (London, 1836).

first introduced to readers when he is caught stealing from the larder of the ship.[67] He soon embarks on exciting adventures with the crew.

At the beginning of the story, Handsome Harry, whose real name is Sir Henry March, is a mysterious character, but readers gradually piece together his life story as the plot progresses. Harry and his twin brother Harold were born in Wiltshire, England and grew up without a father, remembering that their mother was always in mourning. Later, they both fall in love with a girl named Leda Cardio. Knowing how much Harold loved Leda, Harry decides to devote his life to the sea and Harold, with the blessing of Don Salvo, Leda's uncle and guardian, proposes to his beloved. One day Harold tells Harry that a 'Captain Brocken' had asked for Leda's hand in marriage and openly declared that he would have her by any means. On their wedding day, Brocken abducts Leda and kills Harold. Leda subsequently dies of a broken heart on Brocken's ship, the Wild Jaguar. To avenge his brother, Handsome Harry leads his crew from Africa to England to Russia in search of Brocken, fighting pirates, brigands, and slave traders in the process. After a series of betrayals, false accusations, and other adventures, Handsome Harry finally comes face to face with Brocken, but the captain, who turns out to be Harry's father, dies before Harry can kill him, supposedly from a contrite heart.

Nineteenth-century boys' adventure stories such as *Mr. Midshipmen Easy* (1836) and *The Three Midshipmen* (1862) often featured British midshipmen interacting with colourful eccentric characters.[68] Popular eccentric biographies which provided entertainment and moral instruction were read by many children, including Robert Browning and Charles Darwin.[69] The topic was so popular that there was even a periodical dedicated to the subject, called *The Eccentric Magazine, or, Lives and Portraits of Remarkable Characters* (1812–1814).[70] Interest in eccentricity permeated into fiction, where echoes of the eccentric biography could be found in characters such as Charles Dickens's Mr Pickwick.[71] In particular, readers of Victorian boys' adventure stories could expect eccentric characters ranging from the comic to the grotesque to appear in sea stories that were usually full of colourful national types.[72] In the *Handsome Harry* sea story, eccentric Ching-Ching functions mainly as a comic relief character: he 'often

---

[67]   Ibid., p. 8.

[68]   Catherine Gallagher, 'Floating Signifiers of Britishness in the Novels of the Anti-Slave-Trade Squadron', in Wendy S. Jacobson (ed.), *Dickens and the Children of Empire* (New York, 2000), pp. 78–93 (p. 89).

[69]   James Gregory, 'Eccentric Biography and the Victorians', *Biography: An Interdisciplinary Quarterly*, 30.3 (2007): pp. 342–76 (p. 351).

[70]   Henry Lemoine and James Caulfield (eds), *The Eccentric Magazine, or, Lives and Portraits of Remarkable Characters* (London, 1812).

[71]   Even though after the 1860s no new 'eccentric biographies' appeared, reprints and other texts ensured their survival. See Gregory, 'Eccentric Biography and the Victorians', p. 360.

[72]   Gallagher, 'Floating Signifiers', p. 81.

helped to lighten the daily lives of the men of the Belvedere'.[73] In most nineteenth-century adventure stories, Chinese seamen are either presented as pirates or cooks. Ching-Ching however, is neither, because he does not have a particular job to perform on the ship and mainly spins yarns or sings songs while they are at sea. For example, he explains:

> Me born in Pekin. Fader and moder berry rich, but soon die, and leave Ching-Ching to bad oncle [sic]. Oncle beat Ching-Ching – starve him – make dese legs and arms like bamboo cane. Den one day oncle take Ching-Ching into swamp and leave him to die, but sailor come – good sailor – and take Ching-Ching on to his ship. Good sailor's ship taken by the pirate – all killed but Ching-Ching.[74]

According to Michael Anglo, Ching-Ching's speech was a source of great amusement to young readers, who would try it out on each other: 'Drinkee for drunkee, velly goodlers.' 'You comee with me. We both have what foreign devils call a highee spree time. Me likee you velly much for friendlers.'[75] The image of children conversing in Pidgin English and referring to 'foreign devils' as if they were Chinese challenges Kathryn Castle's claim that the Other was regarded as undesirable.[76] Although it cannot be confirmed whether the dialogue described by Anglo actually took place, children, who are fond of communicating with each other using 'secret' languages, probably did try to imitate Ching-Ching's way of speaking.

Anglo's rendering of Ching-Ching's speech follows typical understanding of historical Chinese Pidgin English, used mostly by Cantonese-speaking Chinese to communicate with foreign merchants during the nineteenth century, and often characterized by the replacement of 'l' for 'r' and the appending of 'ee' at the end of words. Although Ching-Ching occasionally replaces 'r' with 'l' such as in the words 'diffelent' and 'memloies', he often adds 'r' after words ending with 'e' instead of 'ee'. For example: 'it hab eber been a sourcer ob grief dat I neber learn it as it am spoker now'.[77] Therefore, strictly speaking he can pronounce 'r's. When Ching-Ching speaks, he usually replaces 'd' for 'th', 'b' for 'v', 'b' for 'f', and 'am' for 'is'. According to Eric Reinders, folklorist Charles G. Leland's *Pidgin-English Sing-Song; or, Songs and Stories in the China-English Dialect* (1876) 'popularized and reinforced Western perceptions of this pidgin [Chinese Pidgin English]'.[78] Although Burrage began writing about Ching-Ching in 1876, the same

---

[73]   Burrage, *Handsome Harry*, p. 131.

[74]   Ibid., p. 9.

[75]   Michael Anglo, *Penny Dreadfuls and Other Victorian Horrors* (London, 1977), p. 104. He does not provide evidence for this claim.

[76]   Kathryn Castle, *Britannia's Children: Reading Colonialism through Children's Books and Magazines* (Manchester, 1996), p. 8.

[77]   Burrage, *Cheerful-Daring-Wonderful Ching-Ching*, pp. 184; 229.

[78]   Eric Robert Reinders, *Borrowed Gods and Foreign Bodies: Christian Missionaries Imagine Chinese Religion* (Berkeley, 2004), p. 79.

year *Pidgin-English Sing-Song* was published, his depiction of Ching-Ching's speech does not adhere to the Pidgin English described in Leland's book.[79]

Burrage writes that Ching-Ching 'has a language of his own, but how acquired nobody can even guess', but in reality, Ching-Ching sounds very similar to the African-American character Samson, who also replaces 'd' for 'th' and 'b' for 'v'. For example, Samson says, 'You call me dat again and I bash your head agin de wall!!' and 'I lib and die for you'.[80] In *Racism on the Victorian Stage*, Hazel Waters discusses the markers of black speech and provides examples such as 'Look on dat ugly picter – den look ob dis' and 'I'll hab revenge'.[81] In addition to replacing 'th' with 'd', the character replaces 'f' with 'b' and 'v' with 'b', which is what Ching-Ching does. Because Ching-Ching speaks in a similar manner to Samson, it is possible that Burrage simply made him a generic ethnic Other in terms of speech without understanding how Chinese Pidgin English was used in China.

Although Ching-Ching is racially Other in terms of physical appearance and speech, readers can identify with his sense of playfulness and penchant for storytelling which transcend markers of nationality. Unlike the silenced marginalized minority who does not have agency to speak, Ching-Ching has an individual voice 'quite distinct from any known people', enjoys freedom of speech, and is capable of verbal anarchy.[82] Ching-Ching helps to 'lighten the daily lives of the men of the Belvedere' with his storytelling. In *Handsome Harry*, readers find many fantastic stories about him. For example, Ching-Ching provides inconsistent stories about his father's death. Initially he attributes it to measles, then starvation, but later claims his father died of grief after a thief chopped off his pigtail. Another tale alleges that his father was sentenced to hanging for stealing a Mandarin's umbrella. In one account, his father supposedly died of heartbreak after his mother succumbed to measles. Regarding his personal life, Ching-Ching claims that he had two wives: 'they were twins, and one wouldn't be married without de oder, so I propose to bof'.[83] He purports they married on a Monday, and on Tuesday he ran away. When he appears before a counsel who commands Ching-Ching to state his age, he replies he is 290 moons old, which the judge calculates to be about 24 years old.[84]

Ching-Ching conforms to the 'archetype of the yarning seaman', which, according to Anthea Trodd, 'imagines a perfect fit of teller and audience'.[85]

---

[79]   See Charles G. Leland, *Pidgin-English Sing-Song; or, Songs and Stories in the China-English Dialect, with a Vocabulary*, 2nd edn (London, [1876] 1887).

[80]   E. Harcourt Burrage, 'Ching Ching and His Chums Chapter I to Chapter II', *Ching Ching's Own*, I.1 (1888): p. 2; Burrage, *Handsome Harry*, p. 1.

[81]   Hazel Waters, *Racism on the Victorian Stage: Representation of Slavery and the Black Character* (Cambridge, 2007), p. 115.

[82]   Burrage, *Cheerful-Daring-Wonderful Ching-Ching*, p. 183.

[83]   Burrage, *Handsome Harry*, p. 44.

[84]   Ibid., p. 252.

[85]   Anthea Trodd, 'Messages in Bottles and Collins's Seafaring Man', *Studies in English Literature 1500–1900*, 41.4 (2001): pp. 751–64 (p. 754).

Despite the outlandish and far-fetched nature of his stories, everyone seems to be captivated by them. In particular, Samson has an eager appetite for Ching-Ching's yarns, and can even forget his painful wound as he looks forward to 'the coming pleasure of listening to another of those truthful and marvellous stories related by Ching-Ching'.[86] Ching-Ching offers a 'new puzzle' for Samson to decipher every day and each is 'a harder nut than the preceding one'.[87] Samson cannot solve any of them: 'His stories ... bordered on the marvellous, but who could doubt when Ching-Ching spoke? Samson and a few others certainly did not hesitate to believe his lightest and heaviest utterances, but took them all as they came as pure, sparkling truth.'[88]

At the end of *Handsome Harry*, Burrage writes to the 'gentle reader' that he is 'pleased' that the adventures have 'been so very popular' and the second part will 'have a new title given to it ['Cheerful Ching-Ching'] in honour of the strange being who has made it what it is – a favourite'.[89] Although Handsome Harry still appears in 'Cheerful Ching-Ching', his name does not appear in the title of the story, suggesting that Ching-Ching has become the main attraction for readers. Following 'Cheerful Ching-Ching', Ching-Ching embarks on other adventures in 'Daring Ching-Ching' and 'Wonderful Ching-Ching: His Further Adventures'. In these early Ching-Ching stories serialized in *The Boy's Standard* and *The Boy's Leisure Hour* (1884–1891) [reissues of *The Boy's Standard*], Ching-Ching is characterized as a kleptomaniac, gambler, drunk, liar, and practical joker who can get away with anything by his flattery and many tricks and stunts (see Figure 3.2). When he is sober he is 'a very diplomatic person', but when drunk, Ching-Ching 'was apt to be reckless'.[90] Ching-Ching may have appealed to readers because unlike the archetypal white hero of boy's adventure stories, he is a mysterious comic storyteller who revels in anarchy but demonstrates the ability to tackle 'members of Tongs, crooks, spies, and sundry other rascals with equal aplomb'.[91]

Although Ching-Ching possesses stereotypical Chinese features, he disrupts the status quo and challenges readers' ideas about 'the Chinaman' in many respects. Writing of the trickster, Lewis Hyde argues: 'When he lies and steals, it isn't so much to get away with something or get rich as to disturb the established categories of truth and property and, by so doing, open the road to possible

---

[86]   Burrage, *Cheerful-Daring-Wonderful Ching-Ching*, p. 247.

[87]   Ibid., p. 308.

[88]   Ibid., p. 298.

[89]   Burrage, *Handsome Harry*, p. 279.

[90]   Ibid., p. 47.

[91]   Anglo, *Penny Dreadfuls*, p. 104. Anglo asserts that Ching-Ching has 'the bland cheerfulness expected of Oriental heroes along with the diabolical cruelty associated with Chinese villains' (104). His assertion of Ching-Ching's 'diabolical cruelty' is not supported with evidence from the texts. I do not believe that Ching-Ching was crueller than Handsome Harry or other characters in the stories, since they all engage in acts of violence against the 'enemies'.

Fig. 3.2   'Samson's unlimited faith in Ching-Ching forbade his interference in many a coarse practical joke', from *Handsome Harry of the Fighting Belvedere* (1876).

new worlds.'[92] Ching-Ching can be regarded as a trickster who relies on cunning manoeuvres to survive in the challenging and dangerous nineteenth-century world. Unlike ordinary men, Ching-Ching 'never walked – he glided; he never ran – he bounded like an india-rubber ball'.[93] Although he is 'light and bony', he is strong, quick, and agile, and manages to escape dangerous situations.[94] Like Bret Harte's Ah Sin, a character in the widely circulated poem 'Plain Language of Truthful James' (also known as 'Heathen Chinee') who, according to Jacqueline Romeo, is like the trickster because he disrupts the status quo by lying, stealing, and behaving subversively, Ching-Ching steals, but 'never appropriated for personal profit'.[95]

---

[92]   Lewis Hyde, *Trickster Makes This World: Mischief, Myth, and Art* (New York, 1998), p. 13.

[93]   Burrage, *Cheerful-Daring-Wonderful Ching-Ching*, p. 183.

[94]   Burrage, *Handsome Harry*, p. 18.

[95]   Although Harry appoints some men to watch over Ching-Ching carefully, he still manages to steal many things from the ship. He steals at least ten times in the story. The poem 'Plain Language of Truthful James' was first published in 1870. For more information on Harte, see Jacqueline Romeo, 'Irony Lost: Bret Harte's Heathen Chinee and the Popularization of the Comic Coolie as Trickster in Frontier Melodrama', *Theatre History Studies*, 26 (2006): pp. 108–36. Burrage, *Cheerful-Daring-Wonderful Ching-Ching*, p. 327.

Despite his many vices, Ching-Ching resists conventional Victorian stereotypes about the Chinese. He does not exhibit meekness or cowardice, but shows 'boldness and bravery'.[96] Ching-Ching, who may seem 'thin to painfulness', is able to surprise and defeat his enemies by first playing into to their preconceived notions of the weak and effeminate Chinese male and then revealing that 'every inch' of him is 'steel'.[97] Through tricksterism he is able to retain his personal autonomy in a world where characters such as Don Salvo hate the Chinese for being 'a cursed, ugly race'.[98] He can dupe those more powerful than him. Instead of being a victim of practical jokes as other stereotypical Chinese characters were, Ching-Ching is more often than not the perpetrator of tricks on others. He is capable of causing chaos but also of restoring order.

Observing Ching-Ching in action is akin to watching a carnivalesque freak show. Because his 'limbs were as pliable as willow', he could also perform amazing tricks such as twisting 'his legs about like elephants' trunks'.[99] When Ching-Ching is in motion, he resembles 'an animated corkscrew' and 'every movement reminded the spectator of a very young and very active eel'.[100] These descriptions also remind one of marionettes on stage and the use of the word 'spectator' heightens the theatrical effect of Ching-Ching's movements. 'A perfect master of a certain class of acrobatic feats', he resembles a comic contortionist because he has 'the power of screwing his face and body into strange shapes, and so to stiffen his pigtail that fairly stood out like a pump handle'.[101] Victorians were obsessed with freak shows and sensation.[102] Since the eighteenth century, Londoners whetted their appetite for the curious by going to see human show creatures 'marked by either superfluity or deprivation'.[103] For example, in 1890, the Ching Goffs, two acrobats who 'excel[led] as contortionists', performed 'some surprising feats in the costume of Chinamen' in Brighton and London.[104] Earlier, in 1863, Kung Costello the Chinese contortionist 'excite[d] the lovers of the wonderful to their heart's content'.[105] From 1865 to 1866, Londoners flocked to the Egyptian Hall to see Chang, the multilingual Chinese Giant, who was approximately eight feet tall, his wife Kin Foo, a three-foot-tall Chinese dwarf

---

[96]   Ibid., p. 230.

[97]   Ibid., p. 312.

[98]   Burrage, *Handsome Harry*, p. 45.

[99]   Burrage, *Cheerful-Daring-Wonderful Ching-Ching*, p. 183.

[100] Ibid., p. 183.

[101] Ibid., pp. 211; 374.

[102] See Matthew Sweet, *Inventing the Victorians* (New York, 2001), pp. 136–54.

[103] For more information on freak shows in London, see Richard Daniel Altick, *The Shows of London* (Cambridge, MA, 1978), p. 43.

[104] 'The London Music Halls', *The Era*, 18 January 1890, p. 16.

[105] 'London Music Halls', *The Era*, 8 March 1863, p. 11.

named Chung Mow, and a dozen other Chinese.[106] Conjoined twins Chang and Eng, better known as the Siamese Twins, performed headstands and other tricks in Edinburgh in the 1860s. According to a contemporary British newspaper, contrary to other 'objects of public curiosity', the twins did not exhibit 'forwardness' nor 'the *mauvaise honte* which would render visitors uneasy in their intercourse with them'.[107] Unlike the Twins, who wore 'gentlemanly' Western suits, Ching-Ching continues to sport his loose-fitting Chinese garb even after settling down in England.

In the early Ching-Ching stories, Ching-Ching's charm attracts women from all parts of the world, albeit mostly lower-class white women or foreign women, suggesting that as a Chinese seafarer he was only suited for females of similar class. He settles down in Carlham, England after marrying Alma Warrenham's maid Annette, who he met in 'Wonderful Ching-Ching'.[108] Annette initially rejected Ching-Ching's advances because she liked 'deferential men' and was angered by his 'all-abounding confidence' and 'unruffled assurance'.[109] Her 'hatred for foreigners' incited her to vilify him as 'a worm, a foreign viper, a thingammy with a pigtail'.[110] It was only when Ching-Ching was feared dead that Annette realized her true feelings for him. Despite admitting her desire to marry Ching-Ching, she wanted to keep their relationship a secret, perhaps because she was worried other people would ridicule her for rejecting him so blatantly before. Her initial rejection of Ching-Ching and subsequent acceptance exemplify the simultaneous repulsion and attraction towards the Other documented by critics such as Robert Young.[111] Back in England, Annette gives birth to Young Ching-Ching, who 'is as much like his father as a son can be, and the effect was heightened by his being similarly attired. The only thing he lacked was the pigtail, which with him was in

---

[106] The 'Chang, the Chinese Giant' show was also staged at the Royal Aquarium circa 1880. See 'Royal Aquarium. Chang the Great Chinese Giant', British Library <http://www.bl.uk/catalogues/evanion/Record.aspx?EvanID=024–000001743&ImageIndex=0> [accessed 19 September 2011].

[107] 'Twins in Edinburgh', *Hull Packet and East Riding Times*, 1 January 1869, p. 7.

[108] After Brocken's death near the end of 'Handsome Harry', Harry sails to South America and marries Juanita, Don Salvo's daughter. However, Don Salvo, who financed the Belvedere because he also wanted to see Captain Brocken dead, snatches his daughter away and forces her into an asylum, claiming that she is an escaped lunatic. In 'Cheerful Ching-Ching', Handsome Harry exhibits 'bravery and coolness' by going to Egypt and Turkey via France to save 'gentle Juanita', who has been locked up in a lunatic asylum in Cairo and disowned by her father because she dishonoured him by marrying Harry and neglecting her duty towards him. After a series of exciting events, Handsome Harry and Juanita travel safely back to England, accompanied by Don Salvo, who has repented of his sin and reconciled with his daughter. See Burrage, 'Cheerful Ching-Ching', p. 2.

[109] Burrage, *Cheerful-Daring-Wonderful Ching-Ching*, p. 383.

[110] Ibid., p. 375.

[111] For more discussion on attraction and repulsion towards the Other see Robert Young, *Colonial Desire: Hybridity in Theory, Culture and Race* (London, 1995).

a budding state, and looked as much like an inverted radish as anything else'.[112] Although Tom True 'never liked a half-caste' in *Handsome Harry*, the fact that Young Ching-Ching is a mixed-race child does not become an issue in any of the stories. In fact, he speaks and acts like a typical naughty British boy, leading other boys to cause commotion at school and wreak havoc around the village.[113]

In *Young Ching-Ching*, Ching-Ching becomes a doting father who constantly tries to bail his son out of trouble, usually by using his 'oily tongue'.[114] In England, Ching-Ching's image is that of a 'Celestial gentleman' and he hosts Christmas parties every year, suggesting he had become Westernized.[115] An illustration of Ching-Ching and his friends enjoying a Christmas feast adorned the cover of *The Boy's Leisure Hour Christmas Number* in 1886. The idea of a Chinese man seated at the head of a table hosting a Christmas dinner in an English village was probably previously unimaginable. Like Herbert/Lyu who sheds markers of his 'Miao-ness' when he settles down with his wife Little Waif in London at the end of *The Wasps of the Ocean*, Ching-Ching gradually becomes an 'upright citizen' and even an authority figure as the Ching-Ching series progress. This is particularly evident in the stories serialized in *Ching Ching's Own*.

Circulation and Readership

Francis Hitchman remarked in 1881 that publishers 'are much the same as other tradesmen – they sell the goods for which their customers ask'.[116] In 1888, responding to the success of 'Handsome Harry', 'Cheerful Ching-Ching', 'Daring Ching-Ching', 'Wonderful Ching-Ching', and 'Young Ching-Ching', Burrage launched *Ching Ching's Own: A Journal that Will Please the Boys* (1888–1893), serving as editor of the weekly paper that featured up to 18 illustrations in each issue. It was touted as 'the best investment for a penny ever put before the world'.[117] Starting from No. 27, it was expanded from an eight-page weekly into a sixteen-page paper ('owing to the large circulation it gained, and by the wishes of its readers') with up to three serials per issue, a weekly novelette, puzzle column, correspondence page, and other features. For example, there was 'Ching Ching's Natural History' column, '[d]ictated by Ching Ching and penned by Eddard during their leisure hours, some years ago'. It provided information such as 'De kangabroo [*sic*] was

---

[112] E. Harcourt Burrage, *Young Ching-Ching* (London, 1886), p. 4.

[113] Burrage, *Handsome Harry*, p. 3.

[114] Burrage, *Young Ching-Ching*, p. 15.

[115] E. Harcourt Burrage, 'Royal Feasting: A Ching-Ching Paper', *The Boys' Standard*, 305 (1881): pp. 268–70. See also 'Ching-Ching's Christmas Party', *The Boy's Leisure Hour*, V (1886): n. pag.; E. Harcourt Burrage, 'Ching Ching's Christmas Number', *Ching Ching's Own*, III.27 (1888): n. pag.; E. Harcourt Burrage, 'A Jolly Christmas Eve: Ching Ching's Own Double Christmas Number', *Ching Ching's Own*, VI.75 (1889): n. pag.

[116] Hitchman, 'The Penny Press', p. 398.

[117] 'Notices', *Ching Ching's Own*, I.7 (1888): p. 55.

firse discobered in Australey, and dere am no reaser to speck dat it eber discobered anywhere elsele, as it am known dat it not an exister in any oder countree ...'.[118] In addition, it was advertised that Ching-Ching would 'relate some new stories of his early life for the edification of the passengers and his chums' in future issues.[119] Many stories serialized in *Ching Ching's Own*, such as 'Ching Ching and His Chums: A Most Mirthful, Moving, and Mysterious Story', 'Young Ching-Ching at School: or, Grand Old Times for the Slapcrashers', 'The Wild Adventures of Jam Josser & Eddard Cutten at Home and Abroad', and 'Ching Ching on the Trail: A New Style of Detective Story' were later published in book form.

As Andrew King points out, circulation figures for most nineteenth-century periodicals are unreliable because 'either they are part of the magazine's or the publisher's self-puffing or they partake in the cultural wars'.[120] I have been unable to locate circulation figures for *Ching Ching's Own*, but evidence of 'self-puffing' can be found in an 1892 article where the editor claimed that 'If all the volumes of "Handsome Harry" and the Ching Ching works issued during the last fourteen years could be collected, and piled on top of St. Paul's, the weight of the binding alone would crush down the sacred edifice and make a pancake of it'.[121] However, in another issue, the editor conveniently forgot his prior 'self-puffing' when he stated:

> This is not a journal in which you will ever read staggering statements of the miles of paper used by us weekly. That sort of thing is got up for the weak and foolish, and no doubt it pays; but it is not pleasant work writing-up such miserable stuff, tongue in cheek, and haunted by the sensation of feeling like an unmitigated humbug. Miles of paper are used in every office of any size daily. A boot-maker might as well bawl out the length of the boot-laces, placed end to end, worn by his customers. It is only during recent years that such puerile calculations have come to the front ...[122]

In terms of actual numbers, a vague estimate of 'many thousands' of subscribers was given in 1890.[123] On 17 August 1889 Burrage informed readers that a Canadian and Australian edition of *Ching Ching's Own* had been published for the colonies

---

[118] E. Harcourt Burrage, 'Ching Ching's Natural History', *Ching Ching's Own*, I.3 (1888): p. 23; E. Harcourt Burrage, 'Ching Ching's Natural History', *Ching Ching's Own*, I.7 (1888): p. 55.

[119] 'Chingy's Own Yarns', *Ching Ching's Own*, II. Novelette No.17 (1888): p. 4.

[120] Andrew King, *The London Journal, 1845–83: Periodicals, Production, and Gender* (Aldershot, 2004), p. 82.

[121] 'Weekly Chat New Series XLIV', *The Best for Boys: Ching Ching's Own*, VI (New Series).72 (1892): p. 102.

[122] E. Harcourt Burrage, 'In the Editorial Room: New Series–LXXXV', *Ching Ching's Own*, X (New Series).120 (1893): p. 47.

[123] E. Harcourt Burrage, 'The Ching Ching Mystery', *Ching Ching's Own*, I–II (New Series).1–14 (1890): p. 88.

and although the readership was not large, it was growing. Later that year, Burrage claimed that on 24 September his agent in Australia 'cabled for the weekly edition to be *increased sixfold*' and remarked on the considerable sales growth of the magazine, 'an amazing fact in the face of the vast number of boys' journals, good, bad, and indifferent, now in circulation'.[124]

The 'vast number' of different boy's journals that competed on the market between 1880 and 1918 has been estimated at over 300.[125] In this highly competitive environment, many magazines folded within a year and others sprang up to replace them. Even the acclaimed boy's journal *Union Jack* (1880–1883), first edited by W.H.G. Kingston and later G.A. Henty, lasted merely three years. To survive among the numerous publications vying for readers' attention, it was important for a periodical to distinguish itself from the others. In the first issue of *Ching Ching's Own*, Burrage proposed to 'go in for variety' and stated his intention 'to try something different from the old thing'.[126] Andrew King has analyzed the significance of a periodical's title, pointing out that the title establishes boundaries and 'producers choose a name in order to imply to purchasers a genealogy'.[127] The title *Ching Ching's Own: A Journal that Will Please the Boys* indicates that Ching-Ching had gained a certain degree of popularity because the producers must have been confident that potential buyers would recognize this name and purchase the periodical based on their interest in the Ching-Ching stories. The periodical changed names twice, first becoming *The Best for Boys: Ching Ching's Own*, then shifting to *The Best for Merry Boys: Ching Ching's Own* possibly because the 'Ching-Ching' name became less well-known over the years. According to the editor, the title was first changed 'in response to the request of a host of our young friends' to 'make it clear to everybody that *Ching Ching's Own* is a Journal for Boys'.[128] Because readers unfamiliar with *Handsome Harry* may not have known whether Ching-Ching was male or female from his name alone, the editor used the new titles to assure boys that this journal was targeted at them. The editor's efforts to 'move with the times and meet the spirit of the age' were reflected in the second change in title.[129] In addition to renaming the paper, the editor decided to have

---

[124] E. Harcourt Burrage, 'In the Editorial Room: Confidential Chats with Our Boys No. 31', *Ching Ching's Own*, VI.71 (1889): p. 96 (emphasis in the original). It is difficult to determine circulation figures for penny dreadfuls. According to Springhall, popular penny dreadfuls probably sold between 25,000 and 30,000 copies per week. See Springhall, 'A Life Story', p. 233. Elsewhere, estimated weekly sale amounts range from 60,000 to two million. See 'The Literature of the Streets', pp. 43; 47.

[125] Kirsten Drotner, *English Children and Their Magazines, 1751–1945* (New Haven, 1988), p. 123.

[126] 'To All Boys Who Speak the English Tongue at Home and Abroad', *Ching Ching's Own*, I.1 (1888): p. 3.

[127] King, *The London Journal*, p. 49.

[128] 'Our New Heading', *Ching Ching's Own*, VII.91 (1890): p. 208.

[129] E. Harcourt Burrage, 'Please Read Carefully', *The Best for Merry Boys: Ching Ching's Own*, VII (New Series).100 (1892): p. 351.

the front illustration printed in colour. However, probably due to high production costs, the magazine eventually merged with a new journal *Bits for Boys* in 1893.

Although *Ching Ching's Own* was defined as a boy's journal, girls were not deterred from reading it, perhaps because in the initial *Handsome Harry* story, Burrage addressed readers as 'my little children – brave boys and girls'.[130] In 1888, to reassure his female readers that they were not in the minority, Burrage wrote in response to a 'brother and sister' from Dublin that 'Of course girls read our Journal – thousands of them, and why should they not?'[131] However, Burrage clearly defined his periodical as a boy's journal because on 8 September 1888 he responded to a female reader that 'a girls' story would be out of place in this journal. The appearance of the first chapters would promptly lead our office being invaded by a host of indignant boys demanding all sorts of compensation for the intrusion of such matter'.[132] According to Burrage, boyhood only lasted for 'five or six years', and 'the child of to-day will be the boy of to-morrow, and in a very little while that boy will be a man'.[133] Therefore, he wanted to convey the impression that adults also enjoyed reading the stories. For example, he included a letter from a reader named Ernest J. Preston in 1888 claiming his parents want to be the first to read *Ching Ching's Own*.[134]

Scholars of periodicals have debated the use of correspondence columns as evidence of 'real readers', questioning the authenticity of the letters published.[135] Burrage himself faced such accusations and addressed this issue in 1889: 'A great many people think it is not genuine, but composed to fill up a column or two … *Ching Ching's Own* requires no padding of that sort. Every answer … is a genuine reply to a letter received.'[136] Although it is impossible to verify whether Burrage penned the letters from imaginary enthusiastic readers or selected only positive responses to include in the correspondence columns, they are still worth examining because as Linda Frost argues, 'these columns indeed constitute bodies of readership, constructions that, imaginary or not, are always also a reflection of an imagined desire within the general population'.[137]

---

[130] Burrage, *Handsome Harry*, p. 143.

[131] 'Correspondence', *Ching Ching's Own*, I.5 (1888): p. 63.

[132] E. Harcourt Burrage, 'Correspondence', *Ching Ching's Own*, I.12 (1888): p. 95.

[133] 'Our New Heading', p. 208.

[134] Ernest J. Preston, 'Correspondence', *Ching Ching's Own*, III.27 (1888): p. 15.

[135] Linda Frost, *Never One Nation: Freaks, Savages and Whiteness in U.S. Popular Culture, 1850–1877* (Minneapolis, 2005), pp. 190–91.

[136] E. Harcourt Burrage, 'In the Editorial Room: Confidential Chats with Our Boys No. 19', *Ching Ching's Own*, V.59 (1889): p. 112. Earlier on 10 November 1888, he informed readers, 'We learn that there are a few people who will not believe that our correspondence is genuine, but assert that the letters appearing in our columns comes from particular friends. We beg to assure our readers that every letter inserted here comes spontaneously from those who are, indeed, our friend, but of whom we have no personal knowledge whatever': E. Harcourt Burrage, 'Correspondence', *Ching Ching's Own*, II. Novelette No. 21 (1888): p. 4.

[137] Frost, *Never One Nation*, p. 191.

Clever mechanisms that Burrage employed to ensure reader participation contributed to sustaining sales figures through the years *Ching Ching's Own* was in circulation. For example, readers could exercise their imagination and artistic skills by submitting their artistic rendering of Burrage's image to the 'Editor Portrait Competition'. Later, a notice appeared in Vol. III explaining that in response to readers who have 'expressed a desire to have a photograph of "their own Editor"', Burrage decided to offer readers a 'cabinet size' copy of his portrait 'post free, for twelve stamps'.[138] Author portraits were popular in the 1890s, and many publishers tried to attract readers by promising free images of their favourite authors. For example, a company reissued George Meredith's *The Tragic Comedians* in 1891 with 'a Photogravure Portrait of the Author' and 'Two other Portraits Engraved on Wood'.[139]

Burrage felt ambivalent towards prize-giving, a common method of attracting readership. In the first issue of *Ching Ching's Own*, readers were informed that 'this journal intends to include a lithographed authentic, full-length portrait of various figures (one with each number), a complete boys' novelette with each number, a complete story, and a silver medal of honour'.[140] The first few issues provided large portraits of Ching-Ching, Eddard, and Samson. During the initial launch of the new magazine, the editor splurged on '100 handsome prize cups, splendidly engraved' for 'boys who have made the best Cricketing and Boating Averages for their respective clubs – town and country'.[141] A reader named James Coombes wrote to the editor from Shottermill, Haslesmere, Surrey calculating that 1,016 Stamps, 41 Cups, 84 Editorial Portraits, 411 Certificates, and 480 Medals were given away from 1 January to 30 March 1889.[142] However, Burrage later condemned the trend of prize-giving, rationalizing that it was not beneficial for readers because 'for every shilling given by the editors of journals, the public pay in paper and stamps a pound'.[143]

Influential publisher George Newnes (1851–1910) initiated several promotional campaigns to increase the circulation figures of his *Tit-Bits*, such as offering a guinea as prize money for submissions to a weekly competition for the 'Prize Tit-Bit'. While Newnes's foray into what Peter D. McDonald terms 'participatory journalism' was successful, Burrage's attempt was less so: although

---

[138] 'Notice', *Ching Ching's Own*, III.34 (1889): p. 126.

[139] For more examples, see Margaret Diane Stetz, 'Life's "Half Portraits": Writers and Their Readers in Fiction of the 1890s', in Laurence S. Lockridge, John Maynard, and Donald D. Stone (eds), *Nineteenth-Century Lives: Essays Presented to Jerome Hamilton Buckley* (Cambridge, 1989), pp. 169–87 (p. 172).

[140] 'To All Boys', p. 3.

[141] '100 Handsome Prize Cups', *Ching Ching's Own*, I.11 (1888): p. 83.

[142] 'Correspondence', *Ching Ching's Own*, V.57 (1889): p. 78. By 20 October 1888, the names of 1,000 readers had already been appeared on Ching Ching's Order of Merit. See 'Ching Ching's Order of Merit', *Ching Ching's Own*, II. Novelette No.18 (1888): p. 4.

[143] Burrage, 'Please Read Carefully', p. 351.

the magazine offered 'small rewards' to amateur authors and artists, the results were 'most disheartening' because the submissions were mostly 'totally unfit for publication'.[144] In 1892, the editor admitted that the 'school of instruction', which aimed to give feedback on readers' writing, was 'a comparative failure' and attributed the reason for this failure to 'the thirst of the rising generation to make money "without any bother"'. He blamed the 'increasing body of unscrupulous editors' for whetting the appetite of readers by 'giving, or pretending to give, prizes of abnormal value'.[145] Whereas this might have been a valid reason for not renewing the system of giving prizes, another possibility might have been simply a lack of finances.

The Ching-Ching characters were not confined to the written word or two-dimensional posters; they 'came to life' in 'The Ching Ching and Chums Marionettes' show at 'School Treats, Foresters' and Temperance Fetes, Flower Shows, and Bazaars' as they toured through the United Kingdom during the spring and summer of 1889.[146] Readers interested in attending the shows were encouraged to contact Ching's Entertainment Department at 42 Essex Street, Strand, London. To strengthen the bond between readers, the editor urged members of the Ching Ching League to wear a piece of yellow ribbon ('Chingy's colours') when attending 'Ching Ching Punch and Judy, Marionette, and Ventriloquial Entertainments' so that 'Eddard may recognise Chingyites among the audience'. Those who wore a ribbon were promised a present after the show.[147] In the 8 June 1889 issue of *Ching Ching's Own*, there was an announcement for readers in the Maidenhead, Abingdon, Oxford, and surrounding area. They were informed that 'Ching Ching Ventriloquist, and Ching Ching Marionettes' would be coming in June and that they would be admitted to the grounds for free if they showed a copy of *Ching Ching's Own* at the gates.[148] On 13 July 1889 the editor responded to a reader named Orlando that he was unsure when the marionettes would be able to come to Colchester, indicating that readers were eager to see the show.[149] In 1910, Ching-Ching appeared on the big screen in a silent film called *Ching-Ching's Revenge* that was distributed by Walturdaw, with the script reportedly based on the stories of E. Harcourt Burrage.[150]

Ching-Ching was so vividly written that some fans believed he really existed. For example, the following letter from a reader named Adam Bridges reveals he wanted to meet Ching-Ching in person: 'My dear Ching Ching – Do you remember

---

[144] Peter D. McDonald, *British Literary Culture and Publishing Practice 1890–1914* (New York, 1997), p. 146; E. Harcourt Burrage, *Ching Ching's Own*, IX.113 (1890): p. 127.

[145] E. Harcourt Burrage, 'In the Editorial Room', *The Best for Boys: Ching Ching's Own*, X (New Series).119 (1892): p. 30.

[146] E. Harcourt Burrage, 'Important Notice', *Ching Ching's Own*, IV.43 (1889): p. 63.

[147] 'Notice to Subscribers', *Ching Ching's Own*, V.57 (1889): p. 78.

[148] E. Harcourt Burrage, 'Announcement', *Ching Ching's Own*, IV.51 (1889): p. 191.

[149] 'Correspondence', *Ching Ching's Own*, V.56 (1889): p. 63.

[150] Alan Goble, 'Ching-Ching's Revenge', *The Complete Index to World Film since 1895* (2009) <http://www.citwf.com/film61907.htm> [accessed 19 August 2010].

when I used to try to see you when the great Ching Ching made his first bow before the public? I was always at the office asking for you, and the only answer I got was that you were not to be seen'.[151] According to A. Harcourt Burrage, 'Often, when a country reader was in town, he would call to see "Mister Chingy" or "Master Sammy" and others, and Eddard Gritten [Cutten] was even honoured thus. The anxious enquirer was generally informed by the editor that these personages were out of town, or gone on another adventure'.[152] Considering that E. Harcourt Burrage concluded 'Cheerful Ching-Ching' by informing readers that 'Ching-Ching lives, Ching-Ching is a real being … and we let our readers know Ching-Ching is still alive', it is not surprising that some readers believed that the Chinese man who lingered around Fleet Street and told people to read *Ching Ching's Own*, 'was in days gone by "Ching-Ching", and honoured him, as they thought, in a very fitting way by "Spin a yarn Ching", "How's Grunt"?, "I say, what a pig Eddard is"'.[153]

The emphasis on friendship was another main reason for Ching-Ching's success. As E. Harcourt Burrage wrote in 1890, 'How many strong friendships we have promoted we cannot say; but we have written proof that their name is legion, and the secret of it is that from the first our journal had friendship for its foundation'.[154] Readers wanted to be Ching-Ching's friend. As W.L. Miller from Glasgow put it, Ching-Ching's 'oily way of winning many friends has also won me'.[155] A distinct 'Ching-Ching culture' existed outside the pages of the stories. The formation of the 'Ching-Ching Brotherhood', characterized by 'peace, jollity, and goodwill', helped create a feeling of affinity among readers.[156] 'Chingyites' received 'a silver medal of honour in handsome leather case' and were given the privilege to append the letters 'C.C.O.G.O.C' ('Cheerful Chum of Grand Old Chingy') after their name. Subscribers were asked to submit 'pithy and humorous reasons' for 'why he thinks he deserves a Medal'.[157] The list of the 100 winners appeared with instructions for successful Chingyites to pick up medals from their newsagents who were asked to display the prizes in their windows.[158] Readers also sent pen-pal requests to the correspondence columns.[159]

---

[151]   Adam Bridges, 'Correspondence', *Ching Ching's Own*, I.5 (1888): p. 39.

[152]   A. Harcourt Burrage, 'Ching-Ching Memoirs', p. 136.

[153]   E. Harcourt Burrage, 'Cheerful Ching-Ching', p. 131; A. Harcourt Burrage, 'Ching-Ching Memoirs', p. 149.

[154]   E. Harcourt Burrage, 'In the Editorial Room: Confidential Chats with Our Boys–New Series–IX', *The Best for Boys: Ching Ching's Own*, I (New Series).9 (1890): p. 134.

[155]   W.L. Miller, 'Correspondence', *Ching Ching's Own*, I.5 (1888): p. 39.

[156]   'Ching Ching's Order of Merit', p. 4.

[157]   'To All Boys', p. 3; 'Notices', *Ching Ching's Own*, I.6 (1888): p. 47. None of the reasons were printed in the periodical however.

[158]   'First List of One Hundred Winners of Ching Ching's Medal', *Ching Ching's Own*, I.9 (1888): p. 71.

[159]   See for example, 'Correspondence', *The Best for Boys: Ching Ching's Own*, II.26 (1891): p. 206.

In addition to the Brotherhood, readers themselves initiated discussion groups. For example, a reader from Aberdeen formed 'The Ching and Eddard' with eight or nine his friends to go over 'all the old series' and discuss 'the adventures of the "famous four"'.[160] Each local Ching Ching Club had the freedom to 'make its own rules' and readers such as James A. Aukrah were reminded 'that the Immortal One will not recognise any club which encourages unthankful men like Eddard'. Once a club was formed, the editor would 'enter the names of its members in the Ching Ching book of Chums'.[161] The Ching Ching Brotherhood represented a community of readers that regarded Ching-Ching not as an inferior repulsive Other but a fellow brother, just as Anne Bowman's St Kassian envisaged the world to be: one in which all men shall be brethren. For these readers then, perusing these stories did not heighten the dichotomy between 'Us' and 'Them' but rather had the potential to break down the barriers between races. In particular, the friendship between Ching-Ching and Samson demonstrates that despite differences in race (Chinese versus African), personality (cunning versus innocent), and physicality (bony versus giant), a strong relationship could be formed between two extremely different individuals. Adhering to his motto 'Never betray a friend', Samson remained faithful to Ching-Ching.[162] Ching-Ching loved Samson above all others: 'He admired and reverenced Handsome Harry, he respected Ira Staines and Tom True, but he loved "Sammy."'[163]

Another reason people continued to read the Ching-Ching stories was possibly because they wanted to uncover the mystery of who this character really was and where he came from. John McBratney asserts that Sherlock Holmes's attraction lies in the fact that he 'remains an insoluble mystery to his fellow human beings, beyond the reach of even those means he uses to solve crimes'.[164] The same argument is applicable to Ching-Ching, who leaves readers baffled as they attempt to solve the mystery of his ancestry, his age, and his language skills, for he is 'as much a puzzle to the nation of China as he is to Britishers'.[165] He evades the Chinese 'type' and is able, like Holmes, to perform the role that 'best assists his art'.[166] In 'Ching Ching and His Chums', one of the characters remarks that the question of who Ching-Ching is 'is the mystery'.[167] The narrator claims the 'Immortal One cannot write, but his is the directing hand' and speaks on behalf of

---

[160] E. Harcourt Burrage, 'Correspondence', p. 95.

[161] 'Correspondence', *Ching Ching's Own*, III.29 (1889): p. 47.

[162] E. Harcourt Burrage, *Handsome Harry*, p. 100.

[163] Ibid., p. 183.

[164] John McBratney, 'Racial and Criminal Types: Indian Ethnography and Sir Arthur Conan Doyle's *The Sign of Four*', *Victorian Literature and Culture*, 33.1 (2005): pp. 149–67 (p. 161).

[165] 'Advertisement', *The Best for Boys: Ching Ching's Own*, VII (New Series).83 (1892): p. 80.

[166] McBratney, 'Racial and Criminal Types', p. 161.

[167] 'Ching Ching and His Chums Chapter I to Chapter II', p. 2.

Ching-Ching when he states that 'If there is no sufficient light to let people know exactly who he was and what he was, Ching Ching is sorry; but he says he can't give more'.[168]

Although he is supposedly from Peking, nobody really knows the truth of Ching-Ching's ancestry, because 'Ching Ching always WAS mysterious'.[169] He originally claims his father was a rich Mandarin, but exaggerates the story further by announcing that his father was the greatest emperor in China, describing him as having worn two pigtails, 'owning 1600 wives, and a few other ladies, and nebber did nothing but sit on an a sackful of gold and eat rice. My moder was his favourite wife, and I am de only chile that he ntake [*sic*] notice of out of the 2716 that he had'.[170] When asked to repeat the number of children his father had, he cannot remember and replies that his father had 'Four thousand eleven hundred and ninety-two'.[171] In 'Cheerful Ching-Ching' he tells Samson that he was not born in Peking but is still 'a true-born Pekinner'.[172] An advertisement in No. 83 of Vol. VII (New Series) states that the 'profound mystery which hovers around his place of birth, notwithstanding the hints he has given from time to time, remains unraveled'.[173] Although readers are informed that Ching-Ching is illiterate when it comes to English, it is not clear whether he is able to read Chinese characters. He confidently informs Samson that 'Chineeser am a speaker languidger, and we am all born to read him'.[174]

'Healthy' Literature

Writing in 1890, Francis Hitchman commented that although publications such as *The Boy's Leisure Hour* and *Ching Ching's Own* were comparatively 'harmless', 'no boy is likely to be the better for reading them. He will derive neither information nor instruction from them, and it may be doubted whether the time spent over them would not be infinitely more usefully employed in cricket and football or some lighter games'.[175] Francis Hitchman probably considered *Ching Ching's Own* harmless because he was more concerned about stories that featured errand boys or young clerks who, discontent with their work, abandoned their jobs to indulge in a life of crime. Because it was assumed that readers of penny dreadfuls were working-class boys with similar backgrounds to the heroes of the

---

[168] 'Our Friends', *The Best for Boys: Ching Ching's Own*, IV (New Series).50 (1891): p. 172; 'Chingy's Own Yarns', p. 4.

[169] 'Ching Ching Debating Society', *The Best for Boys: Ching Ching's Own*, V (New Series).59 (1891): p. 103.

[170] E. Harcourt Burrage, *Handsome Harry*, p. 90.

[171] Ibid.

[172] E. Harcourt Burrage, 'Cheerful Ching-Ching', p. 44.

[173] 'Advertisement', p. 80.

[174] E. Harcourt Burrage, *Cheerful-Daring-Wonderful Ching-Ching*, p. 239.

[175] Francis Hitchman, 'Penny Fiction', *Quarterly Review*, 171 (1890): pp. 150–71 (p. 156).

stories described in them, critics feared that they would imitate the characters and run away to become robbers or pirates.[176] Ching-Ching's antics on the other hand, are too exaggerated to be considered realistic.

Although contemporary critics classified *Ching Ching's Own* as an unedifying journal, Burrage characterized the magazine as a 'wholesome journal issued for boys' 'leavened with earnest records of the doings of the brave and strong' and 'rejoiced' that readers '[gave] up reading abominable murderous literature for Old Chingy', who 'simply aims to amuse' by providing 'good honest, healthy humour'.[177] Burrage emphasized that 'It is NOT a blood and thunder journal/It is NOT filled with injurious rubbish/It is NOT a receptacle for old stories/It is NOT a journal a boy need hide away from his parents/It is NOT connected with any other boys' paper, but stands alone'.[178] Christopher Pittard points out that *The Strand Magazine*'s publisher George Newnes 'described his publications in the context of the health of his readers', frequently making use of the adjective 'wholesome' and its synonyms when discussing his productions.[179] Burrage employed similar descriptions, characterizing *Ching Ching's Own* as a 'wholesome journal' parents 'will rejoice to find'.[180] He explicitly linked *Ching Ching's Own* to health, asserting that '[o]ut of wholesome pleasures come healthy body and strength of mind'.[181] Compared to the other 'injurious' magazines that were full of 'poisonous rubbish and puerile dribblings', *Ching Ching's Own* aimed to 'give the strengthening medium'.[182] This medium was fiction, which Burrage claimed was 'instructive' and taught the reader 'certain codes of honour and morality that ought to govern our lives'.[183] While *Ching Ching's Own* did not contain the overt moralizing or the articles on science that respectable magazines such as the *Boy's Own Paper* did,

---

[176] Dunae, 'Penny Dreadfuls', p. 139.

[177] 'Correspondence', *Ching Ching's Own*, II. Novelette No.15 (1888): p. 4; E. Harcourt Burrage, 'One Word More', *The Best for Boys: Ching Ching's Own*, VII (New Series).101 (1892): p. 368. One reader who gave up reading 'bloods' was Jerry Bott, who wrote 'I was compelled to speculate my week's wages (of younger days) on the so-called Ching Ching's Own. I was very much persuaded not to, having been the victim of papers … tales of "blood and thunder" created a great sensation in the heads of some boys, and I have purchased and purchased in vain with hopes of coming to a good tale, but find they are all of the same description – "end in smoke", but in your paper, thou Immortal One, are two talks that ought to please anyone': Jerry Bott, 'Correspondence', *Ching Ching's Own*, I.8 (1888): p. 63.

[178] 'Our New Heading', p. 208.

[179] Christopher Pittard, '"Cheap, Healthful Literature": *The Strand Magazine*, Fictions of Crime, and Purified Reading Communities', *Victorian Periodicals Review*, 40.1 (2007): pp. 1–23 (p. 2).

[180] 'Correspondence', p. 4.

[181] E. Harcourt Burrage, 'One Word More', p. 368.

[182] Ibid.

[183] E. Harcourt Burrage, 'Confidential Chats with Our Boys No. 48', *Ching Ching's Own*, VII.88 (1890): p. 160.

it nonetheless championed 'honour and honesty'.[184] As Burrage informed a reader named T.T., 'The Immortal One may not be able to put you far on the right road, but he won't lead you into a wrong one'.[185]

Ching-Ching's peculiar personality is toned down in *Ching Ching's Own*, making him more 'wholesome' compared to when he first appeared in *The Boy's Standard*, perhaps because Burrage wanted to project a new image for his magazine and redefine his readership. Burrage downplayed Ching-Ching's troublesome nature in the later stories and transformed him into someone who solves other people's problems. In 'Ching Ching and His Chums; A Mirthful, Moving, and Mysterious Story' (1888), the first serial in *Ching Ching's Own*, Ching-Ching begins his transformation into a detective. Now a widower, he is stricken with financial difficulty when he is 'suddenly' 'robbed of the means of living at ease'.[186] Luckily, 'his services were needed to unravel one of the greatest mysteries of modern days'.[187] With monetary reward in sight, Ching-Ching plunges into the task of helping clear Tom Howard's name and travels to India. The next adventure 'The Ching Ching Mystery' (1890) occurs closer to home, when Young Ching-Ching and his friends disappear and Ching-Ching sets out to find them.[188] Readers were invited to use their deciphering skills to help solve the mystery of Young Ching-Ching's disappearance by scrutinizing the 'few hints' provided and piecing them together to 'produce at least an outline of the facts'.[189] According to the announcement of the winners, only the 41 readers who successfully solved the mystery were rewarded with 'an English timepiece' for submitting an answer along the lines of 'the boys had started ON A TOUR AROUND THE BRITISH ISLES'.[190] When Young Ching-Ching and his friends return safely, Ching-Ching concludes:

> all swell who end swell. Out ob dis lilly fair de boys hab learn a lesser. It am dis. Neber to despise de advisers ob pussons older an' more sperienced den dey are. It am now apelient to 'em dat dey tempted to much; but like truly brabe boys, dey not shamed to own it. One day dey mean to hab anoder go in at somefin, and it am my pillion dat dey will succeed.[191]

---

[184] 'Our New Heading', p. 208.

[185] E. Harcourt Burrage, 'Correspondence', *Ching Ching's Own*, II.Novelette No.17 (1888): p. 4.

[186] E. Harcourt Burrage, 'Ching Ching and His Chums Chapter I to Chapter II', p. 1.

[187] Ibid.

[188] Unlike his father, ten-year-old Young Ching-Ching speaks English like any British schoolboy. Having inherited his father's cunning and charm, he regularly creates disturbances, eventually getting kicked out of school. Like Ching-Ching, Young Ching-Ching also has a 'faithful follower' – a boy named Billy Pink ('a little round-bodied boy'), whose blind devotion to Young Ching-Ching parallels that of Samson: E. Harcourt Burrage, *Young Ching-Ching*, p. 18.

[189] E. Harcourt Burrage, 'The Ching Ching Mystery', p. 88.

[190] Ibid., p. 174.

[191] Ibid., p. 13.

The fact that Ching-Ching discusses 'lessons' that can be learnt from this experience and asks boys to listen to their elders demonstrates how much he has changed because he used to be a prank-playing comic figure 'who never could be serious for twenty-four hours'.[192] Readers could observe 'how Ching Ching had developed with time, how his genius had expanded and grown and grown into a thing of beauty'.[193] Now he was worthy to take on the role of a detective.

Ching-Ching the Detective

Burrage may have decided to reinvent Ching-Ching as a detective after witnessing the popularity of Sherlock Holmes since Arthur Conan Doyle first introduced him to readers in 1887. Although Ching-Ching had exercised his detective skills earlier in 'Ching Ching and His Chums' and 'The Ching Ching Mystery', he only becomes a renowned detective in 'Ching Ching on the Trail: A New Style of Detective Story' (1892) when his 'master mind' is needed to 'fathom a Mystery which our Keenest Detectives of Scotland-yard have hitherto been unable to unravel'.[194] In this story, Ching-Ching's comic relief responsibilities are turned over to characters such as Chaffinch and the Handy Man. Although subtitled 'a new style of detective story' because Ching-Ching was probably the first Chinese detective in Victorian children's fiction, the plot closely adheres to the 'classic paradigm of a detective story' outlined by B.J. Rahn, and, like other serialized detective fiction, 'presents its readers with recognisable and comfortable narrative models'.[195]

First, a murder is committed in a closed environment, which in this case is Rockmount Castle, located near an English village called Tancroft, where the Earl of Rockmount is found poisoned. Second, the puzzled police cannot unlock the mystery and therefore seek help from 'a gifted but eccentric amateur detective with encyclopedic knowledge, intuitive insight, and great capacity for deductive reasoning'.[196] Gibbs and Squirk ask for Ching-Ching's help because he is a 'genius': 'wondrous', 'audacious', 'eccentric', and 'clever'.[197] Moreover, he is very knowledgeable. In the words of Mr Fossil Bone, Ching-Ching is 'uneducated, but

---

[192] E. Harcourt Burrage, *Handsome Harry*, p. 156.

[193] 'Not to Be Flooded Out', *Ching Ching's Own*, I.9 (1888): p. 71.

[194] 'Advertisement', *Ching Ching's Own*, VII (New Series).81 (1892): p. 48; E. Harcourt Burrage, *Ching Ching on the Trail: A New Style of Detective Story* (London, [n.d.]), p. 5.

[195] B.J. Rahn, 'Seeley Regester: America's First Detective Novelist', in Barbara A. Rader and Howard G. Zettler (eds), *The Sleuth and the Scholar: Origins, Evolution, and Current Trends in Detective Fiction* (Westport, CT, 1988), pp. 47–61; Pittard, 'Cheap, Healthful Literature', p. 5.

[196] Rahn, 'Seeley Regester', pp. 49–50.

[197] E. Harcourt Burrage, *Handsome Harry*, pp. 99; 180; 162.

of limitless knowledge'.[198] Often the methods used by these 'eccentric' detectives are unconventional and sometimes baffling, but effective. Ching-Ching's methods are no exception. For example, Gibbs claims that 'Ching Ching will do things his own way or not at all' and 'when his way fails there's no more to be done'.[199] Those who hire Ching-Ching have the utmost confidence in him, believing that 'Ching Ching never yet was mixed up in anything that did not come out right'.[200]

Like the classic detective who arrives at the crime scene to collect evidence and interview witnesses and suspects before formulating a hypothesis, Ching-Ching travels to Tancroft to examine the English country estate and questions some old men who provide 'a great deal of useful information about the servants at Rockmount Castle'.[201] They confide in him because his 'native gentleness won the affections right away of those he visited'.[202] After reviewing the facts and gathering information, Ching-Ching suggests that Benson the butler is the one who poisoned his employer. Furthermore, Benson's brother-in-law Andrew Gorby is impersonating him because his resemblance to the real heir George Beaufoy was so uncanny that they were known as 'the twins' during childhood. Gorby attempts to 'carry out one of the greatest frauds of modern times' and believes nobody would recognize him as an impostor because Beaufoy had left England for Africa to make his fortune in diamonds many years ago.

Upon hearing Ching-Ching's hypothesis, Gibbs comments that 'it was the only reasonable assumption to account for the death of the nobleman'.[203] They fear Beaufoy may be in danger and Ching-Ching embarks on a quest to bring him home safely. Ching-Ching finds George Beaufoy stranded on an island unable to return to England to claim his inheritance because Gorby had murdered everyone on board Beaufoy's boat. Ching-Ching brings him back to England, where he confronts the false heir. Most detective stories preserve the cosmic world view by concluding with the murderer's arrest and the restoration of moral order. Accordingly in this text Andrew Gorby is duly imprisoned. However, before he could be sentenced, he dies from the shock of seeing George Beaufoy 'rise, like a denouncing spirit, in court'.[204]

Before Ching-Ching became a detective, he utilized his cunningness to steal from others and escape punishment. His unreadable face made characters like Samson unsure of whether he was lying or telling the truth. In fashioning Ching-Ching into a detective figure, however, Burrage suggests that nineteenth-century stereotypes of the Chinese as cunning and mysterious, qualities that had been comically evident in *Handsome Harry*, could be put to good use to uphold justice.

---

[198] E. Harcourt Burrage, 'Young Ching Ching at School Chapter XXVIII', *Ching Ching's Own*, II.26 (1888): p. 103.

[199] E. Harcourt Burrage, *Ching Ching on the Trail*, p. 6.

[200] E. Harcourt Burrage, 'Ching Ching and His Chums Chapter I to Chapter II', p. 2.

[201] E. Harcourt Burrage, *Ching Ching on the Trail*, p. 144.

[202] Ibid., p. 143.

[203] Ibid., p. 128.

[204] Ibid., p. 283.

When readers are first introduced to Ching-Ching, they are informed that 'he had plenty of cunning' and later told that he looked like 'a veritable god of cunning'.[205] Furthermore, Ching-Ching can remain expressionless, making it hard for people to read him. In fact, his face 'rarely' showed surprise, and although he 'was occasionally the victim of surprise', 'losing his presence of mind was a thing unknown to Ching Ching'.[206] He remains calm and 'immovable' in the face of danger and kills without batting an eye, able to strangle his enemy with 'a terrible, remorseless grip'.[207]

Like the pipe-smoking Sherlock Holmes, 'the most perfect reasoning and observing machine the world has ever seen', cigarette-smoking Ching-Ching is a good observer and listener: 'his quiet eyes' take in 'everything that could be seen' and his ears absorb 'everything that could be heard'.[208] His eyes are the most striking feature of his 'Mongolian cast of countenance' – 'What a world of cuteness and leeriness lurked in their depths'.[209] His illiteracy is a 'trifling obstacle' because he has 'gifts that might have put him at the head of a state'.[210] Although Ching-Ching is illiterate, he can recognize crucial files. For example, when he observes a man with a bag filled with papers, he notices that there 'was a decided legal appearance' about them and 'had sufficient experience to know that it was an important document'.[211] Hence, he uses his dexterous feet (instead of his hands) to steal this document, which proves to be the Earl of Rockmount's will.

The narrator frequently implies that without luck on his side, Ching-Ching would not have been successful in his detective work. Besides his 'patience' and 'sagacity', 'times and seasons combined to aid him in his work'.[212] Ching-Ching, who 'carries a charm with him that never fails to bring good fortune', relies on both 'instinct' and 'a little good luck' to find and rescue those in need.[213] 'Curiosity' is 'a crowning virtue' of Ching-Ching's, because he could keep it 'well under control, and use it so discreetly'.[214] Collaboration is also important

---

[205] E. Harcourt Burrage, *Handsome Harry*, p. 20; E. Harcourt Burrage, *Ching Ching on the Trail*, p. 38.

[206] E. Harcourt Burrage, *Ching Ching on the Trail*, p. 13; E. Harcourt Burrage, 'Ching Ching and His Chums Chapter XI to Chapter XII', *Ching Ching's Own*, I.6 (1888): pp. 41–3 (p. 42).

[207] E. Harcourt Burrage, 'Cheerful Ching-Ching', 23; Burrage, *Ching Ching on the Trail*, p. 219.

[208] Arthur Conan Doyle, *The Adventures of Sherlock Holmes* ([London]: John Murray, [1930]), p. 1; E. Harcourt Burrage, *Ching Ching on the Trail*, p. 129.

[209] E. Harcourt Burrage, *Cheerful-Daring-Wonderful Ching-Ching*, p. 183.

[210] Ibid., p. 520.

[211] E. Harcourt Burrage, *Ching Ching on the Trail*, pp. 130–31.

[212] Ibid., p. 283.

[213] E. Harcourt Burrage, 'Ching Ching and His Chums Chapter I to Chapter II', p. 2; E. Harcourt Burrage, *Ching Ching on the Trail*, p. 268.

[214] E. Harcourt Burrage, *Cheerful-Daring-Wonderful Ching-Ching*, p. 318.

when solving cases. Just as Sherlock Holmes works with Watson and other associates, Ching-Ching is assisted by a team of friends that he met in *Handsome Harry*. In *Ching Ching on the Trail*, Ching-Ching collaborates with Gibbs, who handles the legal side of the case, using legalities to ensure that Andrew Gorby cannot possess the estate before Ching-Ching discovers and rescues the real heir. To succeed, Ching-Ching must work with someone who can read and write.[215] Detective Ross fulfils this role in the 'Ching Ching Mystery' by deciphering the words on torn-up pieces of a letter.

According to Lawrence Rothfield, Sherlock Holmes's contribution to preserving the structure of British society is in his ability to reveal those who are '"passing" as respectable citizens'.[216] Holmes seeks out the impostors and helps to maintain the desires of the middle and upper classes who wish to be gatekeepers of their society, deciding and controlling who can or cannot enter.[217] Similarly, Ching-Ching preserves the social order by exposing the lower-class Andrew Gorby as an impostor trying to infiltrate the aristocratic world. This image of Ching-Ching as an upright citizen who upholds the law reverses the usual scenario where the perpetrator of a crime is an evil Chinese man, while the detective who brings him to justice is British.

Even before Ching-Ching becomes a detective, he helps to maintain order by participating in the effort to stop Adrian, the villain of *Daring Ching Ching* who aimed for 'the total disruption of society as it is, the destruction of kings, the annihilation of governments', by controlling 'Nihilists in Russia, Socialists in Germany, and Communists in France'.[218] Laura Otis argues that Sherlock Holmes regarded the Orient as a place ready to infect and destroy the British Empire.[219] Although he is an 'Oriental', Ching-Ching is not regarded as a source of foreign 'germs' that will infect Britain. By transforming Ching-Ching into a detective, Burrage has 'sanitized' and tamed the former gambler and drinker, suggesting that Chinese people can maintain and restore order instead of causing disruptions and disorder. However, despite treating the Chinese unconventionally in many ways, Burrage also revealed ambivalent attitudes towards other races.

---

[215] However, in a previous story he had written a note to Handsome Harry. These narrative slippages probably occurred because E. Harcourt Burrage was pressured to grind out several manuscripts each week.

[216] Lawrence Rothfield, *Vital Signs: Medical Realism in Nineteenth-Century Fiction* (Princeton, 1992), p. 139.

[217] Laura Otis, 'The Empire Bites Back: Sherlock Holmes as an Imperial Immune System', *Studies in Twentieth Century Literature*, 22.1 (1998): pp. 31–60; Rothfield, *Vital Signs*, pp. 139–41.

[218] E. Harcourt Burrage, *Cheerful-Daring-Wonderful Ching-Ching*, p. 293.

[219] Otis, 'The Empire Bites Back'.

Burrage's Attitude to Race

By rehashing characters based on national types, Victorian adventure story writers provided readers with a sense of familiarity and simultaneously bolstered their sense of British superiority. Burrage tried to instill pride in his British readers with the following statement: 'If there is one thing which we Britishers have a right to be proud of it is our pluck. Other nations may say what they please, and call this assertion a boast, but it is an indisputable fact that this little isle has more than its share of courage.'[220] According to Laurence Kitzan, Victorian adventure novels 'were often little sermons on power, how the power of Britain gained an empire, and how, in turn, the empire interacted and ensured that Britain would remain powerful and in a position to compete with the other great nations of the world'.[221] Burrage also commented on Britain's rise in power and military might, attributing the Spanish people's antagonistic attitude towards the British to their loss of power or prestige:

> there is no greater hate in this world of hate than the Spaniards hate of the English. The Great Armada has never been forgiven. Once the most powerful nation on earth, and ever the most proud, they mourn over their loss of power, which has been decaying for more than three hundred years. Rightly or wrongly they charge it to us, and say that we have fattened on their ruin. We hold Gibraltar, too, and no wonder that Spaniards at home and abroad hate us.[222]

The Spanish are also described as hating the 'dark races':

> The Spaniards hate the negro, for the terrible vengeance the dark-skinned race exercised in Peru has never been forgotten or forgiven. There the slaves fled from their masters, and, hidden in a wood, lay in wait for them and spared none that they caught ... The negroes had been cruelly treated and goaded to madness. All the Spaniards that were caught were roasted alive, and their hearts eaten – at least, so runs the legend, and the Spaniard believes it to this day. Hence their hatred of the dark races.[223]

Like Bowman's St Kassian, the narrator of 'Cheerful Ching-Ching' is optimistic that less 'civilized' people can progress towards 'civilization': 'The Turk is behind the rest of the civilized world, and nothing more. Gradually lessons in cleanliness, morality, and social duties are taking root in his dogged nature, and if we give him time ... he will grow in grace and virtue as others have done before him.'[224] Of the Portuguese, Burrage writes, 'there is not a more resolute and daring race on earth'

---

[220] E. Harcourt Burrage, *Handsome Harry*, p. 181.

[221] Laurence Kitzan, *Victorian Writers and the Image of Empire: The Rose-Colored Vision* (Westport, CT, 2001), p. 43.

[222] E. Harcourt Burrage, *Handsome Harry*, p. 34.

[223] Ibid., p. 183.

[224] E. Harcourt Burrage, 'Cheerful Ching-Ching', p. 45.

and 'if as a nation they have fallen away in prestige, the fault does not lie with the individual, but with the rulers of that country'.[225]

Burrage has been accused of 'ethnic stereotyping' in one of his other adventure stories 'The Island School' (1895–1896), which, according to John Springhall, includes characters such as 'Lucia di Valo, the proud, revengeful Spanish beauty; Espardo Reonardo, the Invader of the Island ... and Macbeth, Hamlet and Romeo, a trio of Darkies who more or less fill in the whole duty and characteristics of the nigger'.[226] Although Springhall comments that Burrage's 'Darkies' 'fill the duty and characteristics of the nigger', Burrage expressed anger at slave traders, accusing them of knowing 'nothing of the value of life' and caring for 'no loss or suffering but [their] own'.[227] Burrage also protested against slavery in *Handsome Harry* through his character Samson, who 'was particularly furious when the slave question came about, for he had suffered by it'.[228] Samson is infuriated when someone calls him a nigger and threatens to bash his head against the wall if he did it again. In one of the correspondence columns in *Ching Ching's Own*, Burrage criticized the American prejudice towards African Americans in the following response to a reader known as 'Black Boy': 'In this country we do not bother ourselves about riding in the same carriage with a negro. It is in the only land of true freedom, according to their own statement – that of the Americans – that the dark-skinned race is offensively made to feel its inferiority.'[229]

Regarding Africans, the narrator of *Handsome Harry* states that 'ignorant people' might think that they are all 'of the negro type, with low foreheads, thick lips, and flat noses', but they are incorrect. To address this error, he gives an example of the Foolahs, who possess 'exquisitely moulded forms and features' and only resemble 'the ordinary negro' by 'the colour of the skin'.[230] Although he seems sensitive to some Africans, wanting to rectify false impressions about them, his characterization of the African king Matta is quite negative, for he writes that

---

[225] E. Harcourt Burrage, *Ching Ching on the Trail*, p. 215.

[226] Springhall, 'Boys of Bircham School', p. 394.

[227] E. Harcourt Burrage, *Handsome Harry*, p. 78.

[228] Ibid., p. 75.

[229] E. Harcourt Burrage, 'Correspondence Column', *The Best for Merry Boys: Ching Ching's Own*, X (New Series).137 (1893): p. 111.

[230] E. Harcourt Burrage, *Handsome Harry*, p. 77. In 1860, the Foolahs were thus described: 'It is the opinion of modern travellers that the Foolahs are destined to become the dominant people of Negroland, and they have excited more interest and scientific research than almost any other African race. In language, appearance, and history, they present striking differences from the neighboring tribes, to whom they are superior in intelligence, but inferior, according to Barth, in physical development. ... Dr. Barth found great local differences in their physical characteristics, and Bowen describes the Foolahs of Yoru-ba as being some black, some almost white, and many of a mulatto color varying from dark to very bright. Their features and skulls were cast in the European mould': "Foolah," in George Ripley and Charles Anderson Dana (eds), *The New American Cyclopaedia: A Popular Dictionary of General Knowledge* (New York, 1860), pp. 592–3.

Matta would 'sell anything and everything for rum and cutlass'.[231] In addition, stereotypes are used in depictions of Ching-Ching's faithful friend Samson. For example, Samson speaks like a stereotypical African: 'But you once tell me dat you able to read nuffin'.[232] Furthermore, he is described as simple-minded: 'a child in thought' with 'but two heroes in the world–Harry and Ching-Ching. He looked upon the former as the handsomest, noblest, bravest man that ever lived, and the latter as the one true genius which had come to light under the sun'.[233] The narrator asserts that if Ching-Ching

> had declared that he could play skittles with the moon, Samson would have believed him, so great was the faith he had in that most wondrous Chinee ... He might be a little confused over the stories he heard, and find it difficult to reconcile the various anecdotes in connection with the family of that truly remarkable man, but in his simplicity he did not doubt them in the main, and verily believed that they were capable of being reconciled and coming out truthfully bright and clear ... Harry was Samson's star in war, while Ching-Ching was his leading light in peace.[234]

However, Samson is not as simple-minded as he believes himself to be, because he always notices Ching-Ching's inconsistencies. However, because he thinks that 'he possessed a defective memory, he forbore to contradict'. [235]

The Ching-Ching stories are filled with many interesting characters of all races. Initially, the non-Caucasian characters such as Ching-Ching, Samson, and Bill Grunt (the boatswain of African descent) play minor roles, but they increasingly become more prominent in the stories, while Caucasian characters such as Handsome Harry, Tom True, and Ira Staines become less significant. At the beginning of *Handsome Harry*, the more important jobs on the Belvedere were allocated to the 'English, Irish, and Scotch' while the foreigners 'performed the menial offices of the ship'.[236] However, as the Ching-Ching stories develop, this racial hierarchy is gradually reversed. Instead of the white character Eddard Cutten leading the others after Handsome Harry marries and retires, Ching-Ching becomes the 'august' leader.[237]

This phenomenon challenges statements made by critics who claim that late nineteenth-century adventure stories all feature English imperialist heroes defeating evil Others on the outskirts of the Empire. Burrage's treatment of Samson and Ching-Ching also calls into question the Victorian confidence in defining

---

[231] E. Harcourt Burrage, *Handsome Harry*, p. 61.

[232] E. Harcourt Burrage, *Cheerful-Daring-Wonderful Ching-Ching*, p. 239.

[233] Ibid., p. 243; E. Harcourt Burrage, *Handsome Harry*, p. 162.

[234] Ibid.

[235] Ibid., p. 36.

[236] Ibid., p. 3.

[237] '"The Best for Boys" Library', *The Best for Boys: Ching Ching's Own*, II (New Series).15 (1891): p. 30.

people according to 'racial types' because his texts reflect seemingly contradictory attitudes towards the use of 'types'. A tension between appearance and reality is apparent in the Ching-Ching series. In Ching-Ching's polyglot world, there are people such as Sam Rock, who is a Scotsman born in Brazil as well as a pirate chief who 'spoke very good English', but 'did not appear to have an English face'.[238] Not only was it difficult to determine Sam Rock's origin, it was almost impossible to 'guess the nationality of his followers'.[239] The narrator characterizes them as 'a mixed lot, and might be anything. One thing they had certainly in common, and that was their brutal disposition. A more diabolical gang of scoundrels were never gathered together'.[240]

Although some degree of anxiety is expressed over being unable to determine the nationality of these 'scoundrels', no concern is voiced about Ching-Ching, who, as a highly mobile character, is a prime example of a man with indeterminate national identity. For example, 'to look at him [Ching-Ching] he is a Chinaman, but in his speech he is Ching Ching only ...'.[241] Ching-Ching is wholly *sui generis* – in a league of his own. Although some prejudiced characters in the stories make racist statements about the Chinese, readers would probably not have accepted the assertions. For example, Don Salvo declares, 'The Chinese are a cursed, ugly race'.[242] But because he is one of the villains in *Handsome Harry*, his credibility is questionable. Similarly, the cranky white sailor Eddard Cutten insults the Chinese, '"Afore I'd be a yaller Chinnee", ... "I'd be a wampire, or any warmint. There's nothing manly about 'em"'.[243] However, Ching-Ching demonstrates his manliness and proves Eddard wrong by winning their fight.

Ching-Ching's Legacy

Several memoirs and articles from the twentieth century suggest that the Ching-Ching stories were read by adults with as much fondness as they felt in their youth. For example, F.W. Puleston claimed in 1928, 'I do not think there is another one of the old School Writers whose yarns appeal to me nowadays as Mr Burrage'.[244] R.A.H. Goodyear, who sent letters to *Ching Ching's Own* as a child in 1891, wrote as an adult in 1933,

> As a boy I never could finish a story by Jules Verne or G.A. Henty. I turned with relief to 'The Slapcrash Boys', 'Handsome Harry', 'Tom Tartar at School' because they were merry and bright and tinged with natural humour throughout.

---

[238] E. Harcourt Burrage, *Cheerful-Daring-Wonderful Ching-Ching*, p. 267.

[239] Ibid.

[240] Ibid.

[241] E. Harcourt Burrage, 'Ching Ching and His Chums Chapter I to Chapter II', p. 2.

[242] E. Harcourt Burrage, *Handsome Harry*, p. 45.

[243] Ibid., p. 136.

[244] F.W. Puleston, 'Correspondence', *Collector's Miscellany*, 1.1 (1928): p. 5.

Now and then I come across books which dear old E. Harcourt Burrage ... wrote for publishers like Partridge and Sampson Low: they read tamely by comparison with his robust Ching Ching series, than which nothing livelier was ever produced for boys.[245]

Barry Ono (1876–1941), a famous collector of penny dreadfuls, remembers that growing up in the late Victorian era, 'when everything but the good little boys' *Boy's Own Paper* was sweepingly designated a "penny dreadful" or "pernicious literature"', he 'used to buy the *Boy's Own Paper* and with the title very ostentatiously displayed outside', and read his 'current number of "Sweeny Todd", "Handsome Harry" or "Spring Heeled Jack" inside'.[246] Sir J.A. Hammerton (1871–1949), author and editor of reference works, describes a bully in his school named Harry whose looks reminded him of the pictures of 'Handsome Harry of the Fighting Belvedere', and that it 'led to that long-sustained boys' "penny blood" being a favorite with my playmates'.[247] Ben Winskill recalls in 'The Penny Dreadful Offices' that he collected posters of the penny dreadfuls and that the 'old yellow posters with page illustrations from Turnpike Dick, Sweeny Todd and Ching-Ching delighted [him] most'.[248]

Conclusion

In 'Get Out of Gaol Free, or: How to Read a Comic Plot', John Bruns argues that comic characters such as Falstaff, Don Quixote, or Mr Pickwick 'seem to exist as comic entities outside the pages of their respective works'. For example, because Falstaff appears in three Shakespeare plays, he is not defined by a single plot, and has freedom of movement to 'walk the earth wherever he pleases'.[249] Parallels can be drawn between Falstaff and Ching-Ching, who both steal, lie, and consume a great deal of alcohol. Most importantly, like Falstaff, Ching-Ching is a comic character who is not confined by the pages of the stories. Bruns argues that while readers of novels join 'the march towards resolution', readers of comedy join 'the endless dance'.[250] He asserts that readers are more interested in finding

---

[245] Goodyear received the following response in *Ching Ching's Own*: 'R.A.H. Goodyear – We have enough cons. in hand to last three months. We will keep yours in hand. 2. you might have sent the card to him. It would have been an act of courtesy': E. Harcourt Burrage, 'Correspondence', *Ching Ching's Own*, II (New Series).17 (1891): p. 62; Goodyear, 'Stories I Liked the Most – and Least', p. 46.

[246] Barry Ono, 'Camouflaged Blood Titles', *Collector's Miscellany*, 7 (1933–1934): pp. 9–10 (p. 9).

[247] J.A. Hammerton, *Books and Myself: Memoirs of an Editor* (London, 1944), p. 9.

[248] Ben Winskill, 'The Penny Dreadful Offices', *Vanity Fair*, 17.2 (1925): pp. 47–9 (p. 47).

[249] John Bruns, 'Get out of Gaol Free, or: How to Read a Comic Plot', *Journal of Narrative Theory*, 35.1 (2005): pp. 25–59 (p. 28).

[250] Ibid., p. 28.

out how Falstaff manoeuvres from one situation to the next than what happens to him in the end. Likewise, readers of the Ching-Ching stories join in the dance as Ching-Ching glides from one adventure to the next, wriggling himself out of one difficulty after another. Instead of laughing *at* Ching-Ching, readers laugh *with* Ching-Ching. Ching-Ching's physical and linguistic markers of Otherness were not regarded with repulsion and derision by young Victorian readers. On the contrary, they considered him a 'Guide, Friend and Councillor'.[251]

Children's texts on China are a product of their historic moment. Because Burrage was writing during a time when the number of Chinese immigrants in Britain was fairly low, his stories reflect a sense of ease about Ching-Ching's presence in England. Children considered Ching-Ching a friend because he was a non-threatening character who more or less assimilated to British culture after marrying Annette. Furthermore, his criminality was never on the same level as the daring highwaymen or murderous barbers associated with infamous penny dreadfuls. Readers may not have learned many 'facts' about China and the Chinese from *Ching Ching's Own* because it rarely included articles about the country, but they were presented with the idea that a Chinese person could be their friend.[252]

In *Handsome Harry*, the narrator comments that Ching-Ching's 'nature has so many contradictions in it that one scarcely knows what he is – I, the writer of his history, fail to fathom him, and it may be that he was even a puzzle to himself?'[253] This comment suggests that during the course of the serial story, Ching-Ching came to take on a life of his own and refused to be typecast. Although Burrage began his career as a penny dreadful writer, he did not adhere strictly to the conventions of the genre. Ching-Ching may have been created as a lying kleptomaniac who fulfilled the role of a comic foreigner, but he evolved into a distinctive character that challenged generic conventions. Because penny dreadful stories were published weekly, Burrage was free to invent stories about Ching-Ching as he went along. Ching-Ching's illusive quality made him appealing and his knack for spinning yarns was particularly suited to the genre of serialized fiction because mini-digressions bearing no direct relevance to the plot could be included each week. The fact that readers were not given details of Ching-Ching's past when he first appeared on the Belvedere also allowed Burrage creative space to continually devise amusing anecdotes about this character. Had Burrage been a novelist, he would probably have been more restricted in terms of how he could develop the Ching-Ching character.

---

[251] A. Harcourt Burrage, 'Ching-Ching Memoirs', p. 136. At the beginning of the article, A. Harcourt Burrage quotes a poem from a reader named G.H. which ends with 'Guide, Friend and Councillor – Farewell! FAREWELL!'

[252] For articles on China, see 'The Chinese "Cangue"', *The Best for Boys: Ching Ching's Own*, I (New Series).10 (1890): p. 148; 'The Place for Boys', *The Best for Boys: Ching Ching's Own*, II (New Series).15 (1891): p. 20; 'Boys and Girls in the Flowery Land', *The Best for Merry Boys: Ching Ching's Own*, X (New Series).127 (1893): p. 159.

[253] E. Harcourt Burrage, *Handsome Harry*, p. 162.

Ching-Ching's transformation from an outlandish globetrotter to a serious intelligent detective residing in England also challenges the idea of the image of the Other as fixed and unchanging. Considering that cheap periodicals were easily digested and disposed of and many did not survive for more than five years, Ching-Ching's 17-year 'literary career' was remarkable. In 1891, Burrage asserted that 'the day is far distant, we believe, when a generation will arise that knows not Chingy'.[254] In fact, four decades after Ching-Ching first appeared in 'Handsome Harry of the Fighting Belvedere', Ching-Ching's popularity was mentioned in one of the *Boy's Own Paper*'s correspondence columns.[255]

Although Ching-Ching is presented as a borderless individual with freedom to travel anywhere he pleases, this mobility is not perceived as a threat, unlike in later children's stories such as Captain Brereton's *The Dragon of Pekin* (1902) in which Chinese immigration is seen as dangerous.[256] The next two chapters will focus on novels related to major historical events in Anglo-Chinese relations which contain more negative images of the Chinese. Chapter 4 will examine the representation of the Taiping Rebellion (1850–1864), while Chapter 5 will investigate narratives of the Boxer Uprising (1899–1901).

---

[254] 'Correspondence', *The Best for Boys: Ching Ching's Own*, III.30 (1891): p. 110.

[255] The editor responded to a reader named H.T. Painter that 'The character you mention was so popular among its readers that the same publisher issued "Ching Ching's Own", which has also ceased. To give it a start a competition was devised, the prize being a semi-detached house. The house, which was in Leathwaite Road, Battersea Rise, was called Ching Ching's Villa, and bore the name for some years': 'Correspondence Column', *Boy's Own Paper*, 40 (1917–1918): p. 391. There is a reference to Ching Ching's Bower and Harmony Hall in *Ching Ching's Own*, but not a Ching Ching's Villa.

[256] Brereton writes, 'China is the question of the future. If we are not careful her spare millions will swamp the world, for the Chinaman has taken to emigrating, and wherever he goes he prospers. He accepts a wage which to others is not a living one, and for it his vast fund of energy allows him to labour all day long. His living costs him next to nothing, for John Chinaman enjoys a feast from the leavings of other nations ... Ay, I have seen him in Australia, in America, and in Burma; and everywhere he is the same, -well dressed, thriving, and full of dignity and prosperity': F.S. Brereton, *The Dragon of Pekin: A Tale of the Boxer Revolt* (London, 1902).

Chapter 4
Heroes and Hostile Hordes: Representing the Taiping Rebellion (1850–1864)

> Every opportunity is taken of putting into the mouths of the characters long descriptions of the usual kind, of Chinese manners and customs, none of which, however, throws any new light on the subjects dwelt on.
> —Review of *The Mandarin's Daughter* in *Athenaeum* (1876)[1]

Samuel Mossman's *The Mandarin's Daughter: A Story of the Great Taiping Rebellion, and Gordon's "Ever-Victorious Army"* (1875) was one of the few Victorian novels that featured the Taiping Rebellion (1850–1864). In addition to novels, Mossman wrote non-fictional work such as *China: A Brief Account of the Country, Its Inhabitants and Their Institutions* (1867).[2] He was the second editor of the influential *North China Herald*, the Shanghai newspaper started by Henry Shearman in 1850. In the preface of *The Mandarin's Daughter*, Mossman writes: 'Where the salient points of these memorable events [Taiping Rebellion] are narrated, the facts recorded in their history are strictly adhered to; so also are the secondary features of the narrative, in describing the customs and manners of the Chinese – consequently the amount of fiction is infinitesimal'.[3] Like William Dalton, Mossman utilized plot twists enabling his characters to travel to many parts of China so that he could introduce places such as the Grand Canal, the Yellow River, and the Porcelain Tower, as well as curiosities such as outdoor barber shops, the 'punishment of the kang [cangue]', and 'a physiognomist who studied the characters of his customers by their features, to which he added a little fortune-telling by means of palmistry …'.[4] Even though Mossman boasted of his credentials as someone 'who has resided in [China] for some years; and who made it his study to understand the extraordinary people who inhabit it, their history, and institutions', his understanding of China and the Chinese did not impress the reviewer in the *Athenaeum* who stated that none of the long descriptions of Chinese manners and customs in *The Mandarin's Daughter* sheds 'new light on the subjects dwelt on'.[5] As the reviewer's comment indicates, while the information

---

[1] 'Book Review', *Athenaeum*, 2515 (1876): p. 53.

[2] *North China Herald* became *North China Daily News* in 1864. Samuel Mossman, *China: A Brief Account of the Country, Its Inhabitants and Their Institutions* (London, 1867).

[3] Samuel Mossman, *The Mandarin's Daughter: A Story of the Great Taiping Rebellion, and Gordon's "Ever-Victorious Army"* (London, 1876), p. v.

[4] Ibid., p. 322. Further page references are given after quotations in the text.

[5] Mossman, *China*, p. iv; 'Book Review', p. 53.

about China imparted in *The Wolf Boy of China* was considered 'little-known' in Dalton's time, by 1875, it had become familiar and 'usual' due to the expansion of knowledge and the large number of new books that introduced China to the general public. Like *The Wolf Boy of China*, *The Mandarin's Daughter* was also marketed as a Christmas book, but it received mostly negative reviews. While Dalton was praised for bringing the 'peculiarities' of the Chinese to readers in an 'entertaining and agreeable manner', Mossman was criticized for putting forth material 'in such a dry, dreary way that it becomes rather a matter of labour than of interest to read beyond a few chapters'.[6] These negative book reviews suggest that while Dalton's formula for introducing China to the young may have been praiseworthy in the 1850s, it was much harder to rehash this familiar format successfully when writing about China in the 1870s. It also illustrates how critics expected children's literature to be more imaginative and entertaining after the publication of Lewis Carroll's *Alice's Adventures in Wonderland* in 1865, which heralded what has become known as the first 'golden age' of children's literature.

Although the customs and manners included in Mossman's book may have been recycled from familiar material, its information on the Taiping Rebellion was not. A reviewer in *The Times* remarked that 'Mr. Samuel Mossman, speaking through the mouth of a Sergeant of Engineers, tells the story of the Taiping Rebellion, and the "ever-victorious Army" of "Chinese" Gordon [Charles Gordon], concerning whom we fancy some boys, and for the matter of that their elders, do not know quite so much as they might'.[7] As *The Times* review suggests, although the book is for boys, older readers would be able to glean information about the Taiping Rebellion from it. Because the story was originally serialized in *The Leisure Hour: An Illustrated Magazine for Home Reading* (1852–1905), a weekly 'family journal of instruction and recreation', it is not surprising that Mossman addresses his book to both 'the rising generation' and 'adult readers' in his preface (v).

According to Claudia Nelson, the number of historical tales published between 1870 and 1914 was greater than those that appeared between 1820 and 1870, and most of them were intended for children.[8] Adults believed that historical fiction could make history interesting for young readers because instead of memorizing important dates by rote, they would be able to gain more understanding of the events and obtain moral lessons from the past by reading a story set during that period. Many parents and teachers hoped that children might be inculcated with national pride and be inspired to emulate the great historical figures they learned about because

---

[6]   'The Wolf-Boy of China', *Bentley's Miscellany Review*, 42 (1857): p. 424; 'Children's Books for Christmas', *Pall Mall Gazette*, 22 December 1875, p. 12.

[7]   'Christmas Books', *The Times*, 28 December 1875, p. 10. Born in Woolwich to a Scottish military officer in 1833, Charles George Gordon ('Chinese' Gordon) became the most famous commander of the Ever-Victorious Army, which was called to help suppress the Taiping Rebellion.

[8]   Claudia Nelson, *Boys Will Be Girls: The Feminine Ethic and British Children's Fiction, 1857–1917* (New Brunswick, 1991), pp. 88–90.

the stories of their lives would, according to a Board of Education Circular of 1905, 'furnish the most impressive examples of obedience, loyalty, courage, strenuous effort, serviceableness, indeed of all the qualities which make for good citizenship'.[9] For example, readers of *Simple Stories from English History for Young Readers* (1898) are told that '[e]very boy and girl should be proud that Gordon was an Englishman, and should say to themselves: "I will also be a hero as Gordon was"'.[10] Titles such as G.A. Henty's *With Clive in India* (1880) and *With Kitchener in the Sudan* (1900) exemplify the trend of writers for boys of placing their adolescent protagonists alongside noteworthy historical figures such as Robert Clive (1725–1774) and Horatio Herbert Kitchener (1850–1916) so that their reader, bypassing age and class hierarchies, could participate vicariously in real historical events. By allowing their heroes to experience adventures set in different time periods, authors such as Henty hoped to make history 'go down with the boys' and that readers would aspire to be as courageous as the heroes were.[11] Victorian journalist and children's literature critic Edward Salmon presented this idea in 1888 when he stated that when a boy reads, 'It is the God-fearing courage of a Gordon which his reading should engender, not the ignoble daring of a Ned Kelly'.[12] The 'God-fearing' military hero Charles Gordon (1833–1885) was presented as a self-sacrificing Englishman willing to devote everything to help the less fortunate 'primitive Other'.[13]

As the title of Mossman's book suggests, Gordon, the most famous commander of the Ever-Victorious Army, was one of the historical figures that figured prominently in British recollections of the Taiping Rebellion. In addition to Gordon, Mossman also incorporated the American adventurer Henry Burgevine (1836–1865), the Chinese statesman Li Hongzhang (1823–1901), and other key figures of the Rebellion into the story. In 1901, Bessie Marchant (1862–1941), a popular girl's adventure story writer known as the 'girl's Henty' or 'female Henty', revisited the Taiping Rebellion in *Among Hostile Hordes: A Story of the Tai-ping Rebellion*.[14] Like Mossman's story, Marchant's also included real

[9] Quoted in Eric Evans, 'The Victorians at School: The Victorian Era in the Twentieth-Century Curriculum', in Miles Taylor and Michael Wolff (eds), *The Victorians since 1901: Histories, Representations and Revisions* (Manchester, 2004), pp. 181–97 (p. 182).

[10] *Simple Stories from English History for Young Readers* (New York, 1898), p. 186.

[11] G.A. Henty, 'Writing Books for Boys', *Answers* (1902): p. 105.

[12] Edward Salmon, *Juvenile Literature as It Is* (London, 1888), p. 237.

[13] Brook Miller, 'Our Abdiel: The British Press and the Lionization of "Chinese" Gordon', *Nineteenth-Century Prose*, 32.2 (2005): pp. 127–53 (p. 127).

[14] D.L. Murray, 'Bessie Marchant', *Times Literary Supplement*, 15 November 1941, p. 569. See also Sally Mitchell, *The New Girl: Girls' Culture in England, 1880–1915* (New York, 1995), p. 116. Elizabeth (Bessie) Marchant was born on 12 December 1862 in Petham, Kent to William and Jane Marchant. Not much is known about her education, except that she attended Petham County Primary School. Despite her literary fame, she suffered financial difficulties which forced her to borrow money and even consider selling her furniture. See Alan Major, 'Bessie Marchant: The Maid of Kent whose Exciting Stories Thrilled Thousands of English Children', *This England*, Winter (1991): pp. 30–33 (p. 31).

historical figures, namely, Charles Gordon, Henry Burgevine, and Hong Xiuquan (1814–1864), the leader of the Taiping Rebellion. As John Stephens has argued, historical fiction is 'the discoursal product of firm ideological intentions, written and read in a specific, complex cultural situation'.[15] Therefore, although both *The Mandarin's Daughter* and *Among Hostile Hordes* deal with the same events and incorporate similar historical figures into their narratives, there were many differences between the stories because of the 25-year gap between the two novels' publication dates.

The Taiping Rebellion (1850–1864)

Mossman specified in his preface to *The Mandarin's Daughter* that he aimed to 'convey a truthful account of the most gigantic insurrection and foreign war that ever occurred in that disturbed empire' (v). The Taiping Rebellion, which has been described by a modern historian as the 'longest, fiercest and most destructive war of the nineteenth-century world', started in Guangxi under the leadership of Hong Xiuquan, a former schoolteacher from Guangdong.[16] In 1836, Hong had travelled to Canton to take an examination to obtain the *xiucai* degree. While he was in the port city, he received a copy of *Quanshi liangyan* ('Good Words Exhorting the Age'), a nine-volume booklet containing a collection of Bible passages translated by British missionary Robert Morrison (1782–1834) and brief commentaries compiled by Liang Afa (1789–1855), a Chinese evangelist working for the London Missionary Society.[17] Hong did not read the pamphlets carefully at the time and set them aside when he returned home from Canton. Later, after another failed attempt to pass the exam, Hong fell seriously ill. He claims that during this time, he had visions about an old man in heaven who handed him a sword and urged him to destroy demons. A middle-aged man also appeared in the visions and taught him how to exterminate these demons. These images did not make sense to him until 1843 when he began reading the Christian tracts he had received years before. He began to interpret the visions based on the tracts and declared himself the second son of God and the younger brother of Jesus Christ. Not long after, Hong began preaching and baptized some relatives and friends, including a man named Feng Yunshan, who later formed 'The God-worshippers Society'. The Society's members vowed to destroy their idols and stop worshipping evil spirits. In 1847, Hong journeyed to Canton to receive instruction from the American missionary Issachar J. Roberts (1802–1871). When he came back, he found

---

[15]   John Stephens, *Language and Ideology in Children's Fiction* (Harlow, UK, 1992), p. 205.

[16]   Jack Gray, *Rebellions and Revolutions: China from the 1800s to 2000*, 2nd edn (Oxford, 2002), p. 75. It is estimated that 20 to 30 million people died during the Taiping Rebellion.

[17]   See Jonathan D. Spence, *God's Chinese Son: The Taiping Heavenly Kingdom of Hong Xiuquan* (New York, 1996), pp. 30–31.

the number of God-worshippers had increased dramatically. Soon the Society became political in nature and eventually attempted to overthrow the Manchu government.

During the 1840s, China suffered from the aftermath of several natural disasters, including severe famines in 1849 and 1850. Hong attracted many followers by promising land reform, advocating equality, establishing a common treasury, making plans to overthrow the landlords, and fighting for the expulsion of the ruling Manchus. After adopting the title of *Tianwang* (Heavenly King) in 1851, Hong, with a large following of more than 1,000,000, captured Nanjing in 1853, claiming it as the capital city of the 'Heavenly Kingdom of Great Peace' (*Taiping Tianguo*). Hong's chief subordinates were given titles ending with '*wang*' (king). Two of the '*wangs*', Yang Xiuqing (the 'Eastern King') and Xiao Chaogui (the 'Western King'), who claimed to be spirit mediums possessed by God and Jesus, respectively, became particularly powerful men within the leadership. Part of the Taiping army headed north in an attempt to take over Peking, but the Manchu imperial troops (known as 'Imperialists' in much of the contemporary literature) stopped them. However, the Taipings maintained control of Nanjing and much of the lower part of the Yangzi Valley for over ten years.

When news of the Taiping insurgents first reached England in the early 1850s, the British were divided over whether to support or condemn them.[18] Some believed that the Taipings were Christians who should be encouraged, while others disagreed, arguing that the conversion of the Chinese was too good to be true.[19] Most missionaries originally supported the Taiping movement because they heard that many idols were being smashed to pieces by Hong's followers, making them optimistic about the likelihood of China becoming a Christian nation under the Taipings. In their minds, this would then lead to the abandoning of barbarous customs such as foot-binding, the banning of opium-smoking, and the encouragement of trade. As Mossman noted in his preface to *The Mandarin's Daughter*, there was 'hope that it might have been the means of regenerating China, through the spread of Christianity' (vi). However, by 1862 missionaries were railing against the destructive and blasphemous nature of the rebellion.[20] British readers felt disturbed by reports of the Taipings because they represented the nightmare of a proselytizing mission gone horribly wrong. As Hong's distorted

---

[18]   According to Clarke and Gregory, Westerners only gained a more informed picture of the Taiping movement in early 1853 when direct contact was made between the British and the Taipings. See Prescott Clarke and J.S. Gregory (eds), *Western Reports on the Taiping: A Selection of Documents* (Canberra, 1982), p. 4.

[19]   In 1857, the *Saturday Review* argued that if the Taipings prevailed, 'Christianity would have less chance in China than under present circumstances': 'Exeter Hall on the Chinese War', *Saturday Review*, 9 May 1857, pp. 422–3 (p. 422).

[20]   J.S. Gregory, *Great Britain and the Taipings* (Canberra, 1969), p. 137. In 1853, missionary S.W. Williams stated that the Taiping religion was a 'mixture of Christianity, Mohammedanism, fanaticism, and idolatry in their books': Quoted in Ssu-yu Teng, *The Taiping Rebellion and the Western Powers: A Comprehensive Survey* (Oxford, 1971), p. 192.

interpretation of Morrison's Bible tracts revealed, once Christianity was in the hands of the Chinese, there was no knowing what monstrosity would come of it. Instead of helping expunge 'savagery' from China, the missionary efforts indirectly sparked a rapacious rampage on a massive scale in the southern part of the country.

The Taiping Rebellion in Children's Literature

Little about the Rebellion appeared in contemporary children's texts, perhaps because it was regarded as a civil war and because more attention was paid to the American Civil War (1861–1865) at the time. The few texts that mention the insurrection were written by missionaries who were interested in the Taipings' understanding of Christianity. For example, an article in the *Juvenile Missionary Magazine* in 1853 describes Liang Afa distributing 'Good Words to Admonish the Age' at the examination hall in Canton where Hong received a copy. The author was optimistic about Hung Seu Tsuen [*sic*], who is presented as a 'great chief' of the Chinese rebellion, and his ability to transform China into a Christian country.[21] By 1862 however, the tone among children's writers had changed. Aunt Helen [Helen Collins], a missionary's wife, wrote that Hung-siu-tsuien [*sic*] reads the Bible and professes to believe 'that it is the word of God; but he has many wrong notions'.[22] His followers 'overrun the country, drive out the inhabitants of the walled cities, and are very cruel to those who resist them'.[23] Aunt Helen concludes that '[c]ivil war is very terrible; and we must feel for the poor Chinese, and pray that God will be pleased to bring good out of this evil'.[24]

Many others accused the Taipings of being 'savages' and 'marauders' who used Christianity as a means of gaining sympathy from foreigners.[25] The *Saturday Review* sums up the attitude that many British had about the 'Heavenly Kingdom of Great Peace': 'It proclaimed universal peace, and employed a lawless banditti to inaugurate it.'[26] The Taipings were seen as evil criminals who turned against their own people and 'made the land a desert' wherever they went. Innocent people who could not escape from their homes in time were forced into unpaid labour or 'massacred out of hand'.[27] The British decision to intervene came after much debate. After 1862, the British decided to support the Imperialist troops mainly because they felt the need to protect their foreign settlements in Shanghai and

---

21 'The Rebellion in China', *Juvenile Missionary Magazine*, 113 (1853): pp. 220–24.

22 Helen Collins, *China and Its People: A Book for Young Readers* (London, 1862), p. 30.

23 Ibid., p. 29.

24 Ibid., p. 30.

25 Teng, *The Taiping Rebellion*, p. 182.

26 'China', *Saturday Review*, 6 August 1864, p. 182.

27 Ibid.

future trade interests in China: in the words of the *Saturday Review*, 'unless order could be restored, the ruin of the whole trade of China seemed inevitable'.[28] British newspapers soon published reports on the movements of the Imperialist forces, particularly after Charles Gordon became commander of the Ever-Victorious Army on 24 March 1863, three years after his arrival in China.

Gordon had been preceded by two Americans, Frederick Townsend Ward (1831–1862) and Henry A. Burgevine. After General Ward was killed in action near Ningbo in September 1862, the Ever-Victorious Army came directly under the control of Li Hongzhang, who, under the strong recommendation of the United States minister Anson Burlingame appointed Burgevine as the next leader. However, Li dismissed Burgevine after learning that he had assaulted the Army's treasurer for money. The Army was composed of around 3,500 to 4,000 men, including soldiers from England, Germany, Spain, France, and America, as well as Chinese volunteers and former members of the Taiping forces. These soldiers were known for their undisciplined nature, a fact that Gordon biographers repeatedly emphasized to extol his ability to lead the troops to victory under unpromising circumstances. For example, the *Aberdeen Weekly Journal* asserted that 'under the sway of his genius', Gordon's troops 'soon became a formidable army'.[29] The Taiping Rebellion ended not long after Nanjing was captured in 1864. Not only was Gordon extolled as a great military hero for the part he played in quelling the Rebellion, but he was further praised for his refusal of monetary rewards when he rejected the 10,000 taels offered to him by the Emperor of China for his service. He reportedly left China as poor as (or even poorer) than when he arrived because he donated much of his money to the needy Chinese.

According to Prescott Clarke and J.S. Gregory, nineteenth-century Westerners wrote a great deal about the Taiping Rebellion, perhaps as much as the Chinese did at the time, because they were interested in the quasi-Christianity of Hong and his followers.[30] T.T. Meadows's *The Chinese and Their Rebellions* (1856), Theodore Hamberg's *The Visions of Hung-siu-tshuen, and Origin of the Kwang-si Insurrection* (1854), Captain Thomas Blakiston's *Five Months on the Yang-tsze* (1862), and Andrew Wilson's *The 'Ever Victorious Army', A History of the Chinese Campaign under Lieut.-Colonel C.G. Gordon, C.B., R.E., and of the Suppression of the Tai-ping Rebellion* (1868) are just a few of the numerous books dedicated to the subject. Periodicals such as the *Saturday Review*, *London Review*, *Blackwood's Edinburgh Magazine*, and *Pall Mall Gazette*, newspapers such as the *Illustrated London News*, *The Times*, and *North China Herald*, missionary publications such

---

[28] 'The Rebellion of China', *Saturday Review*, 1 October 1864, pp. 418–19 (p. 419). For more information on the debates regarding British intervention, see Gregory, *Great Britain and the Taipings* and Teng, *The Taiping Rebellion*.

[29] 'Career of General Gordon', *Aberdeen Weekly Journal*, 14 February 1885, p. 8.

[30] Clarke and Gregory (eds), *Western Reports on the Taiping*, p. xvi.

as the *Chinese Repository* and *Missionary Magazine and Chronicle*, and consular officer government reports all contained information on the Taiping Rebellion.[31]

Samuel Mossman's *The Mandarin's Daughter*

As editor of the *North China Herald*, Mossman gained his information about the interior of the Taiping quarters in Nanjing, the condition of Taiping women, and Taiping weddings from articles contributed by an interpreter for the British consular service named R.J. Forrest. Forrest's reports were later included in Blakiston's *Five Months on the Yang-tsze*.[32] *The Mandarin's Daughter*, which reflects the intersection between history, journalism, and fiction, is narrated by Sergeant Cameron, a member of the Royal Engineers. At the beginning of the story, he sails from Melbourne to Hong Kong because all available British forces were ordered to join the army and fleet assembling there towards the end of Second Opium War (1856–1860). Cameron falls in love with Loo A-lee, one of the Empress's maids, after saving her amid the ruins of the Summer Palace (*Yuanmingyuan*), which was burned down by the foreign powers in 1860, an act he justifies as retribution against the cruel treatment of British captives. Cameron escorts Loo A-lee to her father's luxurious mansion within the walls of Peking and becomes a frequent guest of the Loos, who are both Christians (though not of the Taiping kind). However, Foong Cut-sing, an emissary from the Taipings who is responsible for recruiting new members to the 'Heavenly Kingdom', also falls in love with A-lee and convinces her father Meng-kee to travel to Nanjing to meet with Tien Wang [Hong Xiuquan]. Instead of conversing with Tien Wang in person however, Meng-kee meets with Kan Wang [Gan Wang, Hong Ren'gan] and is sent to engage in treaty talks with the English in Shanghai.[33] Along the journey, he witnesses the destructive nature of the rebellion and concludes that these self-proclaimed Christians are 'hypocrites and deceivers' because they 'gloried in robbing their industrious countrymen' and engaged in activities such as 'burning and sacking the shops and houses' (183; 260). He withdraws from the cause but misfortune strikes and he would have starved to death in a temple had it not been for Cameron's miraculous appearance.

---

[31]   See for example, 'The Taepings and Their Remedy', *Blackwood's Edinburgh Magazine*, XCIII.DLXVIII (1863): pp. 135–42; 'Disturbances in Kwangsi', *Chinese Repository*, XIX (1851): p. 462; 'Taeping Rebellion in China', *Illustrated London News*, 12 March 1864, pp. 261–6; 'Imperialist Expedition to Fungwha', *Illustrated London News*, 7 February 1863, p. 150.

[32]   R.J. Forrest, 'The Taipings at Home', *North China Herald*, 19 October 1861. Quoted in Thomas W. Blakiston, *Five Months on the Yang-tsze; with a Narrative of the Exploration of Its Upper Waters, and Notices of the Present Rebellions in China* (London, 1862), pp. 44–55.

[33]   Hong Ren'gan (1822–1864), Hong Xiuquan's cousin, held an important position in the Taiping Kingdom.

After hearing Meng-kee's story, Cameron helps him obtain a post with the staff officers and interpreters working for Gordon. Meanwhile, Foong Cut-sing forces A-lee to accompany him to Suzhou. Gordon's army takes the city, the rebels surrender, and Tien Wang commits suicide. The successful suppression of the Taiping Rebellion is characterized as 'one of the most brilliant campaigns of modern warfare in the far East, in which British valour and generalship maintained its supremacy in the field' (*MD* 335). When the Taipings are negotiating with Gordon, Cameron encounters A-lee again and saves her from Foong. Even though as a native wife A-lee 'could not secure the privileges of an English one, and that any children from such a union would be debarred from the hereditary rights of property', she marries Cameron and they settle in Nanjing (*MD* 339). The story concludes with hints that their son will be born not long after.

While the love between Captain Richardson and Sang in *The Wolf Boy of China* and the adoration of Louis Segnier for Fan-si in *The Travels of Rolando* was acceptable in the 1850s, attitudes towards interracial marriage had changed by the 1870s, because the *Athenaeum* reviewer writes:

> The wide gulf that separates us from the Chinese in everything that is distinctive in the two nations would, under any circumstances, render it extremely difficult to write a love story, having any resemblance of probability or even possibility, in which the hero should be an English soldier and the heroine a Mandarin's daughter.[34]

Although Mossman tries to make this marriage believable by emphasizing that A-lee resembled an English lady in that she 'had a complexion as fair as the ordinary run of her sisters in England', that her eyes were not 'so acute in the angle of the eyelids as we see Chinese eyes generally represented' and 'her feet were of the natural size, not having been bandaged into a stump', the perceived differences between the two cultures had formed a chasm so wide that the love between an Englishman and a Chinese woman was unable to bridge it (*MD* 76). Events that contributed to creating the seemingly impassable gulf between the two countries include the Tianjin Massacre of 1870 when a number of foreigners and Chinese Christians were killed and the Margary Affair of 1875 when Raymond Augustus Margary, a British vice-consul, was murdered in Yunnan province on his way back from an expedition in Burma.[35] In particular, the Wusong Railway dispute of 1876 caused much discontent because the Chinese were angry that the British built the railway from Shanghai to Wusong without authorization and without regard for fengshui principles.[36]

---

[34] 'Book Review', p. 53.

[35] For more information, see Immanuel C.Y. Hsu, 'Late Ch'ing Foreign Relations, 1866–1975', in Denis Twitchett and John King Fairbank (eds), *The Cambridge History of China* (15 vols, Cambridge, 1980), vol. II, part 2, pp. 70–141.

[36] For more information on the history of the Railway, see David Pong, 'Confucian Patriotism and the Destruction of the Woosung Railway, 1877', *Modern Asian Studies*, 7.4 (1973): pp. 647–76.

Like Dalton, Mossman was aware of racial tensions in China and informs his readers that there is 'animosity that subsists between the pure Chinese and their Tartar rulers' (*MD* 48). To illustrate this, he incorporates one of the authors he consulted, Robert Swinhoe, into the story, quoting (without acknowledgment) from Swinhoe's reported conversation with an old Chinese gentleman in *Narrative of the North China Campaign of 1860*. The man expresses hatred of the Tartars, calling them 'a wretched, filthy horde of men from the wilds of Mongolia, who love to oppress the people, and steal from them all they possess' (*MD* 47). Like Anne Bowman's Ki-chan, this Chinese man is an advocate for trade relations between China and Britain, claiming that both nations would benefit from these ties:

> We felt sure that your object in coming here was for the purposes of trade, and surely that was a boon for both countries! But these Tartars, who acquired this country themselves by treachery, are naturally jealous of every other nation, because they are suspicious, and think that the main object of all other people is to wrest away from them by treachery what they won by the same base means. (46)[37]

He does not object to the foreign presence in China and even claims that the British troops 'must eventually conquer the world' (*MD* 47). The Chinese are presented as inferior people who need to be saved from oppression and are willing to accept foreign dominance if it could alleviate the suffering caused by the Tartars. By implying that this conversation is representative of the majority view of Chinese people, the narrator seems to be providing a justification for British imperialist ambitions in China in terms of a major trading relationship which would be more beneficial to Britain than China.

At the beginning of *The Mandarin's Daughter*, Gordon asks one of the interpreters in her Majesty's consular service in China whether he has seen anything of the 'Great Flowery Land'. The 'accomplished naturalist' replies:

> Yes, I have had a walk into the country, among those hills on the northern shore. 'What a delightful spot for a botanist!' you exclaim to yourself as you scramble up the hill side and put your foot accidentally on a lovely pink, or scratch your fingers in grasping at a rosebush, on which dozens of large bright red flowers cluster, at once gladdening the eye with their tints, and delighting the sense of smell with their fragrance, you at last attain the summit of the hill, and look proudly down on the fine fleet of ships sleeping lazily below, on the calm still waters of the bay, with no perceptible signs of life save here and there small specks of boats hastening to and fro. (*MD* 33)[38]

---

[37] The entire conversation can be found in Robert Swinhoe, *Narrative of the North China Campaign of 1860* (London, 1861), pp. 159–61.

[38] This description appears in ibid., pp. 15–16.

This picturesque description, which is similar to Bowman's depiction of China, contrasts greatly with the scenes of massive destruction that Meng-kee witnesses later in the southern parts of China: 'Words cannot convey any idea of the utter ruin and desolation which marked the line of Taiping march from Nanking to Soochow [Suzhou]' (*MD* 278).

Similarly, many of the *Boy's Own Paper* travel narratives and stories related to the Taiping Rebellion describe how the rebels destroyed the beautiful Chinese landscape. The authors frequently juxtapose the fertility of the unscathed land to the barrenness of the earth after the Taiping soldiers stormed through the provinces. For example, one could witness their 'cruelty and riot' throughout 'the richest and most fertile districts of China'. Suzhou and Hangzhou, 'great historical cities', were becoming 'desolate ruins in their possession'.[39] In 'A Trip up the Yang-tze Kiang' (1897–1898), John Morrison confirms that all the places 'which had been overrun by the Taiping rebels' invariably became scenes of 'ruin and desolation'.[40] All the way up to Nanjing and beyond, 'the same aspect of ruin and desolation prevailed', and 'not a living thing, not even a cultivated field, was to be seen'.[41] Wuhu, which had been 'well occupied and fertile' in the hands of the Imperialists, fell to the same fate when the Taipings raided the city some months later.[42] Morrison's description echoes that of Captain Blakiston, who writes in *Five Months on the Yang-tsze*, a book aimed at adults, that the Taiping rebels left behind nothing but devastation and dilapidation: 'The scene of desolation was as complete as at Nanking or Chin-kiang [Zhenjiang], and the whole distance from the suburb to the town was one heap of ruins ... the population appeared to be in a starving condition.'[43]

If destruction of landscape was lamentable, loss of human life was even more so. Meng-kee sees '[h]uman remains were lying about in all directions' and the 'number of dead bodies that continually met the eye was indescribably sickening to the heart' (*MD* 277). The narrator of 'A Ticklish Trip in a Chinese House-Boat' (1897) describes similar scenes he and his friend witnessed during the midst of the Rebellion from 1859 to 1861, such as the canals being 'choked with dead bodies'.[44] On their way up the river, they find the cities burned and the surrounding country (prior to the Rebellion, one of the 'finest and most cultivated' areas) 'practically a jungle'.[45] The next day they are sickened to discover dead bodies lying about the ruins of what used to be a pretty village. The scenes of death coincide with

---

[39]   'Chinese Gordon', *Boy's Own Paper*, 6 (1884): p. 487.

[40]   John Morrison, 'A Trip up the Yang-tze Kiang', *Boy's Own Paper*, 20 (1897–1898): p. 27.

[41]   Ibid.

[42]   Ibid.

[43]   Blakiston, *Five Months on the Yang-tsze*, p. 58.

[44]   'A Ticklish Trip in a Chinese House-Boat', *Boy's Own Paper*, 19 (1896–1897): p. 488.

[45]   Ibid.

Wesleyan missionary Josiah Cox's reports in 1862, where the canal was 'covered with dead bodies at some distances from the city of Su-chau [Suzhou]' so thick was the 'pack of human bodies' and so strong the stench that travellers were forced to change route to reach the city.[46]

In terms of descriptions of death there is little difference between the texts written for children and for adults. The Taiping rebels are portrayed as reckless, impulsive, and uncontrollable people who need civilizing. Mossman writes that the 'scenes of starvation, death, and worse' Meng-kee observed 'are unknown in European warfare – frightful as they sometimes are' (*MD* 268). Even worse, '[s]uch was the destitution that human flesh was greedily devoured, and inhuman butchers actually went about selling it by weight' (*MD* 268). A biography for children entitled *General Gordon and Lord Dundonald: The Story of Two Heroic Lives* also describes scenes of cannibalism and terror:

> Hundreds of gaunt and starving wretches were seen wandering about living on refuse, or human flesh, amongst the ruins of their villages. In one place were found fifty men, women, and children, either with heads cut off or throats cut. Flaying alive and pounding to death was a common punishment at the hands of the rebels.[47]

These horrific descriptions are shockingly confronting images of the brutality of war. Anthony Kearney has argued that Victorian descriptions of the savage and barbaric were 'seen to have further positive uses in reinforcing a sense of civilized values (Saxon and Protestant) when, as was usually the case, the ultra-horrific was associated with alien practices – that is, those belonging either to the remote past or to countries safely beyond Europe'.[48] This is apparent in the way that both Mossman and *Boy's Own Paper* authors associate the Taiping Rebellion with bloodshed, destruction, desolation, and ruin, leaving young readers with a gruesome impression of the Taiping rebels, who are represented as much more vicious and inhumane than the Europeans. Another, possibly inadvertent, effect of such representations however, is to draw attention to the brutality and destruction intrinsic to imperialism in general.

Writing in 1890, Edward Salmon asserted, '[t]here is now none of the writing down to the child's intelligence or supposed intelligence, which used to degrade equally the writer and the reader'.[49] His statement is supported by the fact that descriptions of the Taiping Rebellion for children and the reports on the Taipings

---

[46] Clarke and Gregory (eds), *Western Reports on the Taiping*, p. 309.

[47] *General Gordon and Lord Dundonald: The Story of Two Heroic Lives* (London, [n.d.]), p. 19.

[48] Anthony Kearney, 'Savage and Barbaric Themes in Victorian Children's Writing', *Children's Literature in Education*, 17.4 (1986): pp. 233–40 (p. 234).

[49] Edward Salmon, 'Should Children Have a Special Literature?', *The Parent's Review*, 5 (1890), pp. 337–44, repr. in Lance Salway (ed.), *A Peculiar Gift: Nineteenth Century Writings on Books for Children* (Harmondsworth, 1976), pp. 332–9 (p. 334).

intended for adults are indistinguishable from each other, suggesting that children were not being written 'down to' and were expected to respond intelligently to these terrible graphic descriptions of human suffering. Reading these stories in Britain, they were reassured of their own safety in 'civilized' society and made aware of the 'wide gulf that separates us from the Chinese' referred to by the reviewer of *The Mandarin's Daughter*.

Between the publication of *The Mandarin's Daughter* in 1875 and the appearance of Bessie Marchant's *Among Hostile Hordes: A Story of the Tai-ping Rebellion* in 1901, no other full-length children's novels focusing on the Taiping Rebellion emerged. In Jules Verne's *The Tribulations of a Chinaman in China* (1879), the Taiping Rebellion is mentioned in passing as a 'formidable uprising' that 'threatened the reigning dynasty'. Had it not been for 'the Viceroy Li, and Prince Kong, and especially the English Colonel Gordon', the narrator states, the Emperor would not have been able to save his throne.[50] Gordon is also an important figure in Marchant's *Among Hostile Hordes*, which the *Academy Christmas Supplement* of 1901 recommended as a book for readers aged 8 to 14.[51]

Among Hostile Hordes: A Story of the Tai-ping Rebellion

A review in the *Athenaeum* characterizes *Among Hostile Hordes: A Story of the Tai-ping Rebellion* as a 'thrilling romance' and informs readers that the book 'takes us into the heart of China, and shows us what befalls the intrepid "foreign devils" – traders, doctors, missionaries – who take their lives in their hands and venture to carry the things of the West into the Middle Kingdom'.[52] The statement suggests that *Among Hostile Hordes* is not so much a text about 'discovering' the Chinese (as was the case in Bowman and Dalton's novels) as it is about the experience of the now established Western community in China. Because there was a much larger group of foreigners residing in China at the turn of the century compared to the mid-century when China had just been 'opened', Marchant was more concerned with depicting the lives of these residents rather than introducing the manners and customs of the Chinese. She uses the novel to discuss the 'work' being done in China, particularly missionary endeavours. In *Among Hostile Hordes*, she focuses on three major categories of Westerners in China: missionaries, military men, and merchants.

At the beginning of the story, which is set during the final months of the Taiping Rebellion, when 'Tien Wang's power was on the wane', John Armstrong, an employee of a Shanghai shipping company and his 13-year-old son Don

[50] Jules Verne, *The Tribulations of a Chinaman in China* (New York, 1879), p. 21.

[51] 'Books for Boys and Girls', *Academy Christmas Supplement*, 61 (1901): pp. 555–9 (p. 556).

[52] 'Books for the Young', *Athenaeum*, 3872 (1902): p. 47.

attempt to travel from Shanghai to Nanjing by boat.[53] Their safety is threatened by 'hordes of Tai-ping rebels' who have been 'ravag[ing] the land in search of prey' (7). When river pirates attack and their boat becomes stuck in mud, they are forced to travel to Nanjing on foot. Unfortunately, because Don is very weak and needs immediate medical attention, his anxious father decides to seek help from an American medical missionary named Margaret Hayes.

Prior to meeting John and Don, Margaret had travelled to the small town of Kum Lu in the province of Jiangsu to attend to Yang, the only son of Bo, the owner of a teashop. She was called because when price negotiations between Bo and a greedy Chinese doctor named Loo Choo had turned sour, Bo's customers told him about the 'woman barbarian' who could cure illnesses for a small fee. Margaret diagnoses Bo's son with pneumonia and stays the night to watch over him. The next day, Margaret thinks she witnesses the murder of her servant Ting Lang, an alleged member of the Brotherhood of Death secret society, who she had sent home the previous night.

When the perplexed Margaret returns home, she is shocked to discover Ting Lang alive and to find two 'foreign barbarians' (the Armstrongs) waiting for her. After examining Don, Margaret informs John that his frail son requires adequate rest and suggests that he leave the boy in her care. John reluctantly agrees and continues on his business trip with Ting Lang acting as his guide. Thus, as in *The Wolf Boy of China*, father and son are separated. To John's disappointment, most of the people he meets are 'too indifferent to trouble themselves in the least about commerce, other than as they already understood it' (135). Along the way, John and Ting Lang are caught and locked up by yamen-runners and would have been killed by a local mob had they not been saved by a strange red-robed man known as the 'Nameless One' who apparently possesses magic powers. He surgically removes all traces of Ting Lang's affiliation with the Brotherhood of Death from his scar-ridden face. The Nameless One shows John a Bible that he had retrieved from an injured female missionary who, before dying, gave thanks and smiled. The man concludes that the Bible must be 'a charm which helped her to die without shrinking when the torture pressed her sore' and asks John to explain the teachings in it (194). Although John has not opened a Bible in a long time, he recalls his childhood catechism lessons and attempts to preach Christianity to the Nameless One. He rediscovers his faith in the process.

Meanwhile, Margaret hears from her compatriot Dr Fletcher that the Taiping leader Tien Wang has issued an order for all English men, women, and children in the area to be killed within the next ten days. Fearful for Don's safety, Margaret implores one of her previous patients, Tien Wang's chief wife Kwei-wha, to shelter him for the time being. Kwei-wha agrees and they disguise Don as a Chinese boy by dyeing his hair black, fastening a pigtail made of horse hair on his head, and forcing him to wear many layers of coats. In Tien Wang's house, Don overhears

---

[53] Bessie Marchant, *Among Hostile Hordes: A Story of the Tai-ping Rebellion* (London, 1901), p. 48. Further page references are given after quotations in the text.

a plan to kill his hero General Gordon. He bravely steals the poison meant for Gordon and escapes to warn the General of Tien Wang's murderous scheme. After he finds Gordon and informs him of the plan against his life, Don is invited to join the Ever-Victorious Army as caterer-in-chief. The boy is eventually reunited with his father after John relinquishes his job and joins the Imperialists to fight against the Taipings.

The third subplot of the novel involves Margaret, who had incited the wrath of Loo Choo when she 'stole' his patient from him. Loo Choo devises a plan to seek revenge but Bo intervenes and rescues Margaret. In her flight, she is aided by her faithful servant Blossom and a fellow American named Burgevine, in who Margaret loses confidence when he reveals that he has defected to the Taipings. Fortunately, John arrives to save her and soon Burgevine surrenders. Not long after, Gordon and his troops bombard Suzhou, the power of the Taipings speedily declines, and Tien Wang commits suicide, 'preferring death rather than submission' (329).[54] Margaret Hayes becomes Mrs Armstrong and the family temporarily lives in Shanghai but plans to return to Nanjing after rioting ceases. The story concludes with a visit from Bo and the fully recovered Yang. When Bo hears that Don plans to go to Edinburgh to study medicine and come back to settle in China after obtaining his M.D., he suggests that Yang accompany Don so he can also receive a foreign education.

Considering that Marchant was a popular author who penned some 150 girl's and boy's novels and numerous magazine stories, it is surprising that few contemporary scholars have devoted in-depth attention to her work. Sally Mitchell, Cedric Cullingford, and Donald Hettinga have discussed some of Marchant's heroines, known for their 'zest for adventure and gay, indomitable courage' and ability to remain 'mistress[es] of [their] fate in the face of every adversity'.[55] More recently, Michelle Smith has examined the heroines in some of Marchant's pre-First World War novels and argues that they 'display elements of the mythologized war-time nurse'.[56] She states that there is not much 'significant interaction' between the heroines and the indigenous peoples in Marchant's books, but this is not true of *Among Hostile Hordes* because Margaret interacts with Blossom, Ting Lang, Bo, Kwei-wha, and other Chinese characters.[57]

---

[54]   Although British sources such as the *Saturday Review*, *Daily News*, and *Birmingham Daily Post* note that Hong committed suicide, according to one historian, Hong died from illness rather than suicide on 1 June 1864. See Spence, *God's Chinese Son*, p. 325.

[55]   'For Girls: Adventurous Heroines', *The Times*, 25 November 1941, p. 9; 'For Girls', *The Times*, 4 December 1935, p. 20. See Mitchell, *The New Girl*, pp. 116–18; 127; Cedric Cullingford, *Children's Literature and Its Effects: The Formative Years* (London, 1998), pp. 120–22; Donald R. Hettinga, 'Bessie Marchant', in Donald R. Hettinga and Gary D. Schmidt (eds), *Dictionary of Literary Biography: British Children's Writers, 1914–1960* (Detroit, 1996), pp. 166–9.

[56]   Michelle Smith, 'Adventurous Girls of the British Empire: The Pre-War Novels of Bessie Marchant', *The Lion and the Unicorn*, 33.1 (2009): pp. 1–25 (p. 10).

[57]   Ibid.

Sharon Ouditt, Michael Paris, and Mary Cadogan and Patricia Craig have discussed Marchant's heroines' experiences during the Great War, while Suzette Starmer and Judith Rowbotham have analyzed their role in the expansion of Empire, but detailed analysis of Marchant's historical fiction is lacking.[58]

Questions of Genre

Among Hostile Hordes is a distinctive book in Marchant's oeuvre because she was known predominantly for reigning 'supreme in tales of travel and adventure for girls'.[59] Generically, the book is difficult to define because it combines elements of biography, conversion narrative, and adventure story. Marchant's decision to feature an adolescent boy and two adults in *Among Hostile Hordes* results in a book that resists the traditional categories of 'boy's' and 'girl's' fiction and raises the question of whether it is an adventure story for children or a romance for adults. If we focus on the character of Don, who is characterized by the *Athenaeum* as 'a plucky little English lad', *Among Hostile Hordes* may be categorized as a boy's adventure story.[60] Don, whose 'pluck' impressed Gordon, wishes to fulfil the role of a traditional adventure-story hero. He aspires to 'be the first and the bravest of the lot' and pictures himself 'a hundred times in fancy dashing along that narrow passage inside the walls, charging through the torturous, winding streets, and, with his own hand, flinging wide the gate for the besieging force to enter' (220). Don's dreams of glory resemble those described in Joseph Conrad's *Lord Jim* (1900), where Jim, preoccupied with immortalizing himself through heroic acts, often sees himself

> saving people from sinking ships, cutting away masts in a hurricane, swimming through a surf with a line; or as a lonely castaway, barefooted and half naked, walking on uncovered reefs in search of shell-fish to stave off starvation. He confronted savages on tropical shores, quelled mutinies on the high seas, and in a small boat upon the ocean kept up the hearts of despairing men – always an example of devotion to duty, and as unflinching as a hero in a book.[61]

---

[58]   See Sharon Ouditt, *Fighting Forces, Writing Women: Identity and Ideology in the First World War* (London, 1994), p. 85; Michael Paris, *Over the Top: The Great War and Juvenile Literature in Britain* (Westport, CT, 2004), pp. 122–30; Mary and Patricia Craig Cadogan, *You're a Brick, Angela: A New Look at Girls' Fiction from 1839 to 1975* (London, 1976), pp. 57–9; Suzette Starmer, 'Well I Never, It is a Girl! Fiction and Empire', *The English Review*, 12.4 (2002): pp. 30–33; Judith Rowbotham, *Good Girls Make Good Wives: Guidance for Girls in Victorian Fiction* (Oxford, 1989), pp. 203–19.

[59]   'Christmas Books for Girls at School and on Holiday', *The Times*, 8 December 1939, p. 4.

[60]   'Books for the Young', p. 47.

[61]   Joseph Conrad, *Lord Jim: A Tale* (London, 1900), p. 5.

Whereas Conrad uses the genre of the adventure story to challenge and critique the overly optimistic and arrogant British attitude towards Empire, Marchant expresses the confidence in British superiority that most writers of the genre reflected in their works. For example, Don vocalizes the British imperialist mentality when he speculates that the sight of Gordon would 'teach [the Chinese] how to behave civilly to his neighbours, and the world in general' (80). He has a strong adventurous spirit and 'he would have gone anywhere and done anything for the sake of sharing the risk and the possible glory that might follow' (232). His hopes for glory are fulfilled when he inadvertently discovers an important breach in a wall that ultimately helps Gordon's forces conquer Patachiao [Baodaiqiao]. Don is delighted because the forces are able to capture the town without bloodshed and, 'because he had borne a part in it, there was not in all the wide empire of China a happier boy that day' (234).

Although Don is in many ways the typical imperialist boy hero, one thing that makes him more vulnerable is that he lacks the linguistic competence that other heroes of this genre typically possess. Therefore, although in appearance he may be disguised as a Chinese boy, he must pretend to be deaf and dumb to 'pass' as Chinese. He is literally 'seen and not heard' in Tien Wang's palace, serving 'as an ornament behind the seat of the heavenly king' (277). Don's silence provides security but also sinks him into depression, fast 'breaking his spirit' (125). However, the fact that he is a child enabled him to enter the town where he discovered the breach in the wall because the sentinel at the town gate 'did not challenge Don, probably deeming him an object too insignificant for notice' (211).

Among Hostile Hordes could be considered an adult adventure story if one concentrates on the figure of 35-year-old John Armstrong, the globe-trotting man of the Empire who 'spoke Chinese like his mother-tongue' (50). Prior to travelling to China, John had resided in Japan (where his wife had died) and previously volunteered in India, fighting 'side by side with Sikhs and Sepoys' (93). John's motive for being in China is 'purely commercial': he has been employed to travel up the Yangzi River as far as Yichang to establish as many import stations for foreign goods as he could. However, his life is in jeopardy as he tries to complete this hazardous task because Tien Wang wants to prevent the river from being opened to foreign trade and orders his men to kill John. Like Robert Fortune, the Scottish botanical collector who disguised himself as a Chinese man to gain access to the tea districts of China and obtain knowledge of tea plantations, John tries to accomplish his mission by wearing a native costume. According to the narrator, because John 'spoke Chinese like his mother-tongue, it should have been easy for him to pass unobserved in a crowd' (50). However, because his companion Ting Lang was wearing 14 coats and 6 shirts, people took extra notice of the pair. A man comes closer to ask John some questions, but Ting Lang, trying to 'save his master from being compelled to compromise himself on his nationality', hits the man and infuriates the crowd, who accuse John being a child-eating barbarian spy (51). This incident suggests that having a Chinese servant was not necessarily an advantage for British travellers and that John could have perhaps travelled without being harassed had it not been for Ting Lang.

The crowd refuses to believe John's claims of being a 'peaceable individual travelling in the interests of trade' (53). Ironically, he is far from 'peaceful' when he pulls out his pistol at various points in the novel, resorting to violence or threats of violence to defeat the Chinese. For example, he demands that Ting Lang explain himself clearly or else he will 'blow out [his] silly brains' (72). He also punches some Chinese men and forces them to 'perform some involuntary kow-towing (head-knocking) in the gutter' (102). This reference to kow-towing reminds the reader of Lord Macartney's refusal to kow-tow to the Qianlong Emperor during the Embassy to China in the late eighteenth century. John's ability to force the men to kow-tow symbolizes British power over the Chinese, who will ultimately be defeated and finally bow down to the British. These experiences make John feel young: 'under pressure of the excitement, John Armstrong felt himself a boy again, and showered out blows, kicks, and cuffs with as much zest and energy as ever he had displayed in a playground encounter in the years that were gone' (100). This description also presents the idea of Empire as a playground where the best sportsman or strongest athlete wins.

If we focus on Margaret Hayes, the novel could be seen as a girl's adventure story or a missionary story. Anthony Kearney points out that from 1860 to the Second World War, children's literature, biographies, and real-life adventures frequently featured missionaries.[62] Considering that Marchant was known for her 'deep religious fervour' (she reputedly sang a doxology every time she finished a novel), it is not surprising that the most sympathetic character in the story is the Kansas-born missionary Margaret Hayes.[63] Marchant may have amalgamated the experiences of various medical or female missionaries she had read about into the figure of Margaret, who could not have been in China during the Taiping Rebellion, because the first woman medical missionary to China Dr Lucinda L. Coombs (1849–1919) only arrived in 1873, a decade after the Taiping Rebellion ended.[64] According to Judith Rowbotham, biographical missionary texts featuring the experiences of women missionaries were common from the 1870s onwards.[65] Considering that Marchant was listed in *Who's Who in Methodism* (1933), it is highly likely that she had read about the work of Dr Coombs, who was supported

---

[62]   Anthony Kearney, 'The Missionary Hero in Children's Literature', *Children's Literature in Education*, 14.2 (1983): pp. 104–12 (p. 104).

[63]   Major, 'Bessie Marchant', p. 33.

[64]   See Ann White, 'Counting the Cost of Faith: America's Early Female Missionaries', *Church History*, 57.1 (1988): pp. 19–30. The first American medical missionary Dr Peter Parker (1804–1888) opened Canton Hospital in 1835 and founded the Medical Missionary Society of China in 1838.

[65]   Judith Rowbotham, '"Soldiers of Christ"? Images of Female Missionaries in Late Nineteenth-Century Britain: Issues of Heroism and Martyrdom', *Gender & History*, 12.1 (2000): pp. 82–106 (pp. 84–5).

by the Philadelphia Branch of the Woman's Foreign Missionary Society of the Methodist Episcopal Church.[66]

Having 'penetrated into many a dangerous place, where the foot of an elder woman might well have feared to tread', Margaret is an example of the 'New Woman' of the *fin-de-siècle* who embodies independence, intelligence, and bravery (24).[67] Her 'wit and courage' are coupled with traditionally feminine character traits, such as a 'sympathetic womanly instinct' that is 'fully aroused' when she sees Don's suffering (246; 36). Margaret had come to China 'to do, to dare, and to suffer all things if need be, even unto death' (24). Because of the hardships she had to endure since arriving in China two years before, the 25-year-old looks 10 years older than her actual age. Parallels can be drawn between Margaret and Joan of Arc. At an intense point in the story, when she is about to be engulfed by a 'savage mob', Margaret holds them back temporarily by shouting 'in the name of the Lord, touch me not', causing them to feel momentarily 'frightened and abashed' because 'there was something so majestic in the pose of the slight heroic figure, and such a rapt radiance shone from her eyes' (148). A 'resolute' woman living in 'a city of savages', she is prepared to be a martyr: 'ready to suffer, to endure, aye even to die if it need be ...' (46; 248). Margaret does not die, but goes through her own personal 'baptism of fire' when she is placed in a basket and hung from the ceiling of a building which was later set ablaze. Although she is a doctor, Margaret is known as 'Miss Hayes', a title Don finds confusing: 'It always puzzled Don why Dr Fletcher, who was a minister, should be called a doctor, whilst his hostess, who was a qualified practitioner, was known merely as Miss Hayes, but he supposed that this must be the American way of doing things' (60).

Not only does Marchant question women's unequal status in society via Don's thoughts, she also uses the stories of Margaret Hayes and John Armstrong to illustrate the tension that often occurred between missionaries and merchants. In the 1890s missionaries in China were a highly controversial subject, second only to the question of opium.[68] According to Susan Schoenbauer Thurin, 'the cost of supporting missionaries in relation to the number of converts to Christianity, and the misgivings of both the Chinese and Westerners about the justice of altering the beliefs of this ancient culture, all contributed to the difficulties missionaries faced in China'.[69] John, who initially harbours a 'lively and well-developed hatred'

---

[66] Methodist Times and Leader, *Who's Who in Methodism 1933: An Encyclopaedia of the Personnel and Departments, Ministerial and Lay in the United Church of Methodism* (London, 1933).

[67] The term 'New Woman' covered 'independent women of all kinds'. See Matthew Beaumont, '"A Little Political World of My Own": The New Woman, the New Life, and *New Amazonia*', *Victorian Literature and Culture*, 35.1 (2007): pp. 215–32 (p. 221).

[68] Susan Schoenbauer Thurin, 'Travel Writing and the Humanitarian Impulse: Alicia Little in China', in Douglas Kerr and Julia Kuehn (eds), *A Century of Travels in China: Critical Essays on Travel Writing from the 1840s to the 1940s* (Hong Kong, 2007), pp. 91–103 (p. 96).

[69] Ibid.

towards missionaries, represents the viewpoint of many merchants in China who believed missionary work interfered with their commercial interests (40). Marchant reflects the difficulty in sending missionaries to China during times of 'perilous portent' when Margaret laments the fact that no one could be dispatched to assist the aging Dr Fletcher because 'civilised consecrated human life is too precious to be wantonly flung away' (146).

At various points in the novel, the different outlooks that merchants and missionaries held about China are highlighted. For example, when Don comments with 'an old-fashioned shrewdness that he had doubtless learned from his father' that China is 'a horrid place to live in ... but there's money to be made out of it if you only know the right way to go to work', the narrator notes that because money-making was not 'an important factor in the life of Miss Hayes, this side of Chinese enterprise failed to appeal to her with any sort of impressive force' (83). Miss Hayes is clearly the more admirable one because she has chosen to devote her life to the people of China without expecting any monetary rewards. Critics have pointed out that although Marchant's heroines engage in thrilling adventures around the world, they usually become housewives at the end of the book. This does not apply to Margaret however because after her wedding, she continues working as a medical missionary. Throughout the novel she demonstrates that she is a competent self-sufficient woman and would have thrived in her work even if she had not met John Armstrong. In fact, it is John who has changed, because after his conversion and marriage to Margaret, he chooses to return to Nanjing with her so that they could 'devote themselves to the improvement of the place and the people' (331). Armstrong's story represents the 'taming' and transformation of an aggressive type of British imperialist into a God-fearing philanthropist. The conclusion reflects Marchant's hope for all merchants to become devout Christians and work together with the missionaries. She suggests that not only did the Chinese need Christianity, but merchants and traders in China should be converted as well.

In addition to helping the Chinese medically, many female missionaries wanted to improve the condition of their 'sisters' abroad. Besides the issue of foot-binding in China, raised earlier by Anne Bowman, another major concern was female infanticide. For example, Mrs Bryson of the London Missionary Society notes in *Child Life in China* (1900) that 'Not unfrequently [*sic*] when a little girl is born, its parents will drown it rather than have the trouble of bringing it up. Some women have destroyed as many as five or six little girls in this way'.[70] Because her husband was a minister and she was a teacher in a church-run school, Marchant would have been familiar with Mrs Bryson and read publications such as *He and She from O'er the Sea: Missionary Recitations and Hymns for Twelve Boys and Girls*, which include lines such as: 'I am a Chinese boy. How glad I am that I'm not a girl! In my country there is a proverb which says that "boy is worth ten times

---

[70]   Mary Isabella Bryson, *Child Life in China* (London, 1900), p. 20.

more than a girl.'"[71] Another character named Cherry Blossom states, '[t]hey did not want me very much, but when my little baby sister came my parents would not keep her, and I never saw her again. How often and often I used to go into the Temple and ask the old god to turn me into a boy …!'[72]

In *Among Hostile Hordes*, Kwei-wha has 'tiny, bound feet' (89) and another old woman 'hobbl[es] … on her bound, mis-shapen feet' (121). While Marchant does not explicitly protest against foot-binding as Bowman did, she, like Bowman, alludes to the importance of educating Chinese women when she describes the ladies in Kwei-wha's house discussing the supposed death of Margaret with an 'air of keen relish which ignorant and ill-fed minds always display for the horrible and ghastly' (123). She also highlights the inferior status of females in traditional Chinese society. When the customers at Bo's tea shop are arguing about whether Bo should accept Loo Choo's unreasonable fees, Su Sen urges Bo to pay 'for the sake of the boy; had it been a girl now, or even a wife, it would have been different' (20). Bo believes his first two children were daughters because he was cursed. The only reason he kept them is because he thought 'that they might prove useful later on, in cleaning and minding the tea-hong' (144). In presenting the plight of Chinese girls to her readers, Marchant may have been urging them to be thankful and to sympathize with their Chinese sisters. On the other hand, this information might have also made them reflect on their own subordinate status in British society.

Unlike Samuel Mossman, Bessie Marchant never travelled to China. From the publication of her first novel *Under Clearer Skies* in 1892 to her death in 1941, she wrote prolifically from her home in Charlbury, Oxfordshire.[73] Although Marchant never left Britain, being 'a traveller only on the enchanted carpet of imagination', she has been praised for 'handling local details with care' in her numerous adventure stories set in places such as Australia, China, India, Canada, Borneo, Persia, South America, and Russia.[74] According to Alan Major, Marchant acquired knowledge about other countries by conducting research in the Bodleian Library, reading *The Geographical Magazine* and gathering information from letters sent by her overseas readers.[75] Considering that between 1899 and 1940, she produced three to four novels a year, Marchant probably did not have much time to conduct in-depth research on the subject of the Taiping Rebellion, regardless of the volumes of work on the subject at her disposal in the Bodleian Library.

---

[71] J.M.B., *He and She from O'er the Sea: Missionary Recitations and Hymns for Twelve Boys and Girls* (London, [1900]), p. 2.

[72] Ibid., p. 5. The *Juvenile Missionary Magazine* also conveyed similar information. See 'Babes in China', *Juvenile Missionary Magazine*, XXI.239 (1864): pp. 91–2; 'A Peep at a Chinese Family', *Juvenile Missionary Magazine*, XXII.254 (1865): pp. 313–20.

[73] Major, 'Bessie Marchant', p. 33.

[74] Murray, 'Bessie Marchant', p. 569; Hester Janet Colles, 'Books for Girls: Australian Stories', *The Times Literary Supplement*, 8 December 1921, p. 127.

[75] Major, 'Bessie Marchant', p. 33.

In fact, besides *Among Hostile Hordes*, a total of seven other Marchant novels were published in 1901.[76]

Despite Marchant's time constraints, it is clear from the 'Notes' section at the beginning of *Among Hostile Hordes* that she researched Chinese language usages and meanings to produce a simple glossary of Chinese terms used in the book. She may have included this page to bolster the validity of her work as an educational historical novel. In addition to explaining words such as 'hong' in tea-hong (meaning 'a shop' or 'any place of business'), Marchant mentions in the 'Notes' that names ending in 'chau, chow, or chou' all denote the residence of an inferior official. She also writes that 'hien' and 'hsien' had the same meaning. Marchant probably felt the need to create this glossary after consulting different sources on the Taiping Rebellion and trying to reconcile disparate romanizations of Chinese place names. Therefore, she most likely had more knowledge of Chinese than William Dalton, who used 'Kwei-chou' and 'Koei-cheou' to refer to Guizhou but did not inform readers that they denoted the same province. However, some words in the 'Notes' are defined incorrectly. For example, readers are told that 'Hang' means 'above' such as in 'Hangchau' [Hangzhou] and 'Su' means 'below' such as in 'Kiang su' [Jiangsu]. Although the word 'Su' could mean 'to revive' or refer to a type of Chinese basil, when used in Jiangsu it does not mean 'below' but denotes a place.[77] The 'hang' in 'Hangzhou' does not mean 'above' but also denotes a place.[78] Despite these mistakes, the 'Notes' page is an important feature of *Among Hostile Hordes* that distinguishes it from other texts examined in this book.

General 'Chinese' Gordon

Because Marchant does not specify her sources, it is unclear whether she read Mossman's *The Mandarin's Daughter*, but it is likely that she consulted his edited book *General Gordon's Private Diary of His Exploits in China* (1885) because her story describes Gordon writing in his 'private diary which he had kept so carefully all through the campaign' (275). In addition, her description of an incident 'at the little village of Chanzu' coincides with an event that happened 'some eighteen

[76]   For a full bibliography, see Anne Commire (ed.), *Yesterday's Authors of Books for Children: Facts and Pictures About Authors and Illustrators of Books for Young People, from Early Times to 1960* (2 vols, Detroit, MI, 1978), vol. 2, p. 245.

[77]   The name for Jiangsu province is a result of combining the first word of the names of the two provincial governments, Jiangning and Suzhou, which were established in this territory in ancient times. The mistake could be due to a misinterpretation of the famous Chinese saying '*shang you tiantang, xia you shuhang*' [there is heaven above and there is Suzhou and Hangzhou below].

[78]   'Hang' could mean 'boat' but in 'Hangzhou' it denotes a place. See *Zhonghua dazidian* (Xianggang: Zhonghua shu ju, 1977), p. 227.

miles from Chanzu' recorded in Mossman's edition of Gordon's diary.[79] Another possible source for her novel is *The Story of Chinese Gordon* (1884) by Alfred Egmont Hake (1849–1916), a relative of Gordon's who hailed the General as a positive moral example for all British readers. Hake's book, which was so popular that by mid-1884 it had already gone into a sixth edition, is just one of the numerous hagiographic biographies of Gordon.[80] Even more accounts of his life pervaded the market after his death in the Sudan in 1885, an event that shook the British public and led them to further romanticize and idealize Gordon as a Christian martyr and loyal soldier.[81] In 1886, the *Birmingham Daily Post* stated, 'there have been many biographical books, and books dealing with the episodes in the life of our greatest modern Knight, General Gordon' and listed nine such works.[82]

Rev. W. Binns, who delivered a message on the death roll for 1885 in the Charing Cross Unitarian Church, Birkenhead, eulogized that 'Gordon's life was a poem; his memory will be an inspiration'.[83] Indeed, many poets wrote panegyric verses lauding Gordon's courage, charisma, and chivalry. For example, John Stuart Blackie's 'Chinese Gordon' (1886) portrays him as a hero who 'laid the hot-brained pig-tailed rebel low' but 'sought no praise from men' and John Farrell's 'Charles Gordon' (1905) describes him as the 'man who swayed fierce pagan hordes / With kind, strong wisdom in a time of flame / When China swooned in horror without name / Of brother-hate and blindly plunging swords' but 'turned from all reward'.[84]

Not only was Gordon lionized in poetry, he was also idealized in children's literature. Gordon biographies for children, with titles such as *General Gordon: The Christian Soldier and Hero* (1898) and *For Honour, Not Honours: Being the Story of Gordon of Khartoum* (1896) became popular Christmas books and school prizes, even until 30 years after his death. For example, in 1917 in the context of a later war *General Gordon: The Christian Soldier and Hero* was given as a Sunday

---

[79] See Samuel Mossman (ed.), *General Gordon's Private Diary of His Exploits in China* (London, 1885), p. 217; Marchant, *Among Hostile Hordes*, p. 320.

[80] Miller, 'Our Abdiel', p. 148.

[81] In 1884 the British government sent Gordon to Sudan to evacuate Egyptian forces from Khartoum, which was threatened by Sudanese rebels. He was killed on 26 January 1885, when the rebels broke into the city. News of his death surprised the British public, who immediately remembered him as a martyred warrior-saint. For more information regarding Gordon and the Sudan, see Robert H. MacDonald, *The Language of Empire: Myths and Metaphors of Popular Imperialism, 1880–1918* (Manchester, 1994), pp. 83–8 and Dennis Judd, 'Gordon of Khartoum: The Making of an Imperial Martyr', *History Today*, 35.1 (1985): pp. 19–25.

[82] 'Memorials of General Gordon', *Birmingham Daily Post*, 26 April 1886, p. 7.

[83] 'The Rev. W. Binns on the Death Roll of 1885', *Liverpool Mercury*, 5 January 1886, p. 7.

[84] John Stuart Blackie, 'Chinese Gordon', 1886, *Literature Online* <http://lion.chadwyck.com> [accessed 24 November 2012]; John Farrell, 'Charles Gordon', 1905, *Literature Online* <http://lion.chadwyck.com> [accessed 24 November 2012].

school prize in Weston-super-Mare.[85] Teachers hoped their students would admire and emulate Gordon's courage, strength, manliness, chivalry, and puritan spirit: qualities typical of the adventure-story heroes of the time. These descriptions could be found in Jeanie Lang's *The Story of Chinese Gordon*, which claims that 'even the rebels who feared his name loved him too. They knew that he was always true and brave, honourable and merciful'.[86] Gordon was also featured in *The Roll-Call of Honour: A New Book of Golden Deeds, The Red Book of Heroes, Heroes in History*, and *Fifty-two Stories of the British Army*. Another reason for Gordon's popularity among children's biographers was his charitable children's work, particularly his kindness towards boys living in poverty at Gravesend, where the words 'God Bless the Kernel [colonel]' could reportedly be found chalked up on doors in the area.[87] Children's periodicals such as the *Boy's Own Paper, The Children's Friend, Chatterbox*, and *Young England* all carried articles on General Gordon.[88] In 'Chinese Gordon', the *Boy's Own Paper* claims that he 'rescued the Chinese Empire from extinction ...'.[89] The statement suggests that the Chinese needed Gordon to save them from their own people, an assertion echoed by Mossman in *The Mandarin's Daughter*: 'But for his skill and perseverance, in all probability the Taiping rebellion would be still raging, and paralyzing the industry of the chief marts of China' (336).

The *Athenaeum* reviewer of *Among the Hostile Hordes* notes that Gordon, the 'ill-fated hero', is 'a conspicuous figure' in the story.[90] Gordon's presence can be felt even before he appears. Kwei-wha describes him as the 'arch-barbarian' who 'wins his victories by black magic' (67). Marchant weaves popular legends surrounding Chinese Gordon into the story. For example, because John travels with a light bamboo cane in his hand, he is mistaken for Gordon, who reportedly only carried a bamboo walking cane (known as his wand of victory) instead of weapons.[91] Later in the story Gordon is seen 'armed as usual only with his small, light cane, which served him in the same fashion as a baton serves the conductor of an orchestra,

[85]   W.J. Reader, *At Duty's Call: A Study in Obsolete Patriotism* (Manchester, 1988), p. 50.

[86]   Jeanie Lang, *The Story of General Gordon* (London, 1900), p. 54.

[87]   Ibid., p. 56.

[88]   See for example, J.L., 'General Gordon', *The Children's Friend*, LIII (1913): pp. 2–3; 'Stories from the Lives of Famous Men No.4 (Charles Gordon)', *Chatterbox*, XXIII (1892): pp. 179–81; 'Gordon's Generosity', *Chatterbox*, XLIX (1901): p. 390; 'Anecdote of Gordon', *Chatterbox*, III (1907): p. 22; '"Chinese Gordon": A Brief Sketch of a Wonderful Career', *The Boy's Journal*, 7 (1913): p. 207.

[89]   'Chinese Gordon', *Boy's Own Paper*, p. 487.

[90]   'Books for the Young', p. 47.

[91]   Gordon's 'wand of victory' is mentioned in many children's texts. For example an article in *Young England* states that 'He was never armed, carrying only the small cane which his troops styled "Gordon's magic wand of victory"': Horace G. Groser, 'General Gordon', *Young England*, 6 (1885): pp. 176–8 (p. 176). See also Cicely Margaret Binyon, 'Gordon: A Hero of Egypt', in *Heroes in History* (London, [n.d.]), pp. 134–44 (p. 137).

which regulates as well as emphasises the tune' (282). In comparing Gordon to a conductor, the narrator creates an image of a peaceful man who makes beautiful harmonic music, downplaying the cacophonic ugly reality of warfare. Interestingly, Don resembles a mini-Gordon because he also holds a 'wand' that helps him to achieve his goal, the silver talisman (a symbol of power) stolen from Boo-Boo the Buddhist monk, which he uses to command the Chinese people he meets.

In Don's mind, Gordon is 'the bravest man' he knows and he would gladly lay down his life for the General because 'a valuable life is always worth guarding' (162; 186). Don notices that Gordon guided 'the crowd of many nationalities that had enlisted in his army' with 'righteous thoroughness' (274). Like E. Harcourt Burrage's multi-national crew of the Belvedere, Gordon's army is 'a cosmopolitan lot', composed of 'men of almost every nationality; there were Jews and Japs, Greeks, Germans, French, British, and Turks – men who fought for money, and not for country or for sovereign' (278). Marchant's patriotism and hatred of greedy mercenaries are evident when she notes that those who complained about Gordon's 'strict discipline' (such as forbidding looting) deserted him and pledged allegiance to Tien Wang, who welcomed 'the floating scum of all nationalities' (125). From these descriptions, readers can see how the 'opening' of China after the two Opium Wars had affected the country because it had become a contested space where people from all over the globe converged to make the most of the new opportunities they had. Most of these people, like the mercenaries in *Among Hostile Hordes*, were motivated by selfish desires and were willing to pledge loyalty to anyone who offered a lucrative incentive. Therefore the China in *Among Hostile Hordes* was hostile not only because of the anti-foreign Chinese population but also dangerous because unscrupulous fickle non-Chinese fortune-seekers could quickly switch sides without warning.

Gordon's image as the model 'muscular Christian' is further bolstered when he advises Don, who kneels before the General on one knee, to 'Bend the knee to God in the future, and to Him alone' (185). Gordon is held in such high esteem that John declares that he is not 'worthy to black that brave soldier's boots' (53). In depicting Gordon as a glorious leader, Marchant adheres to the model-hero formula utilized by many writers of children's biographies. One incident mentioned in almost all Gordon biographies concerns the negotiation with the Taiping 'Wangs' (kings). Gordon promised to treat them mercifully if they surrendered. However, Li Hongzhang went back on his word and allowed General Qing to behead them. The narrator of *Among Hostile Hordes* does not describe Gordon's reaction to the executions, simply stating that General Qing, with the consent of Li Hongzhang, 'quietly murdered' them even after Gordon had been assured they would be shown mercy (329). A letter to the Editor of *The Times* in 1877 uses this incident to illustrate Gordon's 'intense hatred of all lying, treachery, and deceit'.[92] In *Among Hostile Hordes*, Gordon reveals how much he detested treachery, stating that

---

[92] Robert K. Douglas, 'Colonel Gordon – Letter to the Editor', *The Times*, 1 January 1877, p. 8.

'sometimes I think they [the Chinese] must have all been born lacking a moral backbone, there is such a terrible uniformity in their treachery' (277). Not only did Gordon hate betrayal and deceit, he could detect it. According to *The Times*, 'When many thought the Taepings [*sic*] would be the regenerators of China and the propagators of Christianity, Captain Gordon detected the imposture, and revealed their true character and ambition'.[93] Gordon is depicted not only as a great military campaigner, but a detective figure able to uncover the Taiping veil of deception. The Taipings may have been able to 'pass' as Christians for a period of time but ultimately Gordon identified them as impostors and restores order to China.

After joining Gordon's army, Don observes the life of 'the noble-hearted commander' and what he sees 'waken[s] in him a keen zest of emulation' (247). However, despite Don's admiration for Gordon and his desire to perform an act of bravery, it is worth noting that he does not aspire to become a military officer like Gordon but rather a medical missionary like Margaret. He plans to come back to China as a medical missionary and 'do his part in helping forward the civilisation of that vast land, whose souls can only be reached through their bodies, and who turn a deaf ear to teaching that does not carry healing in its train' (330). The narrator implies that as a medical missionary, Don would have a greater chance of sharing his faith with the Chinese.

Henry Burgevine and Hong Xiuquan

Not all of the Western characters in *Among Hostile Hordes* are portrayed in a positive light. In fact, Burgevine is the antithesis of Gordon. Whereas a 'feeling of professional honour will prevent any respectable Englishman or Frenchman from joining the rebels', the *Saturday Review* argues, Burgevine is an adventurer who 'fights for his own hand on behalf of the party which offers him the best prospect of personal advantage'.[94] After being dismissed from the Ever-Victorious Army, Burgevine had switched his loyalties to the Taiping forces in 1863 but a few months later re-defected and surrendered at Suzhou. He secretly joined the remnants of the Taipings in 1865 but was drowned when his boat capsized on the way to Suzhou from Fujian.[95] While Augustus Lindley, a staunch supporter of the Taipings, commented that Burgevine had a 'refined' and 'engaging' manner, most writers labelled him a 'mercenary and filibuster' or 'a self-seeking, hot-tempered American freebooter' with a 'love of violence'.[96]

---

[93]   'General Gordon', *The Times*, 12 February 1885, p. 5.

[94]   'English Policy in China', *Saturday Review*, 5 December 1863, pp. 714–15 (p. 714).

[95]   For more information on Burgevine, see Teng, *The Taiping Rebellion*, pp. 318–21.

[96]   Augustus F. Lindley, *Ti-Ping Tien-Kwoh: The History of the Ti-Ping Revolution, Including a Narrative of the Author's Personal Adventures* (London, 1866), p. 649; Teng, *The Taiping Rebellion*, p. 320; Alfred Egmont Hake, *The Story of Chinese Gordon* (London, 1884), p. 96. For more information on Lindley, see J. Newsinger, 'Taiping Revolutionary: Augustus Lindley in China', *Race and Class*, 42.4 (2001): pp. 57–72.

Burgevine does not play an important part in *The Mandarin's Daughter*: he is only mentioned in passing as the officer who 'was dismissed for disloyalty' (287). However, *Among Hostile Hordes* presents a scathing picture of the 'shifty' and 'untrustworthy' Burgevine (303). When Margaret first meets him, she notices that his manner 'had little of sympathy or even kindness in it', there was a tone of 'bitterness' in his voice, and his laugh was 'short, mocking, and mirthless' (255). After learning he had initially refused to assist her and only agreed to help so that Margaret's servant Blossom would stop following him, Margaret's dislike for him increases. Burgevine, who has 'sold his body and soul to Tien Wang', reveals his 'sinister menace' and his disregard for human life when he reports that he shot his compatriot as he 'would shoot a dog, or a beggarly Chinaman that would not do his work' (255; 268). Margaret dismisses him as a coward as she notices his face turned to 'a ghastly pallor' when he sees Blossom's dead body, prompting her to say, 'You are a soldier, and must have seen death in many forms; how was I to know that you would be afraid?' (286). She grows to dislike and fear the man so much that 'she would prefer to run the gauntlet of every Taiping fanatic in the town, even including Loo Choo in the number, than to be compelled again to avail herself of his unwilling protection' (289). Through the negative portrayal of Burgevine, Marchant is not only able to exalt Gordon to greater heights but also to demonstrate that one's nationality is no guarantee of noble behaviour. Despite being a fellow American, Burgevine was reluctant to help Margaret. On the other hand, the British merchant John risked his life to rescue her.

The Taiping leader Hong Xiuquan is known as Tien Wang in both novels. Hong Xiuquan does not make an appearance in *The Mandarin's Daughter* despite many references to him in the novel. Readers are informed that Hong was 'one of the most blasphemous impostors the world has ever seen' (*MD* 239). Meng-kee is forced to kneel with his face to Tien Wang's empty seat and pray to him, which made him feel 'an air of sham dignity about the whole affair' (*MD* 240). It is not clear how much Marchant knew about Hong Xiuquan and his connection with Christianity. Margaret laments that Tien Wang had converted to Christianity many years ago, but has 'grown old, blood-thirsty, and cruel' (81). Don speculates 'he knew only enough of Christianity to make a hash of it, the same as a good many more enlightened folks do' (82). Having 'long ago forsworn all that he had ever professed and believed concerning the Christian religion', Tien Wang orders his 'soothsayers and magicians' to advise him 'on the best way of defeating the so-called black magic of Gordon' (125; 127).

In the novel, Tien Wang explains that his initial edict to kill the English but not the Americans stems from the fact that he has 'softened to the Americans because of the former years' (91). Later in the story, he recalls that when he was a young man, 'the missionary had told him of evil spirits being cast out of people by a wonderful Man who had come down from heaven to live on earth for a while' (125). This suggests Marchant's awareness of Hong's relationship with Issachar J. Roberts, the American missionary who met with Hong in 1847 and was later offered the role of 'Director of Foreign Affairs' for the Taipings in 1861.

Roberts denied the title, choosing to stay in Nanjing to proclaim his faith but sometimes worked as an interpreter for the Taipings. He persuaded the Taipings to allow missionaries access to territories under their control and obtained permission to build 18 chapels in Nanjing. However, the buildings were never constructed and Roberts left the city in 1862 after falling out with some Taiping leaders. Later, he wrote in the *North China Herald* that he believed Tien Wang was 'a crazy man' who had a 'violent' temper and opposed commerce, murdering those who were caught trading in the city.[97] Marchant may have read Roberts's description of Tien Wang or the works of Josiah Cox, who reported that the Taiping leader had an 'imperious and cruel temper' and reigned like a 'despot' 'without respect to law, or the liberty of the individual'.[98]

Although Tien Wang is 'a dreadful man; a perfect ogre', he is not physically terrifying in the novel, being 'a man of average height, rapidly ageing now, as was evidenced by the haggard lines of care in his parchment-like face and the weary droop of his bowed shoulders' (81; 88). This coincides with Roberts's 1853 description of him as 'a man of ordinary appearance, about five feet four or five inches high'.[99] However, it contradicts J.M. Callery and M. Yvan's descriptions of Tien Wang as 'a man of tall stature', and the assertion of Andrew Wilson, former editor of the *China Mail*, who writes that Tien Wang 'is known to having been of large stature, with a flowing black beard, bright eyes …'.[100] Regardless of his physical stature, Tien Wang does not frighten Don, who thinks he sounds like an 'old toothless dog trying to gnaw a bone' even when he declares his power, claiming that 'blood flowed in rivers through the streets when I willed it so' (90). The leader of the Taipings lacks awareness of personal hygiene: 'Tien Wang never washed himself nor yet gave the slightest attention to his toilet' (126). In including this detail about Tien Wang, Marchant's narrator reflects the Victorian obsession with the 'cult of cleanliness', which could be observed from nineteenth-century advertisements for Pears' soap.[101] As this cult swept through England, sanitation and personal hygiene 'became hallmarks of a civilized society'.[102] Societies that did not prioritize the importance of cleanliness were seen as inferior, which China clearly was in the narrator's eyes.

[97] Clarke and Gregory (eds), *Western Reports on the Taiping*, p. 314. For more information on Roberts and his relationship with the Taiping Rebellion, see Yuan Chung Teng, 'Reverend Issachar Jacox Roberts and the Taiping Rebellion', *The Journal of Asian Studies*, 23.1 (1963): pp. 55–67 and Teng, *The Taiping Rebellion*, pp. 196–202.

[98] Clarke and Gregory (eds), *Western Reports on the Taiping*, p. 312.

[99] Ibid., p. 19.

[100] J.M. Callery and Melchior Yvan, *History of the Insurrection in China, with Notices of the Christianity, Creed and Proclamations of the Insurgents*, trans. John Oxenford (New York, 1853), p. 188; Wilson, *The 'Ever-Victorious Army'*, p. 41.

[101] Anne McClintock, *Imperial Leather: Race, Gender, and Sexuality in the Colonial Conquest* (New York, 1995), pp. 207–31.

[102] Susan Schoenbauer Thurin, *Victorian Travelers and the Opening of China, 1842–1907* (Athens, OH, 1999), p. 190.

In *Among Hostile Hordes*, Charles Gordon, Henry Burgevine, and Tien Wang are essentially two-dimensional characters who exemplify the difference between good and evil, civilized and savage, honourable and treacherous. However, unlike other adventure stories that emphasize the binary of East versus West, the villainous figure of the American Burgevine reveals that simplistic notions of East equals 'bad' while West equals 'good' must be complicated. In addition, Burgevine's defection can be seen as representing America's emerging threat to Britain in the Imperial arena, especially during the period when the book was written. British readers are reminded to be wary of the Americans lest they turn out to be devious characters like Burgevine. Despite incorporating important figures of the Taiping Rebellion into the story and interweaving key events of the Rebellion with the fictional plotline involving Don, John, and Margaret, Marchant's description of the anti-foreign atmosphere in *Among Hostile Hordes* suggests that although she set the story in her recent past, she was reflecting the anxiety brought about by events of her present, namely, the Boxer Uprising (1899–1901). This movement, which was raging in Northern China around the time Marchant was writing *Among Hostile Hordes*, aimed to eradicate all foreigners from the country. As a minister's wife, Marchant would have received reports from missionaries in China describing the Boxer Uprising. Although the subtitle of Marchant's book is 'A Story of the Tai-ping Rebellion', there are several indications that *Among Hostile Hordes* is more of a Boxer narrative than a Taiping story.

Among Hostile Hordes as a Boxer Narrative

The late Qing dynasty was marked by another major uprising at the end of the nineteenth century: the Boxer Uprising. The Yihequan ('Righteous and Harmonious Fists') was a group known as the 'Boxers' because in the eyes of foreigners, their strengthening exercises and martial arts practices (*quan*) resembled shadow boxing.[103] This anti-Qing society initially sought to restore the Ming dynasty. However, in the 1890s, they became an anti-foreign group. By 1899 the Boxers were openly attacking and killing foreigners and Chinese Christians in Northern China. In early October 1899, foreign newspapers began to circulate notices regarding the Boxers and by mid-December, it was reported that the movement was 'spreading like wild-fire'.[104] According to Paul A. Cohen, evidence from various sources suggests that the Boxer movement spread and intensified because of a severe drought that showed no signs of ending.[105] Widely distributed in early 1900, Boxer notices blamed the drought in North China on the presence of foreigners, especially Christians. The notices proclaimed that rain would not fall until all foreigners met their death and their influence had been extinguished.

---

[103] For more information on types of Chinese 'boxing', see Paul A. Cohen, *History in Three Keys: The Boxers as Event, Experience, and Myth* (New York, 1997), pp. 16–17.

[104] Ibid., p. 44.

[105] Ibid., p. 77.

In June 1900, the Qing government showed their support for the Boxers by giving them a semi-official title, the Yihetuan ('Righteous and Harmonious Militia'). The foreign Legations at Peking were besieged from late June to mid-August 1900 and British newspapers were emblazoned with headlines such as 'The Crisis in China'. An international troop freed the trapped residents of the Legations on 14 August 1900 and the uprising eventually subsided.[106]

According to Robert A. Bickers, the Boxer Uprising and other recent events in Chinese history were 'all firmly fixed in the British popular imagination' during the late nineteenth and early twentieth century.[107] In all aspects of British popular culture (children's literature, thrillers, plays, romances), China and the Chinese were noticeably present. On stage, American magician William Robinson, performing as 'Chung Ling Soo', attracted huge audiences with his bullet-catching trick called 'Condemned to Death by the Boxers'.[108] Boxer events were scripted into films such as *Attempted Capture of an English Nursery and Child by Boxers* (1901), *Assassination of an English Citizen by Boxers* (1901), and *Attack on a China Mission–Bluejackets to the Rescue* (1900).[109] Such films influenced children's perceptions of the Chinese, as missionary administrator Harold Hodgkin noted in 1925, relating an incident where the son of a friend claimed to know 'all about Chinamen; they were cruel, wicked people; he had seen lots of them at the pictures'.[110]

Written during a time when the Boxers dominated headlines, *Among Hostile Hordes* is a product of this historical moment for several reasons. First, Marchant's descriptions of anti-foreign antagonism, chaos, madness, and hysteria are more often associated with the Boxers rather than the Taipings, because the Taiping Rebellion was generally not regarded as threatening to the British residents in China.[111] When fierce riots erupt in Kum Lu, Loo Choo is very pleased and declares that 'these outbursts of lawlessness were the best things which could happen to a place, since they *purged it of the hated foreign element*, and gave honest men like himself plenty of work to do' [my emphasis] (109). Loo Choo's anti-foreignism was characteristic of the Boxers' attitude, because they were particularly hostile towards foreign missionaries. Therefore, in writing that John

---

[106] For more information on the Boxer Rebellion see Cohen, *History in Three Keys*. More discussion about the Boxers will be provided in Chapter 5.

[107] Robert A. Bickers, *Britain in China: Community Culture and Colonialism, 1900–1949* (Manchester, 1999), p. 23.

[108] Jim Steinmeyer, *The Glorious Deception: The Double Life of William Robinson, a.k.a. Chung Ling Soo, The "Marvelous Chinese Conjuror"* (New York, 2005).

[109] For a discussion of the first two films, see James Louis Hevia, *English Lessons: The Pedagogy of Imperialism in Nineteenth-Century China* (Durham, 2003), p. 305. For analysis of *Attack on a China Mission*, see Frank Gray, 'James Williamson's "Composed Picture": Attack on a China Mission–Bluejackets to the Rescue (1900)', in John Fullerton (ed.), *Celebrating 1895: The Centenary of Cinema* (London, 1998), pp. 203–11 (p. 207).

[110] Quoted in Bickers, *Britain in China*, p. 23.

[111] Cohen, *History in Three Keys*, p. 15.

holds missionaries 'responsible for every outbreak of barbarian lawlessness and fiendish violence' (54), Marchant was probably alluding to the Boxer Uprising and not the Taiping Rebellion because although the Taipings were not very welcoming of the foreigners, their main goal was not to exterminate them, unlike the Boxers, who brandished flags with the slogan '*Fu* [or *Zhu*]-*Qing mieyang*' (Support [or Help] the Qing, destroy the foreign [or foreigner])'.[112]

In 'Faced by Chinese Rebels: and the Ruse that Outwitted Them' (1900), a Boxer story in the popular boy's magazine *Chums* (1892–1932), the Boxers are characterized as a 'howling mob', 'armed with knives, bludgeons, and iron-tipped bamboos'.[113] According to Ross G. Forman, authors borrowed the 'late-Victorian terminology of the mob' previously associated with Britain's urban working classes to describe the Chinese during the Boxer Rebellion.[114] The 'Hordes' of Marchant's title was also frequently used to describe the Boxers. In addition to 'hordes', the word 'mob' repeatedly appears in Marchant's text. For example, although John Armstrong manages to keep a 'frantic, howling mob at bay' on a boat, he is again confronted with an 'enraged mob' at the yamen (54; 104). Similarly, Margaret finds herself at the mercy of 'one of the most savage mobs the wide world would show', and is later shut up in 'a wild-beast cage of raving fanatics' (147; 303). Elsewhere, the Government is blamed for failing to 'protect its adherents from the frenzy of a mob, maddened by hardship and starvation' (109). Inside Bo's tea shop, the 'howls of the mob' could be heard over the arguments taking place inside and Bo eventually loses customers 'put to flight by the mob which lusted for slaughter' (112). The juxtaposition of a small British army against hordes of Chinese is an image frequently employed by authors of Boxer narratives. Similarly, Marchant writes, 'in point of numbers, the handful of English, with the regiments of native soldiers, were but as nothing in comparison with the hordes of the rebel army, who ... were like the locusts for multitude' (205). The implications of the use of the words 'hordes' and 'mob' will be discussed in more detail in the next chapter which considers Boxer narratives for children.

An atmosphere of anxiety and fears of death pervade the novel. Margaret laments that she simply wants the 'fearful lust of slaughter' to cease but the people seem 'to have no thought, and no ambition beyond killing each other' (82–3). As the situation worsens, she frequently hears 'the terrible shouting of "kill! kill!"' (290). Cries of 'kill! kill!' often appeared in Boxer narratives, such as in *The World's Navies in the Boxer Rebellion (China 1900)*, where the Boxers repeatedly yelled '"Tow-ah!" "Tow-ah!" (Kill! Kill!)'.[115] The threat of imminent

---

[112] Ibid., p. 25.

[113] 'Faced by Chinese Rebels: and the Ruse that Outwitted Them', *Chums*, VIII.413 (1900): pp. 814–15 (p. 814).

[114] Ross G. Forman, 'Peking Plots: Fictionalizing the Boxer Rebellion of 1900', *Victorian Literature and Culture*, 27.1 (1999): pp. 19–48 (p. 27).

[115] Charles Cabry Dix, *The World's Navies in the Boxer Rebellion (China 1900)* (London, 1905), p. 75.

death reaches its peak in the scene where Margaret and Blossom attempt to escape to Suzhou by hiding in two coffins. In describing their flight by coffin, Marchant may have been inspired by the story of Rev. Father Stephanus Sette, who managed to evade the Boxers in Hunan because his Chinese Christian friends carried him in a box resembling a coffin. During the seven-day journey, whenever his friends were stopped and questioned about the box, they could continue on because of the Chinese reverence for the dead.[116]

Secondly, although Marchant tries to educate her child readers about some possible reasons for the rebellion by explaining, in terms similar to descriptions of the Irish Famine, that 'These poor wretches had been taught to believe that foreigners brought bad harvests, blighted the corn, ruined the rice crops, and generally worked havoc and destruction in the land, so it was little wonder that they rose in their misery, and smote the common enemy hip and thigh', the reasons she provides have been mostly attributed to the cause of the Boxer Uprising and not the Taiping Rebellion (112–13). For example, in 1900, *The Review of Reviews* quotes Rev. Roland Allen of the Church of England Mission in Peking who cites 'the force of hunger' caused by the drought in North China as one of the causes which led to the siege of the Peking Legations, claiming that 'the people attributed the calamity to the anger of Heaven caused either by the Empress' highhanded action or by the presence of foreigners'.[117] In addition to written messages, Boxers composed simple jingles such as '*Shale yangguitou, Mengyu wang xia liu*' ('When foreign devils have been killed, A heavy rain will fall'); and '*Yangren shajin, Yu yu huan yu, Yu qing jiao qing*' ('When the foreigners have all been killed off, Rain will come when we call for rain, And it will be clear when we want it to be clear') that were effective in spreading their message.[118]

Third, Ting Lang's story resembles those of the starving residents of Shandong who joined the Boxers because of hunger or fear of anticipated hunger.[119] Although severe drought and famine from 1848 to 1850 also induced impoverished residents in the southern provinces to join secret societies such as the Triads in the hope of being fed by wealthier members of the group, Ting Lang explains that he joined the Brotherhood of Death out of necessity when he was starving in Northern China (74).[120] The text does not mention Ting Lang's hometown, but it is possible he is from northwestern Shandong, a poverty-stricken province particularly susceptible to flooding, where many Boxers originated. Ting Lang explains that members of the Brotherhood

---

[116] Zephaniah Charles Beals, *China and the Boxers: A Short History on the Boxer Outbreak, with Two Chapters on the Sufferings of Missionaries and a Closing One on the Outlook* (Toronto, 1901), p. 120.

[117] The Best Authority in the World, 'What Should be Done in China', *The Review of Reviews*, XXII (1900): pp. 447–9 (p. 448).

[118] Cohen, *History in Three Keys*, p. 85.

[119] Ibid., pp. 30–35.

[120] Teng, *The Taiping Rebellion*, p. 60.

> sell themselves to the rich ones, and for the price that is paid they join themselves
> in the Brotherhood of Death, receiving so many of cash for every scar that is
> written on face and brow. But we are sold for death, and all the appointed ones
> may for to kily [*sic*] us when they meet us anywhere. (74)

His 'hideous' and 'terrifying' face makes him an easily recognizable target for the appointed killers (74). The extent of his repulsiveness is evident in the following assertion: 'his native land could not produce another man so ugly as himself' (48). Incidents involving facial scarring or marking were reported during both the Taiping and Boxer Rebellions. Taiping generals who caught villagers trying to escape would tattoo the characters 'Heavenly Kingdom of Great Peace' on their faces as a warning not to stray again.[121] The narrator of *The Mandarin's Daughter* also alludes to this practice: 'A great many of these men appeared to have been lately pressed into the service, and as a precaution against desertion they had the Chinese character for the Taiping dynasty tattooed on their cheeks' (279). During the Boxer Uprising, some Christians had crosses cut on their forehead by a sword.[122] In envisioning the events of the Taiping Rebellion through the lens of the Boxer Uprising, Marchant creates a historical novel that reflects the imperial anxieties of the *fin-de-siècle*. In initially depicting John Armstrong as a spiritually weak man who had lost his faith, Marchant was mirroring post-Boer War (1899–1902) anxiety about the vulnerability of British imperialism and the fear that Englishmen were becoming degenerate both physically and spiritually.[123] *Among Hostile Hordes* suggests that in order to maintain order in imperial outposts such as China which had become increasingly antagonistic to foreigners, men needed to be transformed as John Armstrong was. At the same time, there was deepening anxiety about the distortion of Christian knowledge by the Chinese, which was absent in Bowman's *The Travels of Rolando* or Dalton's *The Wolf Boy of China* where the key Chinese characters are 'good' Christians.

Conclusion

In 1887, noted Victorian novelist and critic Charlotte Yonge pointed out the importance of 'Historical Tales' in *What Books to Lend and What to Give*, noting that they were suitable for both girls and boys and extolling their 'considerable value' in terms of conveying facts and 'serving as "sugared history"'.[124] However, historical tales about the Taiping Rebellion are not 'sugared history' but bitter stories of turmoil, chaos, and destruction which cannot be romanticized.

---

[121] Spence, *God's Chinese Son*, p. 304.

[122] Cohen, *History in Three Keys*, p. 177.

[123] Maria Davidis, '"Unarm, Eros!": Adventure, Homoeroticism, and Divine Order in *Prester John*', in Philip Holden and Richard R. Ruppel (eds), *Imperial Desire: Dissident Sexualities and Colonial Literature* (Minneapolis, 2003), pp. 223–40 (p. 223).

[124] Charlotte Yonge, *What Books to Lend and What to Give* (London, 1887), p. 55.

The Taiping Rebellion narratives by Mossman, Marchant, and *Boy's Own Paper* authors reveal that from the 1870s onwards, it was no longer possible to hold onto the romanticized view of China presented in Dalton and Bowman's books. The beautiful Chinese landscape on willow pattern plates disappeared after the Taiping rebels ravaged through it. After the publication of *Among Hostile Hordes* in 1901, it was also impossible to imagine Empire as a relatively safe playground for boys to frolic in as Burrage's characters did in the Ching-Ching series. The Taiping Rebellion reaffirmed British stereotypes of the Qing government as incompetent and helpless and the Chinese as inhumane uncivilized people who committed atrocious acts of violence against their fellow countrymen. In Marchant's words, the result of Taiping violence was the 'daily spectacle of hopeless, helpless misery, the scores of impotent sufferers, who perished of starvation in the ditches all around, or fought desperately with each other for a share of some lean dog, who had succumbed to the same death of starvation which menaced themselves' (206).

The China of the Taiping era is a horrific place where nightmarish scenes constantly confront the reader. For example, the narrator of 'A Ticklish Trip in a Chinese House-Boat' describes the drastic measures the Governor of Shanghai took to strike 'terror into the hearts of the Taipings': he ordered 'bunches of human heads to be hung up in all conspicuous places' to serve as a warning to the rebels.[125] Marchant also refers to this practice when Ting Lang sees a dark object swaying high above a town gate and fears his head would be chopped off and placed inside the basket. Although Ting Lang manages to escape this punishment, the guide who lured John and Ting Lang into the town did not. He is executed by a mandarin because he brought strangers into the place and his head 'was hung in a bamboo basket outside the gate of the town' (197). Similarly, Burgevine fears he is also in danger of having his head 'hung out to adorn the town gate' (289). These descriptions are reminiscent of the public executions at the Tower of London of previous centuries, where the accused were beheaded and sometimes also had their heads displayed as a warning to others.

Earlier in the novel, the narrator alluded to England's previous public executions when commenting on Ting Lang's association with the Brotherhood of Death. She asserts, 'the cruelty of gladiatorial combats, the bull-baiting in which our forefathers took such savage delight, the public executions, and all the other manifestations of human lust for blood which ante-dated our modern civilization, paled and waned to absolute insignificance' when compared to the atrocities of the Brotherhood of Death (75). Although she mentions that public executions 'ante-dated our modern civilization', in reality, 'male traitors' in England 'had their heads hacked off and held up to the crowd' as late as 1820 and the public executions were only abolished in 1868, less than 50 years before Marchant's time

---

[125] 'A Ticklish Trip', p. 488.

of writing.[126] Thus, although China was condemned for using outdated torturous methods of administering justice, the situation in nineteenth-century England was not as different as Marchant would have readers believe.

Marchant was aware of the didactic aspect of her novels: in 1931 she wrote to one of her readers that it is 'most thrilling' to 'talk to girls all round the world' and to 'influence them'.[127] Although by 1901 there was much more information about China available to Marchant compared to the number of resources available to Dalton, Marchant presents a more monolithic view of the Chinese compared to Dalton, ultimately promoting the stereotypes of the Chinese as cruel, greedy, dirty, and superstitious in *Among Hostile Hordes*. In her attempt to highlight the cultural inferiority of the Chinese, she emphasizes that Ting Lang's story of Chinese cruelty and the practice of beheading were far removed from contemporary 'civilization', ignoring the fact that horrible forms of punishment and torture were being executed in European colonies around the world. Therefore, although knowledge about China and the Chinese had increased dramatically by the early twentieth century, authors did not necessarily pass on any new information to young readers. Because Sino-British relations had soured toward the end of the century due to conflicting views surrounding railway rights and the building of telegraphs, British authors writing from the 1890s onwards probably had a more negative view of China and the Chinese.[128] For historical fiction writers, the events of the Taiping Rebellion provided a perfect backdrop to highlight the worst aspects of the Chinese character while giving them the opportunity to extol the admirable qualities of the British as exemplified in General Gordon, the model Christian soldier hero and paragon of manliness.

Interest in the Taiping Rebellion has not subsided since Marchant researched the event for her novel in the early twentieth century. For example, in 1904, Charles Halcombe included a lesson about the Taipings in his novel *Children of Far Cathay*. George MacDonald Fraser used the Taiping Rebellion as the setting of one of his Flashman books: *Flashman and the Dragon* (1985).[129] Two children's historical novels set in the Taiping Rebellion were also published in the 1980s: Katherine Paterson's *Rebels of the Heavenly Kingdom* (1983) and

---

[126] V.A.C. Gatrell, *The Hanging Tree: Execution and the English People 1770–1868* (Oxford, 1994), p. 7. Newspapers such as the *Illustrated Police News*, *Leeds Mercury*, and *Reynolds's Newspaper* all reported on the last public execution of Michael Barrett at Newgate in May 1868. See 'Execution of the Fenian Michael Barrett', *Illustrated Police News*, 30 May 1868, p. 2; 'Execution of the Fenian Barrett', *Leeds Mercury*, 30 May 1868, p. 12; 'The Execution of the Fenian Convict, Barrett', *Reynolds's Newspaper*, 31 May 1868, p. 7.

[127] Quoted in Major, 'Bessie Marchant', p. 33.

[128] For discussion of the railway debates, see Ralph William Huenemann, *The Dragon and the Iron Horse: The Economics of Railroads in China, 1876–1937* (Cambridge, MA, 1984), p. 3.

[129] See Charles J.H. Halcombe, *Children of Far Cathay: A Social and Political Novel* (London, 1906), pp. 60–69; George MacDonald Fraser, *Flashman and the Dragon* (Glasgow, 1985).

Laurence Yep's *The Serpent's Children* (1984), which both explore the impact of the Taiping Rebellion from the perspective of Chinese children. Paterson's book deals with the disillusionment of her young protagonists toward the Heavenly Kingdom after they witness firsthand the practices of the Taipings while Yep's novel depicts the suffering among villagers during this period of instability. The next chapter will examine how another period of political instability in China, the Boxer Uprising (1899–1901), was presented for children in the early twentieth century and the genre of historical fiction will also be discussed in further detail.

Chapter 5
China Against the Allies: Interpreting the Boxer Uprising (1899–1901)

> There is not a single passage in this volume that could not have been culled from
> the newspapers, or, at best, a not very illuminating book of travels. Atmosphere,
> in the true sense of the word, there is none. Of course it is possible that Mr.
> Graydon is familiar with China and the Chinese; but, if this is the case, he has
> been at pains to conceal any intimate knowledge of which he is possessed.
> —Review of *The Perils of Pekin* in *The Captain* (1905)[1]

W.M. Graydon's *The Perils of Pekin* (1904), which relates the adventures of two
American boys during the Boxer Uprising (1899–1901), was one of the works
that contributed to 'The Flood of Books about China' that the *North China Herald*
reported on in 1904. The article identified 'the Boxer business of 1900 onwards' as
one of the events that sparked a 'steady stream of booklets, volumes, and tomes in
sets, running to a frightful aggregate'.[2] As noted in the previous chapter, reviewers
of children's novels on China from the 1870s onwards were looking for more
than a book filled with 'facts' on Chinese customs and manners; they hoped to
find new knowledge on China interwoven into an interesting and readable story.
They expected authors such as Graydon to blend fact and fiction seamlessly into
their novels instead of presenting glaring passages that were obviously culled from
newspapers or a 'not very illuminating book of travels'. As a reviewer of *The
Perils of Pekin* complained, although the author attempted to add 'local colour'
by using stock phrases such as 'native Christians', 'impending massacre of
Europeans', 'foreign devils', 'legation soldiers', and 'the allies', the story was 'far
from interesting'.[3] The reviewer speculated that Graydon set the story in China
even though he did not know much about the place, thinking his boy readers would
know even less. The review reveals that authors who wanted to write about China
could no longer assume readers lacked knowledge of the country, for it was no
longer the 'little-known Celestial Kingdom' that Dalton introduced to readers in
the mid-nineteenth century. Therefore, authors needed to demonstrate an 'intimate
knowledge' of China if they wished to produce a quality book.

The phrases 'native Christians', 'impending massacre of Europeans', 'foreign
devils', 'legation soldiers', and 'the allies' that appear in Graydon's novel were
frequently used in books that focused on the Boxer Uprising. These can be divided

---

[1] 'The Perils of Pekin', *The Captain*, XII.70 (1905): p. 340.

[2] 'The Flood of Books about China', *North China Herald and Supreme Court and
Consular Gazette*, 29 July 1904, p. 234.

[3] 'The Perils of Pekin', p. 340.

into three major categories. First, there were narratives about 'legation soldiers' and 'the allies' during the Siege of the Peking Legations, which lasted for 55 days from late June to mid-August 1900. British, Japanese, German, Italian, French, American, Russian, Belgian, Austrian, and other residents were trapped inside the walls of the Legations until an international force known as the 'Allies' rescued them on 14 August 1900. Books in this category include *Diary of the Siege of the Peking Legations, June to August, 1900* (1900), *The Story of the Siege in Peking* (1901), and *Behind the Scenes in Peking* (1910).[4] Secondly, there were missionary survivor stories of the Shanxi massacres and tales of 'native Christian' martyrdom such as *Fire and Sword in Shansi* (1903), *The China Martyrs of 1900* (1904), and the bestselling *A Thousand Miles of Miracles in China* (1904).[5] Books in the third category focused on accounts of the relief column headed by Admiral Seymour (1840–1929) such as *From Tientsin to Peking with the Allied Forces* (1902).[6] Seymour's troops departed from Tianjin heading for Peking on 10 June 1900 in response to a call for assistance from Sir Claude MacDonald (1852–1915).[7] However, they returned to Tianjin on 26 June because they were unable to advance further to Peking. Because Seymour's column consisted of approximately 2,000 soldiers, they were greatly outnumbered by the Boxers, a fact frequently highlighted in accounts of the relief effort. This kind of rhetoric was evident in major British newspapers such as *The Times*, which published the following statement after the relief of the Legations: 'History has repeated itself ... Once more a small segment of the civilized world, cut off and surrounded by an Asiatic horde, has exhibited those high moral qualities the lack of which renders mere numbers powerless.'[8]

The Perils of Pekin is just one of the numerous British children's texts set during this tumultuous period characterized by an emphasis on chaos, commotion, despair, and distress. Some of them emerged almost immediately after the news of the Boxers had reached Europe and America. For example, Charlotte Yonge's

---

[4]   W.M. Hewlett, *Diary of the Siege of the Peking Legations, June to August, 1900* (London, 1900); S.M. Russell, *The Story of the Siege in Peking* (London, 1901); Mary Hooker, *Behind the Scenes in Peking: Being Experiences during the Siege of the Legations* (London, 1910).

[5]   E.H. Edwards, *Fire and Sword in Shansi: The Story of the Martyrdom of Foreigners and Chinese Christians* (Edinburgh, 1903); Robert Coventry Forsyth (ed.), *The China Martyrs of 1900: A Complete Roll of the Christian Heroes Martyred in China in 1900 with Narratives of Survivors* (London, 1904); Archibald Edward Glover, *A Thousand Miles of Miracle in China: A Personal Record of God's Delivering Power from the Hands of the Imperial Boxers at Shan-si* (London, 1904). Christian publications such as *Chinese Recorder and Missionary Journal* were inundated with harrowing reports about murdered missionaries and native Christians, mostly in the Shandong and Shanxi area.

[6]   F. Brown, *From Tientsin to Peking with the Allied Forces* (London, 1902).

[7]   For more information on Seymour's column, see Joseph W. Esherick, *The Origins of the Boxer Uprising* (Berkeley, 1987), pp. 288–9.

[8]   'The Relief of Peking', *The Times*, 2 October 1900, p. 10.

children's book *The Making of a Missionary, or, Daydreams in Earnest* (1900) was published even before the conflict had ended. In her preface, dated 12 June 1900, two days after Seymour's troops were sent to relieve the Peking Legations during a time of great uncertainty over the fate of the trapped residents, Yonge explained that not much was known of 'the cruel persecution by the so-called Boxers' and predicted that 'there will probably [be] much more to lament' by the time the Uprising ended.[9] In the book's final chapter, Mabel, a missionary teacher, is shot in front of her church in a village near Tianjin by a group of about 30 Boxers armed 'with swords and firelocks, yelling: "Death to the foreign devils"'.[10]

Never before had an event in Sino-British relations ignited such an outpouring of fiction for children. Other British Boxer novels include Constancia Serjeant's *A Tale of Red Pekin* (1902), F.S. Brereton's *The Dragon of Pekin: A Tale of the Boxer Revolt* (1902), G.A. Henty's *With the Allies to Pekin: A Story of the Relief of the Legations* (1903), and Charles Gilson's *The Lost Column: A Story of the Boxer Rebellion in China* (1909). In addition to novels, there were several short stories published in periodicals such as the *Boy's Own Paper* and *Chums*, including Rev. Alfred Colbeck's 'Wang T'ien Pin: The Story of the Boxer Rising' (1901–1902) and 'Dodging the Boxers: A True Story of Desperate Days' (1911–1912).[11] It is worth examining how the Uprising is represented in *With the Allies to Pekin* and *The Lost Column* because both were written by well-known boy's writers whose books were consistently popular school prizes and Christmas gifts.[12] These works provide interesting points of comparison: G.A. Henty (1832–1902) never travelled to China while Charles Gilson (1878–1943), who the *Penny Illustrated Paper* claimed was 'the Henty of today' in 1909, spent three and a half years there in the early twentieth century.[13]

Historians and novelists have documented the influence which Henty and Gilson's books on China had on their lives. For example, Graham Greene recalled how reading *The Lost Column* affected his career. He argues that the 'influence of early books is profound. So much of the future lies on the shelves: early reading

---

[9]   Charlotte Mary Yonge, *The Making of a Missionary, or, Daydreams in Earnest* (New York, 1900), p. 5. Most of the action in the book takes place in England – only the last four chapters are set in China, because according to Yonge, she does not have 'sufficient information' on the 'habits of the converts' in China (p. 6).

[10]   Ibid., p. 225.

[11]   For more Christian stories on the Boxer Uprising, see Nell Parsons, *The Little Chinese Girl* (London, 1909), pp. 75–81.

[12]   Gilson's sales figures were lower than Henty's but in 1932, he estimated that over 200,000 copies of his books for boys had been sold. See Charles Gilson, *Chances and Mischances: The Memories of a Writer, a Sportsman, a Soldier and a Wanderer in Five Continents, in War and Peace* (London, 1932), p. 282.

[13]   'P.I.P. Playgoer', *P.I.P.: Penny Illustrated Paper and Illustrated Times*, 17 April 1909, p. 249. Although Gilson does not provide the exact dates he lived in China, it is highly likely that he was stationed there sometime between 1902 and 1905. See Gilson, *Chances and Mischances*, pp. 80–83.

has more influence on conduct than any religious teaching'. To illustrate his assertion, he states that had he never read *The Lost Column*, he would have 'made a false start' in the British American Tobacco Company, who had offered him a post in China when he was 21. Later in life, he 'bought and reread [the book] for old time's sake'.[14] Henty's books, which have been translated into languages such as French, Danish, Norwegian, and Spanish, have sold millions of copies world-wide.[15] Critics have panned Henty's dialogue, plots, and characters for various reasons.[16] However, according to Robert Huttenback, Henty's importance lies not in his originality but rather 'in the extent to which he heightened and tinted with life an already existing stereotype and so colored the attitudes and opinions of future generations of British and, for that matter, American schoolboys'.[17] Novelist Geoffrey Trease portrays himself answering 'Henty's call' to 'march *With Roberts to Pretoria, With the Allies to Pekin* … and … with almost every military expedition from Hannibal and his elephants onwards'.[18] American historian Arthur Meier Schlesinger, who became 'absorbed in Henty' despite his stigmatization as a Victorian imperialist 'in a time of debunking and disillusion', acquired initial knowledge of the Boxer Uprising from *With the Allies to Pekin*.[19]

Just as Bessie Marchant's characters faced 'hostile hordes', the heroes of the Boxer narratives must overcome 'hordes' of Chinese on their journeys. Rex Bateman in *With the Allies to Pekin* successfully makes his way past the 'hordes of Chinese' that lie between Tianjin and Pekin and Gerald Milton Wood in *The Lost Column* finds himself 'in the very midst of the Boxer hordes, the men who were mad to kill'.[20] During the Boxer Uprising, *Punch* published a caricature featuring Japanese, Russian, and other European soldiers heading to

---

[14]   Graham Greene, *A Sort of Life* (London, 1971), pp. 52–3.

[15]   Mark Naidis, 'G.A. Henty's Idea of India', *Victorian Studies*, VIII.1 (1964): pp. 49–58 (p. 50).

[16]   See Stuart Hannabuss, 'The Henty Phenomenon', *Children's Literature in Education*, 24.2 (1983): pp. 80–93 (pp. 81; 87); Nicholas Ranson, 'G.A. Henty', in Laura M. Zaidman and Caroline C. Hunt (eds), *Dictionary of Literary Biography: British Children's Writers, 1880–1914* (Charleston, 1994), pp. 118–33; Kimberley Reynolds, *Girls Only?: Gender and Popular Children's Fiction in Britain, 1880–1910* (London, 1990), p. 71; Claudia Nelson, *Boys Will Be Girls: The Feminine Ethic and British Children's Fiction, 1857–1917* (New Brunswick, NJ, 1991), p. 107.

[17]   Robert A. Huttenback, 'G.A. Henty and the Imperial Stereotype', *Huntington Library Quarterly*, 29 (1965): 63–75 (p. 75).

[18]   Geoffrey Trease, *Tales out of School: A Survey of Children's Fiction* (London, 1964), p. 19.

[19]   Arthur Meier Schlesinger, *A Life in the Twentieth Century: Innocent Beginnings, 1917–1950* (Boston, 2000), p. 67.

[20]   Henty, *With the Allies to Pekin*, p. 81; Gilson, *The Lost Column*, p. 312. The use of the word 'hordes' echoes earlier fears of Mongol hordes invading Europe. See Ariane Knüsel, '"Western Civilization" against "Hordes of Yellow Savages": British Perceptions of the Boxer Rebellion', *Asiatische Studien/Etudes Asiatiques*, LXII.I (2008): pp. 43–84 (p. 46).

Peking dressed as knights of the Middle Ages. As Ariane Knüsel has pointed out, the illustration references 'the crusades or Arthurian legends in which Western (Christian) civilization fought against hordes of (heathen) barbarians'.[21] Just as Charles Gordon was depicted as an Arthurian knight in reports of the Taiping Rebellion and Boer War, the British men involved in the Boxer Uprising were described by Gilson as fighting for 'more than their lives, for brave, pale-faced women and helpless children and the God who loved them all' in this 'twentieth-century crusade'.[22]

It is important to examine Boxer stories for children because as Kim Wilson argues, writers can effectively use historical fiction to highlight certain values that are helpful in forming and perpetuating a national identity.[23] It is also important to consider the authors' backgrounds and how their sources may have influenced the type of 'facts' transmitted. Mitzi Myers points out that '[m]ore than any other juvenile categories, war stories foreground basic questions: what counts as "children's literature" and how does that literature differ from works for an adult audience; what constitutes permissible subject matter ...'.[24] Examining Gilson's and Henty's work brings these questions to the foreground especially when one considers the rhetoric of violence in their two narratives. *With the Allies to Pekin* and *The Lost Column* are a locus for the anxieties and uncertainties about Empire and Britain's position in China that surfaced during the Boxer Uprising.

With the Allies to Pekin and *The Lost Column* have been analyzed in Ross G. Forman's 'Peking Plots: Fictionalizing the Boxer Rebellion' and James Hevia's *English Lessons: The Pedagogy of Imperialism in Nineteenth-Century China*. While Forman's discussions regarding issues of masculinity, economics, politics, and the parallels between discourses on the Boxer Uprising and the Indian Mutiny (1857–1858) are insightful, he tends to regard Boxer fiction as mostly homogeneous rather than heterogeneous. He does not reflect on how the books' publication dates and their chronological proximity to the events may or may not have influenced the depiction of the Boxers. Some of his statements are problematic. For example, he asserts that Boxer fiction can be divided into two types: 'the first, about the events of the Rebellion itself and the heroic efforts of a boy protagonist, disguised in native dress, to safeguard his family members and the European community at large; the second, about the break-up of China and an

---

[21]   Ibid.

[22]   Gilson, *The Lost Column*, pp. 313–14; 362. In his memoir, Gilson writes that during his years in China he felt 'as if we were taking part in a Twentieth Century Crusade': Gilson, *Chances and Mischances*, p. 98.

[23]   Kim Wilson, '"Are They Telling Us the Truth?": Constructing National Character in the Scholastic Press Historical Journal Series', *Children's Literature Association Quarterly*, 32.2 (2007): pp. 129–41 (p. 130).

[24]   Mitzi Myers, 'Storying War: A Capsule Overview', *The Lion and the Unicorn*, 24.3 (2000): pp. 327–36 (p. 333).

ensuing invasion from the East of "yellow hordes"'.[25] This categorization is too simplistic however, because the type of fiction written by authors such Charlotte Yonge, Alfred Colbeck, and Constancia Serjeant which focuses on Christian suffering during the Boxer Uprising was more diverse. Some of Forman's other assertions regarding issues of disguise are questionable, and will be discussed later in this chapter. In *English Lessons*, Hevia asserts that the writers of Boxer fiction for children 'fixed the meaning of the event in clear-cut terms of perpetrator and victim, while providing their young heroes the opportunity to perform the positive masculine virtues of empire builders'.[26] He also posits that in Henty's book, there is 'absolute distinction between civilization and barbarism' and that 'the racial typologies of the era' are reproduced in it.[27] These statements demonstrate the tendency to see this literature in stereotyped terms. Both Henty and Gilson's novels are more complicated however.

Early Boxer Narratives: 1900–1902

Before discussing Henty and Gilson, I want to consider some early Boxer narratives to provide a point of comparison for how images of the event changed over the decade between 1899, when news of the Boxers first reached Britain, and 1909, when Gilson's novel was published eight years after the signing of the Boxer Protocol.[28] In *History in Three Keys: The Boxers as Event, Experience, and Myth*, Paul A. Cohen examines, among other issues, the important role rumours played in fuelling the Boxer Uprising.[29] Two early Boxer stories, Alfred Colbeck's 'Wang T'ien Pin: The Story of the Boxer Rising', serialized in the *Boy's Own Paper* from 1901 to 1902, and Constancia Serjeant's *A Tale of Red Pekin* (1902), reflect how rumours influenced the Chinese perception of foreigners and how they contributed to mutual misunderstandings between the Chinese and the British. For example, in Colbeck's story, Wang T'ien Pin's father initially refused to seek help from a British doctor because he had heard rumours that the foreign doctor's medicine is made from the bones of little boys. Colbeck suggests that the ignorant Chinese people, prone to sensationalism, let their wild imaginations dictate their actions instead of rationally analysing the situation, choosing to believe rumours

---

[25]   Ross G. Forman, 'Peking Plots: Fictionalizing the Boxer Rebellion of 1900', *Victorian Literature and Culture*, 27.1 (1999): pp. 19–48 (p. 40).

[26]   James Louis Hevia, *English Lessons: The Pedagogy of Imperialism in Nineteenth-Century China* (Durham, 2003), p. 303.

[27]   Ibid.

[28]   The conditions of the Boxer Protocol (1901) included an indemnity of 450,000,000 taels of silver and permission for foreign occupation in Tangshan, Tianjin, Qinhuangdao, Shanhaiguan, and Langfang.

[29]   See Paul A. Cohen, *History in Three Keys: The Boxers as Event, Experience, and Myth* (New York, 1997), pp. 146–72.

such as missionaries eating Chinese children and mutilating patients.[30] In *A Tale of Red Pekin*, the Chinese are described as 'ignorant people' who 'are told all kinds of things which they believe, that the Europeans take their little children and kill them, and that it is our [the British] presence here which causes the lack of rain'.[31]

Rumours abound in this story. According to one, houses marked with a 'Red Hand' are cursed. Both the British and the Chinese dread seeing the scarlet imprint and each believe the other is responsible for placing the curse. Mrs Ross fears the inhabitants of the marked houses would be killed by Boxers, while the Chinese accuse the foreigners of smearing the houses red and believe that 'in seven days one of the inmates would go mad, or in fourteen days they would die'.[32] Serjeant borrows this incident from Roland Allen's *The Siege of Peking Legations* (1901), a book praised for its 'simple and straightforward' narrative style and reportage that did not wander off 'into disquisitions on diplomacy or military tactics'.[33] On 13 June 1900, Allen, the Acting Chaplain to H.B.M.'s Legation in Peking, hears from Sir Robert Hart about the 'Red Hand', which he thought was a 'Boxer mark set on houses suspected or doomed'. However, Hart informs him that 'the mark was supposed to be set on the houses by foreigners, and was a charm which caused one of the inmates to go mad in seven days or to die in fourteen'.[34] This incident highlights the mutual distrust between the Chinese and the British and their tendency to believe the worst about the other side.

These early Boxer narratives focus on Christian suffering during the Uprising. Brave, devout, and self-sacrificing, Wang T'ien Pin, who converted to Christianity after medical missionaries healed him, is attacked and beheaded by Boxers when he firmly refuses to renounce his new beliefs. In *A Tale of Red Pekin*, Boxers, 'like devils possessed', start to burn buildings, loot villages, and kill Christians.[35] Mr St John, a medical missionary, urges his wife and children to flee to another city while he stays behind with the Chinese Christians. Twelve-year-old Cecilia St John and her family undergo various trials while trying to escape from the Boxers. Whereas earlier Boxer texts portray the protagonists as innocent victims of irrational hatred, Henty and Gilson's books, which focus more on the military and diplomatic aspects of the event, provide possible reasons for Boxer anti-foreign sentiments.

---

[30] Critics argue that 'The Boxers played upon peasant fears – fables that missionaries collected orphans to eat them, and that their hospitals practiced alchemy through the mutilation of patients': E. Stillman and W. Pfaff, *The Politics of Hysteria: The Sources of Twentieth-Century Conflict* (London, 1965), p. 92.

[31] Serjeant, *A Tale of Red Pekin*, p. 46.

[32] Ibid., p. 47.

[33] 'Allen's (Rev. Roland) the Siege of the Pekin Legations (Book Review)', *Academy*, 60 (1901): p. 441.

[34] Roland Allen, *The Siege of the Legations: Being the Diary of Rev. Roland Allen* (London, 1901), p. 78.

[35] Serjeant, *A Tale of Red Pekin*, p. 6.

George Alfred Henty and Charles Gilson

George Alfred Henty, a Cambridge-educated journalist turned boy's writer, authored over 80 adventure stories for boys, mostly historical novels, written 'to amuse as well as to give instruction in the facts of history'.[36] After leaving his job as war correspondent for the London *Standard* in 1876 due to health reasons, he concentrated on writing and churned out an average of three books a year. Henty gave some interviews during his lifetime that illuminated his writing objectives and practices. In 'Writing Books for Boys', Henty notes that his books were popular among parents because they did not 'deviate in the very slightest degree from historical facts, except where the boy hero is, so to speak, on the loose'.[37] Henty's stated practice was to mix 'a very large amount of personal adventure' in with the history to 'make it [the history] go down with the boys'.[38] Because his didactic intentions were very clear, it is not surprising that in 1906, Caroline M. Hewins (1846–1926), an employee of the Hartford Public Library in the United States, promoted Henty's novels not for their literary merit but because they could help boys cultivate a taste for history.[39]

Charles James Louis Gilson, considered one of Henty's successors, is one of the few authors examined in this book who had lived in China. Born in Dedham, Essex to Charles Rawlinson Gilson and Flora Macdonald, Gilson was educated at Dulwich College, where he excelled in cricket and rugby.[40] Gilson entered the army at the age of 18, was wounded while serving in the Boer War (1899–1902), and began writing during his convalescence. He later served in China, Japan, the South Sea Islands, Australia, Canada, East Africa, and the East Indies. However, at the age of 27, Captain Gilson was invalided out of the army.[41] Back in England, he focused on writing boys' stories and in 1907, *The Captain* published his first full-length serial: 'The Lost Island: A Strange Tale of Adventure in the Far East', a story based on R.L. Stevenson's *Treasure Island* (1883) but which had 'a Chinese setting, because [Gilson] felt at home with Chinamen'.[42] Gilson joined the Naval

---

[36]   See Preface of G.A. Henty, *With Lee in Virginia; a Story of the American Civil War* (London, [n.d.]), n. pag.

[37]   G.A. Henty, 'Writing Books for Boys', *Answers* (1902): p. 105. For other interviews, see G.A. Henty, 'How Boys Books Are Written', *Great Thoughts from Master Minds*, 2 (1902–1903): pp. 8–10; G.A. Henty, 'Interview', *Chums*, 2 (1894): p. 159.

[38]   Ibid.

[39]   See Montrose J. Moses, *Children's Books and Reading* (New York, 1907), p. 175.

[40]   See David Shacklock, 'The Henty Succession', *Henty Society Bulletin*, XI.88 (1999): pp. 17–22 (p. 22); Brian Doyle, *The Who's Who of Children's Literature* (London, 1968), p. 111; Anne Commire (ed.), *Yesterday's Authors of Books for Children: Facts and Pictures About Authors and Illustrators of Books for Young People, from Early Times to 1960* (2 vols, Detroit, MI, 1978), vol. 2, p. 124.

[41]   Gilson, *Chances and Mischances*, p. 25.

[42]   Charles Gilson, 'About My Own Stories', *Boy's Own Paper*, 44 (1921): pp. 21–2 (p. 22).

Division in World War I and was later promoted to the rank of Major. These experiences prompted him to continue writing stories for children's periodicals such as the *Boy's Own Paper*, *Chums*, and *Pluck*, and many of his subsequent serials, such as 'The Mystery of Ah Jim', were published in book form. In addition to writing boys' stories, Gilson also wrote plays and published girls' stories such as *Beyond the Dragon Door: A Story of Adventure for Girls* under the penname Barbara Gilson.

Gilson's memories of China can be found in *Chances and Mischances: The Memories of a Writer, a Sportsman, a Soldier and a Wanderer in Five Continents, in War and Peace* (1932). His knowledge of the Boxer Uprising was much more personal than Henty's because he arrived in China as part of the Allied Army of Occupation when 'the Boxer Rebellion was of more or less recent occurrence'. In his view, China was the 'most interesting part of the world' in those days, because the country had become a 'diplomatic hot-bed'.[43] One of his jobs during that time was to bring a column of 'two hundred infantry and several miles of transport from Tientsin [Tianjin] to Peking by road'.[44] His experience familiarized him with the area between the two cities and the map provided in *The Lost Column* reflects his knowledge of the buildings and streets of Tianjin.

Because Gilson worked in northern China not long after the signing of the Boxer Protocol on 7 September 1901, he most likely had the opportunity to converse with some of the people involved in the Boxer Uprising. He recalls being acquainted with 'Germans, French, Serbian Cossacks, and Indian cavalrymen'– people who may have experienced the Siege of the Legations or participated in Admiral Seymour's relief column.[45] One of his most famous acquaintances in China was *The Times* Peking correspondent George Morrison (1862–1920) who used to dine with Gilson when he came down to Tianjin. It was Morrison who 'strongly advised' him to 'give up the sword for the pen'.[46] During the Boxer Uprising, many journalists believed rumours that everyone in the Peking Legations had been massacred and prematurely published obituaries of key figures such as Sir Robert Hart, Sir Claude MacDonald, and Morrison himself. Gilson recalls Morrison showing him a press-cutting book 'entirely filled with his own *obituary notices*. These appeared in 1900 in all the leading papers of the world, when it was reported that the Peking Legations had fallen to the Boxers and the entire garrison had been massacred'.[47] This incident must have made Gilson more aware of the unreliability of newspaper reports and possibly inspired him to write *The Lost Column* as a more realistic account of how the lives of British residents were affected during the Boxer Uprising.

---

[43] Gilson, *Chances and Mischances*, pp. 82; 98.

[44] Ibid., p. 84.

[45] Ibid., p. 83.

[46] Ibid., p. 159.

[47] Ibid., p. 158 (emphasis in the original). For an example of the obituaries Morrison referred to, see 'Dr. G.E. Morrison', *The Times*, 17 July 1900, p. 4.

With the Allies to Pekin and The Lost Column

Like Marchant's *Among Hostile Hordes*, *With the Allies to Pekin* reflects the concerns of merchants, missionaries, and military men in China. While *Among Hostile Hordes* features a younger boy hero (Don is 13), Henty and Gilson's stories focus on teenagers on the cusp of manhood. Henty's story begins with the hero Rex Bateman leaving China at the age of 12 to receive an education back in England. His father James wants him to retain his Chinese language skills, so he asks his servant Ah Lo to accompany Rex during his sojourn back home. Because elite public schools such as Eton would not permit Rex to take some afternoons off to converse in Chinese with Ah Lo, he enrolls in a local school in the London vicinity. Returning to China in spring 1900, 16-year-old Rex experiences a series of exciting events. First, he saves his two orphaned cousins from Boxer captivity (their missionary parents were murdered) and escorts them to the Peking Legations. Then, he acts as an interpreter for Major Johnson and later for the Japanese troops, rescues 13 trapped Chinese Christians, silences two guns, enters Prince Ching's palace to hand him a letter from the British Minister, delivers a message to Sir Claude MacDonald, helps in the relief of the Legations in several other ways, and saves some women from Russian soldiers. After the Boxers are defeated, Rex acting on his father's advice, purchases many valuable looted goods offered at low prices on the market.[48] He therefore emerges from the Boxer Uprising rich with loot and replete with accolades from his superiors. For example, Major Johnson informs Mr Bateman that he should be very proud of his son because, 'If he had been in the army he would certainly have earned a V.C.' (*WAP* 265). At the end of the book Rex decides to return to England with his family for a few years before coming back to Tianjin to continue running the family business. Ah Lo, 'who refused positively Mr. Bateman's offer to set him up comfortably in a farm in his native village' also sails with them to Europe (*WAP* 353).

Compared to Henty's book, the scale of Gilson's novel is smaller and more focused on the personal level. One reviewer commented on the 'realism' in *The Lost Column* (*LC*), where 'fact and fiction are blended so cleverly by one who knows the people and the places he is writing about that it all reads as if every word of it might have been true'.[49] The scope of this novel is limited to the Tianjin area because Gilson explains that 'The defence of the Peking Legations will live for ever in the memories of the countrymen of those who kept their nations' flags at the masthead through it all. But no less are the defenders of Tientsin deserving

---

[48]   Many critics have commented on the morally questionable depiction of looting in *With the Allies to Pekin*. See for example, Hevia, *English Lessons*, p. 304; David Gunby, 'Henty and the Boxers: Sources and Attitudes', *Henty Society Bulletin*, XI.88 (1999): pp. 2–17 (p. 17); Guy Arnold, *Held Fast for England: G.A. Henty, Imperialist Boys' Writer* (London, 1980), p. 73; Dong Ning Lin, 'Power and Representation in Victorian Discourse on China' (unpublished doctoral dissertation, University of Maryland, 1994), pp. 195–6.

[49]   'The Bookman Christmas: The Lost Column', *Bookman*, 35.207 (1908): pp. 56–7.

of the highest praise ...' (*LC* 134). Because numerous accounts of the Siege of the Peking Legations had already been published by 1909, Gilson perhaps wanted to focus on the 'other' (less well-known story) of the Boxer catastrophe.

The Lost Column investigates the effects of the Boxer Uprising on a merchant family in Tianjin, the Milton Woods, and a group of their friends. Like Rex, Gilson's hero Gerald, who lives in Milton Towers with his brother, mother, and guardian Mr Pannick, is agile, athletic, chivalric, clever, dutiful, generous, honest, modest, self-sacrificial, and has excellent language skills, having been raised by a Chinese nurse and educated by an English governess. At the beginning of the novel, 18-year-old Gerald fights some Boxers, warns his family and friends (Dr Raydon and Jack Carter) of their coming, and protects Milton Towers against the Boxer attacks, only to witness it burn down a few days later. Further, he attempts to find Admiral Seymour's lost column and seeks help from his friend Mr Wang, 'the cleverest detective in the world', to disguise him as a peasant from Gansu province (*LC* 174). Mr Wang, who 'scented' the Boxer trouble in north China all the way from Shanghai, predicts '[m]urder and massacre and war' and tries to persuade Gerald to give up his quest (*LC* 160). However, because Gerald is determined to accomplish his task, Mr Wang keeps an eye on him and saves him in perilous situations: once from an opium den and another time from the formidable villain Jugatai who is head of the Secret Society of Federated Asia, which aims to 'sweep the eastern world of the white vermin' by combining forces with countries such as Japan, India, 'Burmah and the Malay' (*LC* 206; 292).[50] Later, Gerald, like Rex, acts as an interpreter and delivers a despatch for Seymour after the capture of the Western Arsenal. As in the case of Rex, men also shower Gerald with praise: Mr Wang comments that he has 'the makings of the general' in him and another character claims that 'if [Gerald] had been in the service [he] would have got a V.C.' (*LC* 301; 323). Although Gerald is not awarded a V.C., his name appears on the list of honours published in the *London Gazette* (*LC* 358–9). After the Boxer trouble is quelled, Gerald prepares to build a new house in this 'strange land they had learnt to call their own' (*LC* 379). Before analysing Henty and Gilson's novels, I will first point out how previous critics have approached the two books from a position that is less attuned to the nuances of the texts.

---

[50] Jugatai, who is 'many inches taller than the average Chinese', has 'broad and square' shoulders, a 'finely chiseled' aquiline nose, and 'penetrating' coal-black eyes, anticipates the 'tall, lean and feline, high-shouldered' Fu Manchu, who appeared in 1913 as 'the great and evil man who dreamed of Europe and America under Chinese rule' – 'the yellow peril incarnate': Gilson, *The Lost Column*, p. 189; Sax Rohmer, *The Insidious Dr. Fu-Manchu: Being a Somewhat Detailed Account of the Amazing Adventures of Nayland Smith in His Trailing of the Sinister Chinaman* ([n.p.], 1913), pp. 25–6; Sax Rohmer, *The Return of Dr. Fu-Manchu* (New York, 1916), p. 39.

Missed Nuances

With the Allies to Pekin is the subject of one chapter in Dong Ning Lin's Ph.D. dissertation 'Power and Representation in Victorian Discourse on China'. Lin argues that although Ah Lo 'receives the patronage of the honourable English schoolboy and proto-colonialist' because of his 'desirable behaviour', 'the master of the situation' is Rex.[51] However, this interpretation, characteristic of a postcolonial viewpoint, is overturned when one examines the relationship between the two more closely. Rather than being a silenced passive servant who blindly follows his master's orders, 'intelligent' Ah Lo often discusses his ideas with Rex. Contrary to Gerald, who 'had bred a wholesome British contempt for the Chinese', Rex is good friends with Ah Lo and values his opinions.[52] For example, when planning to rescue Rex's cousins, Ah Lo, after analysing the situation carefully, suggests they first head north and provides sound reasoning for doing so. Knowing that Chinese women do not travel much, he also persuades Rex to disguise the girls as boys to avoid arousing suspicion. In addition, he invents a story that gives them an excuse to travel to Peking: if anyone asks why they are going there, they should answer that they want to enlist in the Chinese army and that the 'boys' are going to seek employment. Ah Lo even anticipates they will be questioned about their guns and creates a credible story about how they obtained the weapons. Rex accepts all of the suggestions and praises Ah Lo's 'good plan'. Although Ah Lo is thanked for his role in helping Rex to safety, he rejects the commendations and contests that Rex carried him through because 'He always told me what to do; I did just so and it came out all right' (*WAP* 79). This false statement simply reflects Ah Lo's humility. Rex, confident that Ah Lo 'would go through fire and water' for him, claims that he would trust himself 'anywhere with him' and confides that he has become so accustomed to Ah Lo's company that 'I really don't know what I should do without him' (*WAP* 318). Ah Lo is like Ching-Ching because he is a faithful and loyal friend, reflecting the importance of this trope in children's fiction. The closeness between Rex and Ah Lo is an example of a cross-cultural friendship that transcends the boundaries of a traditional master-servant relationship.

According to Robert H. MacDonald, the 'motif of the Anglo-Saxon hero disguised as a beggar, a Turk, an African, runs through Victorian and Edwardian adventure stories; the Englishman transformed himself into the other and back again in time for tea; there was no tongue he could not command, no gesture or custom outside his knowledge'.[53] Ross G. Forman makes similar observations about British adventure-story heroes employing disguises to successfully pass as Chinese in Boxer stories. In 'Peking Plots', he discusses both *With the Allies to Pekin* and *The Lost Column*, asserting that 'Chinese disguise is always in

---

[51]   Lin, 'Power and Representation', pp. 179–80.

[52]   Henty, *With the Allies to Pekin*, p. 2; Gilson, *The Lost Column*, p. 33.

[53]   Robert H. MacDonald, *The Language of Empire: Myths and Metaphors of Popular Imperialism, 1880–1918* (Manchester, 1994), pp. 32–3.

the costume of a coolie, never a mandarin'.[54] While this may be true in most cases, it does not apply to Gerald because one of his costumes is that of 'a well-to-do young Chinaman of the upper class' (*LC* 298). Secondly, Forman argues that the boys in the Boxer novels are able to pass as Chinese because they 'possess feminine traits often assigned to the Chinese male'.[55] However, Gerald is not always able to successfully pass as Chinese: Jugatai sees through his disguise. When asked how he knew Gerald was not Chinese, Jugatai replies, 'A Chinaman, equally tired, would have slept through a thunderstorm on a heap of broken bones. But you could not, you were not able – because the wall was hard' (*LC* 226).

Forman's analysis fails to note the distinction between Henty's and Gilson's attitudes towards disguise and overlooks the differences in Gerald's various disguises. Whereas Henty's Rex was absolutely confident in the impenetrability of his disguises, Gilson's Gerald realizes no matter how brilliant the disguise in terms of transforming his physical appearance, 'passing' as Chinese is impossible when people like Jugatai are watching. Before meeting Jugatai, Gerald had been certain he would be able to pass as Chinese because he was born in China and spoke Chinese since childhood. He was able to persuade the British naval captain to allow him to go search for Seymour's lost column because he 'understands the customs' and knows 'the manners' of the Chinese (*LC* 152). Gerald believed his knowledge, coupled with Mr Wang's disguise, would certainly guarantee him the 'invisibility' to traverse undetected among the Chinese enemies. However, unlike Lyu's father Captain Richardson, who successfully passed as Chinese to gain crucial information about his son's whereabouts, Gerald is unable to carry out his plan smoothly.

In addition, when Mr Pannick attempts to disguise himself as 'a respectable Chinaman of the lower working class', the narrator states, 'no one could possibly ever mistake him as such' – he was still Mr Pannick, 'disfigured but not disguised' (*LC* 77). Because Mr Pannick is a comic relief character, this incident is meant to be humorous, but the fact that his disguise is a complete failure suggests that the racial differences between the British and the Chinese have become insurmountable. Through the characters of Mr Pannick and Gerald, Gilson questions the trope of disguise so frequently employed by writers of adventure stories. The fact that his characters' disguises are not foolproof signifies an important change in writers' attitudes towards adventure-story conventions. Because he witnessed the repercussions of the Boxer Uprising while stationed in China not long after the conflict, it is not surprising that Gilson provides a darker version of events in *The Lost Column*. The result is a striking contrast to *With the Allies to Pekin* which exhibits confidence in Britain's ability to defeat the Chinese and uphold 'justice' in a turbulent area of the world. Although the Boxer narratives share commonalities, there are subtle differences between the adventure stories that should be pointed

---

[54] Forman, 'Peking Plots', p. 28.
[55] Ibid., p. 30.

out and not glossed over in an attempt to fit all the books neatly into the same category. The next section will consider how differences in the works that authors consulted affected the portrayal of those involved in the Boxer Uprising.

'Good' History?: Historical Accuracy and the Boxer Novels

G.A. Henty claimed that he aimed to 'write good history' and insisted that all of it 'be absolutely unassailable'.[56] One of the strategies he used to give the semblance of unassailable history was through the use of peri-textual material such as the preface in which he specifies his sources. In addition, he cites many statistics and dates throughout the novel to lend a gloss of objectivity, to demonstrate that he has rigorously researched his topic, and to show his stringent adherence to 'facts', perhaps not so much because he wanted readers to remember them, but to reassure parents that their children were being properly educated through fiction. To bolster his claim to fidelity to historical fact, Henty revealed in 'Writing Books for Boys' that he 'equipped' himself for writing by first consulting atlases and encyclopædias for basic information about a country, then receiving ten books from a London library, glancing through them, selecting two that would suit his purpose, and sending for another batch until he acquired all the information he needed.[57] However, scholars have criticized his uncritical use of sources, inaccurate historical details, and his frequent near plagiarism of texts.[58]

According to David Gunby, over one third of *With the Allies to Pekin* is culled from various sources, including newspapers such as *The Times*, and three of Henty's acknowledged sources: Roland Allen's *The Siege of the Peking Legations* (1901), H.C. Thomson's *China and the Powers* (1902), and George Lynch's *The War of the Civilisations* (1901).[59] These sources were tapped by Henty to incorporate mini-history lessons into the novel. Because his lengthy paragraphs punctuate the narrative with digressions that do not advance the plot, they aptly fit into the 'thick chunks of history' category that William Bryce referred to when he described Henty's late historical fiction as being 'like a plate of badly-made sandwiches, and the thin streaks of adventure representing the slices of meat, and the thick chunks of history the all too hefty slices of bread'.[60] Henty created contrived dialogues to achieve his goal of educating his readers on all the major events of the Boxer Uprising. For example, Rex asks midshipman Robinson for a description of the capture of the Dagu forts, Major Johnson for an update on Seymour's column, and Mr Sandwich for information on what occurred in the Legations during his absence. To enhance the reliability of his accounts, Sandwich, who is an interpreter,

---

[56] Henty, 'How Boys' Books are Written', pp. 8–10. Quoted in Arnold, *Held Fast for England*, p. 89.
[57] Henty, 'Writing Books for Boys', p. 105.
[58] Arnold, *Held Fast for England*, p. 89; Huttenback, 'G.A. Henty', p. 64.
[59] See Gunby, 'Henty and the Boxers', pp. 3–4.
[60] William A. Bryce, *Half-Hours with Famous Writers for Boys* (London, [1935]), p. 57.

informs Rex, 'I have kept a journal ever since the siege began, so that I can tell you how everything was done in its right order' (*WAP* 318). This reference to a journal links the information provided by Sandwich to Allen's diary entries in *The Siege of the Peking Legations*, which were checked by the writer against the 'scanty accounts or depatches already made public' to ensure accuracy.[61]

While the number of Boxer accounts might have been 'scanty' in 1901, by 1909 much more information on the Uprising had been made public. With so many books on Chinese history and the Uprising available to Gilson at this point, it is interesting that he chose a general reference book, *The Historian's History of the World* (1904), as his source for the background chapter which outlines the events leading up to the Boxer movement. Chapter 3 of *The Lost Column* is the only place where readers will find a 'history lesson'. In this chapter entitled 'What the Shrieking Madness Is', the narrator first recounts the overthrowing of the Ming dynasty by the 'Tartans [*sic*]', then focuses on the Guangxu Emperor's accession to the throne in 1875 and the rising of the Empress Dowager to absolute power (*LC* 42).[62]

What 'facts' about the Boxer Uprising are presented in these stories? Do the texts reflect the complexity of the politics surrounding this event? The name of the Boxer organization varies in different children's stories, ranging from the 'Society of Boxers', 'Harmonic Heavenly Fisters', to 'I-ho-Ch'uan [Yihequan] or Fist of Righteous Harmony Society'. The first time Gerald encounters the Boxers from Shandong, he notices they were of the 'coolie, or peasant, class', and wore blue with 'red sashes and ankle bands' (*LC* 52). These Boxers, estimated at a hundred in number, carried a 'great red, triangular flag' with black Chinese characters 'I-HO-CHUAN: *We defend with the fist*', 'brandished their weapons in the air', and had eyes 'fierce and bright with the mania to kill' (*LC* 52; 53). Gilson employs the language of nineteenth-century 'racial science' and ethnography to describe the Boxers: they have 'low, receding foreheads' and 'the cruel, cunning, slanting eyes and the high, bony cheekbones of all the Mongol breed' (*LC* 52). These phrases echo the discussion between Montval and St Kassian in Anne Bowman's *The Travels of Rolando* where Montval asserts 'you can make out no affinity between the Caucasian, the Mongolian, and the Ethiopian' while St Kassian argues that 'a slight difference in the formation of the skull does not militate against the poæssibility of civilization and education producing that agreement and harmony which constitute brotherhood' (*TR* 4). Sceptical of St Kassian's optimism, Montval insists that 'the long narrow skull, the low forehead, and coarse animal structure of the Ethiopian did not contain the mind to project or accomplish the glorious works of art which enriched Egypt' (*TR* 5). However, whereas Montval associates low foreheads with the Ethiopians, Gilson has allocated this description to the Mongolians. He does not point out the distinction between the ruling Manchus and the Boxers who were mostly Han Chinese.

---

[61]   Allen, *The Siege of the Legations*, p. viii.

[62]   Gilson derived the information from Henry Smith Williams (ed.), *The Historians History of the World: Volume XXIV: Poland, the Balkans, Turkey, Minor Eastern States, China, Japan* (London, 1904), p. 552.

Both Gilson and Henty attempt to provide some reasons for the Chinese loathing of foreigners and Chinese Christians. According to Gilson, because the secret society in China has always been an 'outlet for discontent', the 'Society of the Fist of Righteous Harmony' is a 'brotherhood that has the power to bring the shrieking madness to life' (*LC* 45). The society bonded together because of 'a common grievance': the interfering Europeans, who forced themselves 'upon a country that had done well enough without him for forty centuries' (*LC* 40; 146). The Europeans used six-inch guns to force China to 'accept the mushroom civilization of a day'. It is difficult for the Chinese to accept this, because when 'Europe was wild and barbarous and dark', the Chinese 'had their own learning, their own customs, history and civilization'. Therefore, Gilson writes 'there was reason and justice enough in all they said' (*LC* 146–7).

Similarly, Henty's Mr Bateman feels 'no personal animosity towards the Chinese' because he thinks the British have 'given them ample grounds for endeavouring to get rid of us' (*WAP* 84). This sentiment echoes the thoughts expressed by H.C. Thomson in his preface to *China and the Powers* where he states that he has tried to present 'the Chinese view of the different matters in dispute equally with that of the Powers' because he believes the Boxer tragedy was not fully caused by one side.[63] According to Rex's father, the Opium War, the opening of the treaty ports, and missionary abuse of power all contributed to the Chinese people's 'ingrained hatred of foreigners' (*WAP* 82). While both Henty and Constancia Serjeant consulted Allen's *The Siege of the Peking Legations*, Serjeant portrays the missionaries sympathetically in *A Tale of Red Pekin* while Henty presents them in a more negative light in *With the Allies to Pekin*. A character in the latter novel comments that missionaries wanted to sell looted objects to finance the chapels and mission-houses which had been destroyed. However, these actions directly defied the treaty that forbade 'the ill-treatment of private persons, the forcible entry into their houses, [and] the taking of their goods' (*WAP* 343).[64] Despite being critical of certain missionary activities, Henty also includes a quote from the Vicar Apostolic of the Roman Catholic Mission at Peking which describes the great suffering of the Christians in the Northern Cathedral: 'The suffering was so great that one has to go back to the siege of Leyden for a parallel. The defenders, when relief arrived, were almost skeletons, living spectres scarce able to drag themselves along …' (*WAP* 335). These different perspectives illustrate Henty's ambivalent attitude towards the missionaries.

According to Gail S. Clark, while Henty's racial stereotypes are trite and his descriptions of race reflect attitudes of superiority held by Anglo-Saxons, this does not mean that he did not make distinctions between racial and national groups.[65] In *With the Allies to Pekin*, two national groups are portrayed in a particularly

---

[63] Thomson, *China and the Powers*, p. vi.

[64] Henty is referring to the Hague Conventions of 1898 and 1899.

[65] Gail S. Clark, 'Imperial Stereotypes: G.A. Henty and the Boys' Own Empire', *Journal of Popular Culture*, 18.4 (1985): pp. 43–51.

negative light: the Germans and the Russians. Most readers would have learned that the Boxer movement originated in Shandong province and was triggered by the murder of two German missionaries (Franz Nies and Richard Henle) and the subsequent German seizure of the port of Jiaozhou to seek compensation. Rex's father claims that the Chinese reaction to the 'monstrous' seizing of Jiaozhou is understandable because it is a 'preposterous price to pay'. He also condemns the 'shocking' 'game of grab' that the Powers are engaged in (*WAP* 28; 83). The scramble for China is also mentioned in Chapter 3 of *The Lost Column*. The narrator attributes the defeat of 'the old mildewed Dragon' by Japan in the Sino-Japanese War (1894–1895) to China's incompetence due to 'corruption' and effeteness rendered by 'the rust of endless time' (*LC* 43). Other countries jostled to take over parts of China, noticing the country 'was falling to pieces at last ... all Europe was going to be there to pick up as much as she could' (*LC* 29).

While Germany's territorial ambitions are denounced by Mr Bateman, Britain's own economic activities in China are supported by Ah Lo, who explains to his father that the British are 'great traders' who only fight when 'their trade is interfered with' (*WAP* 51). In using the character of Ah Lo to voice support for British trade interests, Henty utilizes the same technique that Bowman and Mossman used in their novels, where Chinese characters are portrayed as advocates for increasing Sino-British trade relations. Thus, Henty embeds his critique of the Powers within a narrative that endorses the superiority of the British.

While Henty presents a more realistic portrait of countries interested in protecting their trade and territorial strongholds on China, Gilson rewrites history however, changing the troubled reality into a rosy-picture of unity and communal solidarity. Although Henty writes that there are 'all sorts of bickerings and jealousies' between the international forces and deplores the conduct of Russian, Belgian, German, and French soldiers, Gilson presents a contrary view, stating that 'past rivalries' between the nations were 'forgotten in one great common cause – Humanity' (*WAP* 283; *LC* 362). Differences in the depiction of the international forces and racial politics may be attributed to the authors' different sources. H.C. Thomson, one of Henty's sources, mentions that 'the force was made up of bitterly jealous nationalities', while W.A.P. Martin, one of Gilson's sources, writes that the motive that compelled the Powers to 'bury their political animosities and unite in one expedition' is 'Humanity'.[66] The tensions, rivalries, and jealousies that characterized the complex dynamics between the international powers are effaced by Gilson when he writes that the Russians, Americans, and British, who came 'together from the North and the East and the West', worked for a common cause – 'humanity', which is 'what their enemies mostly lacked' (*LC* 152). He paints a portrait of the Allies bonded in unity when in reality the countries disagreed on many issues.

---

[66] Thomson, *China and the Powers*, p. 20; William Alexander Parsons Martin, *The Siege in Peking: China against the World* (Edinburgh, 1900), p. 14. Martin (1827–1916) was an American missionary who witnessed the siege.

Throughout *The Lost Column*, the polarity between civilized and uncivilized, human and inhuman (at one point the narrator describes the enemies as 'inhuman foes'), rational and irrational, is constantly evoked. The shrieking madness of the Boxers is juxtaposed against the 'humanity' of the Allies. The narrator explains that although 'there was much to justify their [the Boxers'] wrath', there was 'nothing to excuse the ends to which it carried them' (*LC* 148; 147). These excessive 'ends' are the result of Boxer fanaticism and madness. In 1900, 'the shrieking madness could not long be stayed' because it had set the Boxers' 'brains on fire' (*LC* 54).

'Shrieking Madness' and Boxer Fanaticism

Gilson uses sensational language, particularly the phrase 'shrieking madness', throughout *The Lost Column*. This madness is linked to infection and disease: 'this old same madness has spread across the paddy fields and laid hold upon the people like the plague, spreading infection, until whole provinces are up in arms and crying out for revenge' (*LC* 41). Although there have been times of peace in China, the narrator claims that 'the germ of the shrieking madness is always there', and all through the 'four thousand years of civilization' China has frequently 'been devastated and the soil dyed with the blood of scores of millions whom the shrieking madness has seized' (*LC* 41). Thus, Gilson presents the idea of an essential Chinese 'madness' that transcends history and lies dormant until something triggers it.

To demonstrate how 'the madness had taken root', the narrator cites reports that at 'Yung-ching, in the same province as Tientsin, two English missionaries were murdered brutally; at Tung Chow there was a wholesale massacre' (*LC* 131).[67] Earlier in the novel, he describes the 'shrieking madness' taking a hundred Chinamen by the throats, and 'howls of rage and death' could be heard when Boxers appeared (*LC* 75; 82). Whereas the predominant rhetorical feature in *The Lost Column* is 'shrieking madness', this trope is not so evident in *With the Allies to Pekin*. Only once does the topic of madness appear, when Rex states that the Chinese 'seem to go mad' and 'take up swords and muskets ... and blindly fall upon the whites' because they hear '[h]ideous stories ... that they [the whites] have killed and eaten children or sacrificed them in some terrible way' (*WAP* 14).[68] The Boxers in Gilson's novel are never deemed courageous, but Henty describes them showing 'great courage' and 'extreme bravery'.[69]

As Knüsel and others have pointed out, British accounts of the Boxer Uprising frequently portrayed the Boxers as people who have given their souls over to

---

[67]   His source of information is Charles Cabry Dix, *The World's Navies in the Boxer Rebellion (China 1900)* (London: Digby, Long & Co., 1905), pp. 14–17.

[68]   The 'good' Chinese in Henty's novel, however, rationally dismiss these rumours. For example, Ah Lo's father asserts that unlike many villagers who believe in tales of foreigners stealing little children to sacrifice to their gods, he refutes these false stories.

[69]   Henty, *With the Allies to Pekin*, pp. 98; 230; 268; 267.

demonic spirits. Both *The Times* and the *Daily Mail* dehumanized the Boxers in their reports, describing them 'as diabolical, "demons in human form", and vermin'.[70] Occult power seemed to have taken hold of their bodies making them unable to control themselves. According to Lanxin Xiang, the first reference in print to the 'Boxers' appeared in the *North China Herald* on 9 October 1899: 'A sect has risen whose only reason for existence is their hatred for foreigners and the foreign religion. For some occult reason they have taken the name of "Boxers."'[71] The link between the Boxers and the occult can also be found in *The Lost Column* when Gerald witnesses Boxers, led by men who possessed 'occult power', throwing themselves into 'a kind of trance' (which he was 'at a loss to understand') and when 'they came back from their self-inflicted faints, these men were like fiends incarnate. They sprang to their feet, shrieking oaths, and, with swords on high, rushed headlong through the streets, out of the gates and over the open plain' (*LC* 201). They are 'madmen' seemingly 'possessed of almost supernatural strength' (*LC* 202). This description of the Boxer ceremony resembles Sir Robert Hart's report on the ritual where Boxers

> bow to the south-east, recite certain mystical sentences, and then, with closed eyes, fall on their backs; after this they arise, eyes glazed and staring, possessed of the strength and agility of maniacs, mount trees and walls and wield swords and spears in a way they are unable to at other times.[72]

Just as the Thuggees in early nineteenth-century India, known for murdering by strangulation, were represented as being changed by the *goor* (consecrated sugar) they ate during their rituals, the Boxers were portrayed as becoming fanatical after their incantations.[73] According to the *Oxford English Dictionary*, 'fanatic' is defined thus: 'Such as might result from possession by a deity or demon.'[74] Therefore, it is not surprising that Gilson writes that the Chinese man has 'become the most merciless, most pitiless, most relentless fanatic in the world' (*LC* 41).

---

[70] Knüsel, 'Western Civilization', p. 61.

[71] Quoted in Lanxin Xiang, *The Origins of the Boxer War: A Multinational Study* (London, 2003), p. 112.

[72] Robert Hart, *"These from the Land of Sinim": Essays on the Chinese Question* (London, 1903), pp. 7–8.

[73] According to Edward Thornton, 'The effect of the consecrated sugar or goor is believed to be irresistible. Captain Sleeman, having reproached some of the fraternity on account of a murder marked by many ferocious and unmanly features, one of the party replied: "We all feel pity sometimes; but the goor of the Tuponee changes our nature: it would change the nature of a horse. Let any man once taste of that goor, and he will be a Thug, though he know all the trades and have all the wealth in the world."' Edward Thornton, *Illustrations of the History and Practices of the Thugs* (London, 1837), p. 66.

[74] 'Fanatic', *Oxford English Dictionary*, Oxford University Press, 2nd edn, 1989; online edn <http://dictionary.oed.com> [accessed 19 August 2012].

For Gerald Milton Wood, the Boxer presence is very real and their 'occult power' instills fear in him: 'the Boxers, with their haunting songs and threats, and weird, mystic ceremonies, chilled his blood and brought the cold moisture out in beads upon his brow' (*LC* 312). The song that Gerald hears 'called together the brothers of the Long Sword and those of the Fist of Righteous Harmony … They would drive the barbarians into the ocean; and the tragic Sisters of the Red Lantern would bring up the rear to see that all were gone' (*LC* 200).[75] The Boxers have a nightmarish effect on him: 'it was all a nightmare, fearful and fantastical' (*LC* 202). Later, in an opium den, Gerald fell into a dreamy state of consciousness, 'wherein he saw all China swept by frenzied men, shouting for blood and brandishing naked arms' (*LC* 236). There are parallels between the rhetoric of hallucination that Gilson uses and discourses of the Indian Mutiny, because according to Christopher Herbert, 'the insistence on the dreamlike, fantastic, hallucinatory character of the events of the time' was a basic trope of Mutiny discourse.[76]

Gerald is much more disturbed by the Boxers than Rex is. He feels like he was 'back at the birth of the Middle Ages: the rise of the Goths …' (*LC* 188). Compared to Gerald, Rex does not live in constant fear of death and does not anticipate any difficulty in carrying out his plans against the Boxers. Similarly, one of the men in the Peking Legations claims confidently that 'I have not a shadow of fear that we shall not be able to beat off the Boxers and regular troops too'. In fact he is more 'afraid of hunger' than anything else (*WAP* 117). He is never frightened of the Boxers who, believing in their invulnerability, 'fight with fanatical fury', set fires, torture Christians, and loot villages (*WAP* 93). There are no descriptions of the Boxer incantations performed 'preparatory to murdering' (*WAP* 115). Therefore even though the Boxers are labelled as fanatics by Henty, they are not as vividly depicted as such.

The Chinese phrase 'Tow Ah! Tow Ah!' is repeated several times in the novel. Whenever the Boxers appear, Gerald could hear their cries of '"Tow Ah! Tow Ah!": "Kill the Christian!" "Kill the foreign devil!"' (*LC* 53).[77] As these chants reveal, the Boxers not only wish to kill foreigners, but also plan to murder Chinese Christians and anyone who sympathizes with the enemies. Gilson calculates that during June and July 1900, 'one hundred and thirty-three Protestant missionaries

---

[75]   For more information on the Red Lanterns, see Cohen, *History in Three Keys*, pp. 138–45.

[76]   Christopher Herbert, *War of No Pity: The Indian Mutiny and Victorian Trauma* (Princeton, 2008), p. 276.

[77]   According to Dix, the Boxers 'just came on a trot yelling "Tow-ah!" "Tow-ah!" (Kill! Kill!) with a calm disregard of death which was as absurd as it was pathetic': Dix, *The World's Navies*, p. 75. Because it is uncertain whether the Boxers were speaking Mandarin Chinese or some other dialect, it is hard to pinpoint the exact meaning of this phrase. It might refer to 'tou ah'. 'Tou' means head and 'ah' is an expletive so in the context the best translation would probably be 'off with his head'. It could also mean 'tao' which means to eliminate or cleanse.

and forty-eight children, and over thirty thousand native Christians were ruthlessly put to the sword' (*LC* 131).[78]

Gerald's first encounter with the Boxers as a 'defenseless boy' forced to defend himself against a 'mob' sets the pattern for later events in the novel (*LC* 55). His experience foreshadows the Boxer attack on Milton Towers where Gerald and his small group of loved ones try protect his home from the 'maddened, seething mob' and later Admiral Seymour's small group of soldiers fighting 'hordes' of Chinese (*LC* 107). The image of Milton Towers being surrounded by an angry mob raging on every side of the stone garden walls can be seen as a symbol for a mini Peking Legations struggling to defend itself against barbarity and savagery. Dr Raydon comments that they are 'a handful of Europeans in the midst of a race that is civilized with only a civilization of its own' facing a 'whole country' that was against them (*LC* 32). The fact that Milton Towers is described as 'nearly resembl[ing] a church' adds to the image of Christendom versus heathenism (*LC* 95). In addition, Midshipman Tite uses Biblical references when he compares Gerald's task of trying to find Seymour's column to Daniel entering the den of roaring lions and notes that he would 'ten thousand times rather go into a lion's den than into the fuming, surging city' (*LC* 177). Also in keeping with Christian imagery, the narrator describes the Europeans gathered 'like flocks of frightened sheep' in Tianjin, the Peking Legations, and the Beitang Roman Catholic Cathedral (*LC* 131).

Discourses of Violence in *With the Allies to Pekin* and *The Lost Column*

The interaction between the characters (both adults and children) and the Boxers in *With the Allies to Pekin* and *The Lost Column* is characterized by violent aggression. John Cech points out that violence in children's literature has existed since the emergence of early nursery rhymes and folktales, but the violence in the Boxer narratives is more severe and excessive compared to earlier adventure stories set in China.[79] According to Roy Turnbaugh, Henty portrays Empire as 'a theatre for aggression' and the combat scenes in his books are 'distinguished by fantasies of slaughter'.[80] Turnbaugh is struck by 'the casual level on which violence is handled' in the novels and uses Rex as an example, commenting that he 'kills his enemies with the utmost ease and composure'.[81] Considering that Henty's biographer G. Manville Fenn asserted that the writer 'had a horror of a lad who

---

[78]   The same information is given in Charles Henry Hamilton Wright and Charles Neil, *A Protestant Dictionary: Containing Articles on the History, Doctrines, and Practices of the Christian Church* (London, 1904).

[79]   John Cech, 'The Violent Shadows of Children's Culture', in Nancy E. Dowd, Dorothy G. Singer and Robin Wilson (eds), *Handbook of Children, Culture, and Violence* (London, 2006), pp. 135–48.

[80]   Roy Turnbaugh, 'Images of Empire: George Alfred Henty and John Buchan', *Journal of Popular Culture*, 9.3 (1975), pp. 734–40 (p. 739).

[81]   Ibid.

displayed any weak emotion and shrank from shedding blood, or winced at any encounter', it is not surprising that Rex, the typical Henty hero, would be able to 'annihilate' 12 Boxers in just two minutes and not feel disturbed by it (*WAP* 91).[82] Later Rex describes how he 'polished off' a Boxer while rescuing Christians as if he had done something as simple as polishing off an apple (*WAP* 144). Further, Rex shoots a Boxer 'through the head' and feels no qualms about holding the man by the head to drag the dead body out of a house (*WAP* 205). Helping Rex to save some women from Russian soldiers, Ah Lo chokes the life out of one of the fighters and uses his rifle to 'put a ball into the man's head' just to make sure that he was really dead (*WAP* 347). When Rex's cousins express horror at his account of shooting some Boxers, he tells them that they do not need to grieve for the dead Boxers. He reassures Jenny and Mabel that these people deserved to die because they 'no doubt' took part in some massacres (*WAP* 70). Rex views his aggressive actions as a form of justified vengeance for the monstrous acts of violence committed by the Boxers, such as massacring all the wounded who had been left between the arsenal and the river near Tianjin. The British felt it 'necessary' to 'inflict a terrible lesson upon the Chinese troops' because they had killed 'thousands, if not tens of thousands' of their own countrymen suspected of being favourable to the Allies (*WAP* 278).

While Rex seems to rely mostly on his gun, the characters in *The Lost Column* usually use their physical strength to overcome their enemies. Physical combat is vividly described in various parts of the novel. For example, although Gerald is armed, he uses his hands to choke a Chinese priest until his face 'turned slowly to a ghastly greeny-blue. Then his jaw dropped open; and he lay quite motionless and mute' (*LC* 224). However, unlike Rex who does not feel 'the slightest regret at having to kill', Gerald tells Jugatai that he is not an assassin and refuses to kill a priest even though he would be in less danger if the man were dead (*WAP* 347). During the Siege of the Milton Towers, Dr Raydon uses the butt of his rifle to deliver a 'shivering blow' to the first Boxer that opposed him, resulting in the man's head 'crack[ing] like a hazel nut' (*LC* 110). Earlier, he had taken a Boxer 'by the throat, and hurled him back against the wall with such sudden violence that his neck broke like a rotten bough' (*LC* 77). Gerald and Mr Wang dispose of two dead bodies by throwing them 'like coals going down a chute' (*LC* 258). Considering many of the characters' callous attitudes towards death and the extent of violence perpetrated against the Chinese, it is ironic that Dr Raydon characterizes his own civilization as one full of 'Christian teachings of mercy, charity, sympathy, sincerity and love' (*LC* 32). There is an inherent contradiction between the retributive acts of violence and the supposed virtue of compassion in the British character.

These stories bear no resemblance to the 'sugared' history that Charlotte Yonge recommended for young readers in *What Books to Lend and What to Give* (1887),

---

[82] George Manville Fenn, *George Alfred Henty; the Story of an Active Life* (London, 1907), p. 334.

especially considering that mutilation or threat of mutilation appears frequently in the Boxer narratives. Contemporary sources on the Boxer Uprising reported that 'stories of the killing of the wounded and the mutilation of the dead were in the mouth of every soldier'.[83] Henty's characters witness dead people lying on the streets, 'for the most part horribly slashed and mutilated' (*WAP* 103). In *The Lost Column*, Dr Raydon fears for the Woods not because he was afraid they would be killed but because of 'the fearful form in which that death was sure to come' (*LC* 117).

Stories of Chinese cruelty date back to the sixteenth century, when the Portuguese merchant Galeotto Perera recorded the tortures that Chinese people inflicted on their prisoners. Although terrible punishments were also a common feature in European culture during this time and even continued until the nineteenth century, readers are later 'informed that torture was a Chinese specialty, and it was proof of the intrinsic Chinese cowardice and cruelty'.[84] The Chinese had become well-known for their infamous torture techniques since the publication of George Mason's *The Punishments of China* in 1801, a popular illustrated work which had gone into five editions by 1830.[85]

In 1804, John Barrow described the Chinese laws as being so cruel that they 'exclude and obliterate every notion of the dignity of human nature'.[86] Authors of Boxer narratives in the late nineteenth century continue to endorse his views. In a short story set during the Uprising called 'The Scarlet Hand: A Thrilling Tale of Adventure in China' (1911–1912), Gilson mentions 'the Chinese death of a thousand cuts', 'the most fiendish torture that has ever been invented by the faculties of man'.[87] According to Harold Isaacs,

> [i]mages of the Chinese torturer and executioner ... made their most vivid impact on a wider public during the events of the Boxer Rebellion of 1900. In the popular press and along the more intimate channels of missionary-church communications passed vivid accounts and pictures of the descent of Boxer fanatics on foreign and Chinese Christians, of brutal killings and tortures, among them the celebrated 'torture of a thousand cuts'.[88]

---

[83] Lynch, *The War of the Civilisations*, p. viii.

[84] Adrian Hsia, 'Introduction', in Adrian Hsia (ed.), *The Vision of China in the English Literature of the Seventeenth and Eighteenth Centuries* (Hong Kong, 1998), pp. 3–25 (p. 8).

[85] For more information, see Timothy Brook, Jerome Bourgon and Gregory Blue, *Death by a Thousand Cuts* (Cambridge, MA, 2008), p. 171.

[86] John Barrow, *Travels in China* (London, 1804), p. 179.

[87] Charles Gilson, 'The Scarlet Hand: A Thrilling Tale of Adventure in China', *The Captain*, XXVI (1911–1912): pp. 386–94 (p. 392). Gilson reveals in his memoir that he once owned some photographs of the *ling-chih* process, 'a revolting and inhuman spectacle', but gave them away to a criminologist in a Midland town because they were 'too revolting to keep': Gilson, *Chances and Mischances*, p. 128.

[88] Harold Robert Isaacs, *Scratches on Our Minds: American Images of China and India* (New York, [1958]), p. 106.

Even the catalogue for the popular exhibit 'Ten Thousand Chinese Things' at Hyde Park in 1842 describes *lingche* [*lingchi*], which was the punishment for treason, parricide, or sacrilege.[89] These horrific descriptions of torture left a deep impression on young readers. For example, a man Isaacs interviewed recalls 'accounts of the Boxer time which he had read as a boy', such as a story by Ralph D. Paine called 'The Cross and the Dragon' (1911) from *The Youth's Companion* that aroused in him a 'sensation of terror'. The pictures in that story still haunted him even though 30 years had already passed since he laid eyes on them.[90]

Echoes of the Indian Mutiny

Closely related to discourses of violence are comparisons between the Boxer Uprising and the Indian Mutiny (1857–1858) when atrocities committed against women were widely reported in the British media.[91] In *The Lost Column*, the European husbands in Tianjin, imitating British husbands during the Indian Mutiny, were prepared to kill their wives and daughters if the Boxers entered the city, because 'death, even from the hands of loved ones, was more welcome than the clemency their foes were like to show. The horrors of Cawnpore would pale before the ferocity of the Chinese' (*LC* 147). In *With the Allies to Pekin*, the behaviour of the females, both British and Chinese, echoes that of the women who committed suicide during the Indian Mutiny to avoid being violated. For example, Rex's teenage cousins would rather shoot themselves 'than fall into [the Boxers'] hands again' (*WAP* 107). Forman interprets these acts of planned suicide as a response to fears of Chinese torture rather than sexual violence, but it is unclear in *The Lost Column* what 'the ferocity of the Chinese' refers to.[92] Perhaps Gilson wanted to allude to sexual crimes but could not do it explicitly because of the taboo against this kind of writing in children's literature.

Yixu Lü observes that in German reports on the Boxer Uprising, the same act of men committing suicide and murdering their wives and children to avoid a worse fate is encoded very differently depending on who was involved in the act. When Europeans killed their families, the reader is faced with a heroic version of events which render the act admirable. However, when the Chinese did the same to their wives and children, they are described as 'barbarous' and all of the gruesome details of the process are provided.[93] According to the narrator of *With*

---

[89]   See William B. Langdon, *Ten Thousand Chinese Things*, 19th English edn (London, 1842), p. 260.

[90]   Isaacs, *Scratches on Our Minds*, p. 106.

[91]   For the reports and rumours about violence against British women during the Indian Mutiny, see Jenny Sharpe, *Allegories of Empire: The Figure of Woman in the Colonial Context* (Minneapolis, 1993).

[92]   Forman, 'Peking Plots', p. 34.

[93]   Yixu Lü, 'Germany's War in China: Media Coverage and Political Myth', *German Life and Letters*, 61.2 (2008): pp. 202–14 (pp. 208–9).

the Allies to Pekin, Chinese women, sometimes holding their children in their arms, 'threw themselves out of windows or drowned themselves in wells' because they had 'an intense fear of the foreign devils' (*WAP* 299). Henty's description probably came from his reading of Lynch, who describes the Allies observing 'many curious sights' and 'not the least curious was the number of houses where the inhabitants had committed suicide just before their arrival'.[94] Lynch reports that when the Chinese heard the guns of the invaders they thought 'the time had come for their wives and sisters, as well as for themselves, to save themselves by suicide'. He is critical of Western 'civilisation' but remarks, 'There are things that I must not write, and that may not be printed in England, which would seem to show that this Western civilisation of ours is merely a veneer over savagery'.[95] Henty also criticizes the 'civilization' of some Allies in his depiction of Russian soldiers who 'gave themselves entirely to looting, rapine, and crime of every kind' (*WAP* 299).

Attitudes Toward War

Some critics have argued that adventure-story heroes regard war zones as fun playgrounds where excitement never ceases. Before arriving at the Peking Legations, Rex claims:

> it would be a splendid thing to go through the siege. It is not like an ordinary siege in an ordinary war. They have attacked us and perpetrated the most horrible massacres all over the country; they have lied through thick and thin; they are treacherous and cruel brutes, who will certainly show no mercy if they capture the place, so that I shall feel that I am fighting in a good cause, and that these men deserve all they will get. (*WAP* 90)

Although Rex may have craved adventure and excitement in the Peking Legations, before he reaches the Legations, 'His love of fun had entirely left him, and his face was as stern as that of the oldest soldier' (*WAP* 282). War might have seemed a game at first, but the toll it has on boys can be seen on their solemn faces. According to Mitzi Myers,

> The platitudes that war books fascinate young readers because they provide risk-free real events more exciting than any make-believe, yet appealingly predictable because the audience knows who 'won'; that they evade serious moral issues or reduce these to the good guys versus the bad, thus serving as conduits for national ideologies; or that they are usually escapist (combat books from 'over there' for boys) or gendered (domestic contribution stories for girls on the home front) need scotching.[96]

---

[94] Lynch, *The War of the Civilisations*, p. 141.

[95] Ibid., p. 142. For a similar discussion of British awareness of their own savagery against the Indians during the Indian Mutiny, see also Herbert, *War of No Pity*.

[96] Myers, 'Storying War', p. 328.

Kimberley Reynolds has shown that in children's writing before World War I, 'mass-circulation of boys' fiction was not dominated by accounts of stirring battles and a patriotic call to arms' and argues that 'the tendency to identify boy's stories as the well-spring of a mythos and instrument of a recruitment campaign that ended with boys on the battlefields of the First World War is simplistic'.[97] These statements are particularly telling when one considers Dorothea Flothow's argument that Gerald's experiences in *The Lost Column* resemble 'a game of hide-and-seek in which Gerald always manages to outwit his opponent. The same motif, which again trivializes war by linking it to children's play, is frequently used in novels of the First World War'.[98] She links Gilson's depiction of war to children's play, but fails to point out that despite the author's descriptions of Gerald's exciting exploits there is a serious anti-war undertone in the novel.

Michael Paris asserts that popular culture of the late nineteenth century 'legitimized war, romanticized battle and portrayed the warrior as a masculine ideal'.[99] Depictions of battle are less-than-romantic in *The Lost Column*, however. For example, the wounded members of Seymour's Column, who used to be strong men, lay

> all but lifeless, and green and drawn with pain; faces of men who see but dimly and have not the power to speak, flushed hot in fever as though in pride of health; sheet-white faces with blood-stained bandages bound about the brows, and tall men carried in comrades' arms like helpless babes. (*LC* 362)

War is a traumatic experience where strong men are reduced to helpless babes and boys are forced to grow up fast. Because of the Boxer Uprising, the transition from adolescence to manhood has accelerated: the narrator laments the loss of childhood when he describes Midshipman Tite and Gerald as 'two English boys, far away from England, playing the parts of men for England's sake' (*LC* 176). Gerald oscillates between feeling like a man and a child in the novel. Setting off to search for Seymour's lost column, he 'felt he was about to do something worthy of the doing; for the first time in his life he felt himself a man' (*LC* 154). Not long after, he prepares to say goodbye to his mother, thinking he 'was a man and her guardian and protector'. However, as soon as she took him in her arms, 'he was again a child' (*LC* 155).

In addition to presenting the non-romantic side of war, Gilson suggests that battles on the outskirts of Empire are something those sitting safely back home in

---

[97]   Kimberley Reynolds, 'Representations of Soldiers and Conflict in Writing for Children before World War I', *Children's Literature Association Quarterly*, 34.3 (2009): pp. 255–71 (pp. 266; 270).

[98]   Dorothea Flothow, '"Train Yourself to Defend Your Country": British Children's Novels in the First World War', in Andrew R. Wilson and Mark L. Perry (eds), *War, Virtual War and Society: The Challenge to Communities* (Amsterdam, 2008), pp. 3–20 (p. 10).

[99]   Michael Paris, *Warrior Nation: Images of War in British Popular Culture, 1850–2000* (London, 2000), p. 13.

Britain will never be fully able to comprehend. Although the capture of the Western Arsenal was reported in British newspapers, it 'is very doubtful whether those who sit at home and read in cold, half-damp print the brief account of some such petty victory as this ever dream for a moment of what it all has meant' (*LC* 337). The capacity of language to describe events accurately is called into question. British civilians read the headlines proclaiming success in the capture of the Arsenal, and 'feel in some small measure a certain glow of pride in their country, their navy and the men who are paid by them ... By the time full details have reached them the affair is a thing of the past, though once again, perhaps, they feel this glow of pride' (*LC* 337). The time it takes for information to be sent back home also reduces the impact of the story. The 'glow of pride' in Great Britain is fleeting – it is a 'little, pleasing, passing emotion', nothing when one thinks in the midst of this that '"the men they pay" have left the world' (*LC* 337). Those who sit by the fireplace enjoying the newspaper have probably never been through war and no matter how many reports they read, they ultimately fail to understand it. The victories in China were won by bloodshed and left some men 'maimed for life', but when these events are reduced to words in a newspaper column they seem to lose meaning (*LC* 148). This is a reflection on the trauma of war and the failure of language to represent adequately war's grim reality.

In contrast to Gilson's description of Seymour's wounded troops, Henty, describing the same scene, writes: 'The head of the column was just coming in. A portion of the relief force led, and then Admiral Seymour's men, many of them carrying the sick and wounded on stretchers, doors, and other make-shifts' (*WAP* 260). The condition of the wounded and sick is not described. Similarly, when Henty reports that the troops decided to withdraw to Tianjin, he merely notes that the wounded were 'carried down and placed on board some junks that had been captured on the previous day' (*WAP* 271). In comparison, Gilson's description is much more disturbing: 'From the junks, moored to the river banks, the groans of the wounded sounded loud and almost unearthly in the night; a man and a horse in pain let out inhuman cries' (*LC* 327). When he was wounded in the Boer War, a devastating conflict that resulted in thousands of British deaths, Gilson probably lay awake listening to the 'inhuman cries' throughout the night in the nursing stations.

In *With the Allies to Pekin* Henty lists the casualties in each battle, but they are simply numbers on a page that have little personal impact on the reader. Henty presents a much more sanitized and unrealistic vision of war. For example, Rex does not seem to feel any pain even when 'a bullet entered just above the wrist and ran up to [his] shoulder' (*WAP* 271). Although Rex feels 'horrified' by the dead peasants lying in the captured villages and expresses great 'grief' at the 'awful' destruction in the towns, detailed descriptions of these scenes is lacking (*WAP* 293; 328; 337). War-torn villages are quickly cleaned up: 'the troops set to work to render the town habitable. Great numbers of dead were removed from the houses that had been destroyed by shell fire, and from the streets, and in a very short time the town was brought into a satisfactory sanitary condition' (*WAP* 268).

While all of the British characters in *With the Allies to Pekin* are courageous and contribute their best efforts to resisting the Boxers, this is not the case in *The Lost Column*. Gilson destabilizes the notion of the staunch British hero in the character of Mr Pannick. Although he is supposed to be Gerald's guardian, the war affects him in such a way that child/adult roles are reversed. Instead of being a brave father-figure to Gerald, he behaves like a comic coward who 'sought to hide his emotion by bravado, in which he was assisted, as it seemed by an additional expanse of waistcoat' (*LC* 64). The narrator asserts that war 'takes men in two ways: it either excites them or makes them morose' (*LC* 68). The latter adjective applies to Mr Pannick. True to his name, he panics and his face becomes 'as white as his waistcoat' when he sees the Boxers' printed notices demanding 'death to the Christians, death to the foreign devils, death to man and woman and child' (*LC* 36–7). Before the Boxer Uprising, Mr Pannick proclaims that if the Chinese did rise against the British, 'we'd wipe the lot of them off the face of the earth', and that he 'did not mean to "miss the fun"' (*LC* 31). However, the narrator notes that what Mr Pannick thought and 'what he actually said were two entirely different things' (*LC* 64). When Milton Towers is attacked, he hides in a stove instead of fighting, proving his unreliability and cowardice. At the end of the story, he is reluctant to return to England however, because in Tianjin, 'he was a man of some importance. In England he would be no one: he would not be admitted to society, and he knew it; if he had been a little richer than he was, possibly he might be tolerated' (*LC* 375). Mr Pannick's situation reflects the dilemma many expatriates face: they are 'stuck' in an in-between space, belonging to neither China nor England. Even though 'England was the only land they loved', people like Mr Pannick are not necessarily accepted back home (*LC* 379).

Conclusion

Children's historical fiction based on the Boxer Uprising far outnumbered the stories dealing with the Taiping Rebellion, because the Taipings were regarded as rebels attempting to overthrow the Chinese government, whereas the Boxers directly threatened the safety of foreign residents in northern China.[100] Caught in the Boxer Uprising, the young protagonists of these stories which were usually more plot-driven than character-driven, perform courageous acts, such as volunteering in Admiral Seymour's relief column, or disguising themselves as Chinese in order to pass on messages between Peking and Tianjin after telegraphic communication between the two cities had been cut by the Boxers. In one of the early Boxer stories, Charlotte Yonge writes that the Boxers were 'not fanatics' but 'more political enemies'.[101] However, the label 'fanatic' is frequently used in association with the Boxers in later narratives for children. Because of the

---

[100]　Henty, *With the Allies to Pekin*, p. 114.

[101]　Yonge, *The Making of a Missionary*, p. 225.

Boxers' perceived 'fanatical' hatred for the British, authors seem to feel justified in describing the excessive violence that their young heroes resorted to in dealing with their enemies. As Rex puts it, they 'deserve all they will get' (*WAP* 90). For many, the language of force was the only means of communication with the 'irrational' Boxers. Even though more than half a century had passed since the opening of the treaty ports and 'floods' of books had been written about China, the distinction between Western civilization and Chinese barbarity was starker than ever. The knowledge that readers of Boxer narratives gained from the stories was about an essential Chinese 'madness', which is very different from the picturesque views of China provided in Bowman and Dalton's works and the carefree humour of Ching-Ching.

Throughout this book, I have highlighted the necessity of looking at the images of the Chinese in relation to their historical moment. From the optimism expressed by Bowman not long after the opening of the treaty ports in the 1840s and 1850s to the intense fear caused by the hostile Boxers at the turn of the century, the shift in representation is significant. The Boxer Uprising was a pivotal event that marked the beginning of 'yellow peril' fever and the trend of distinctly vindictive diatribes against the 'evil, fanatical' Chinese who were characterized by unconscionable cruelty.[102] However, while a stream of invective from many authors of the Boxer narratives may be apparent, this does not mean that injustices against the Chinese were not acknowledged.

Gilson asserts in his memoir that 'there are no half-measures about the juvenile critic. What you give him is either "ripping" or "rotten". And once you gain his attention, you are certain of a safe, if moderate, income, for your books sell from year to year and go on selling, instead of being sold off as remainders'.[103] Like Henty before him, Gilson had found a formula for ensuring that his stories would be considered 'ripping' by juvenile critics and stuck to it throughout his career as a children's author. Although both authors employed conventional plots involving young heroes defeating evil Boxers who reacted antagonistically to Western involvement in China, Henty criticizes some of the Allies, in particular Germany and Russia while Gilson emphasizes the solidarity between the Powers. Therefore, Hevia's statement that Henty's novel 'fixed the meaning of the event in clear-cut terms of perpetrator and victim' needs to be reconsidered. Not all of the Europeans were victims, and neither were all the Chinese perpetrators of violence. In fact, some innocent Chinese village women would have been preyed upon by Russian

---

[102] For example, Gilson's Secret Society for Federated Asia may have been inspired by H.G. Wells's 1907 invasion story *The War in the Air* which describes India, Japan and China forming a Federation to attack Europe and America. Gilson's ambitious Jugatai paves the way for children's invasion novels such as *When East Meets West: A Story of the Yellow Peril* (1913) and a story about the yellow peril in Australia, *The Invisible Island* (1910). See Percy Francis Westerman, *When East Meets West: A Story of the Yellow Peril* (London, 1913); Alexander Macdonald, *The Invisible Island* (London, [1910]).

[103] Gilson, *Chances and Mischances*, p. 25.

soldiers had Rex not arrived at the right moment to save them. Through this incident, Britain's superiority over the other Powers is highlighted. Even some of the Boxers can be regarded as victims because in certain villages, young men join the group because they fear that if they do not, 'evil will befall them' (*WAP* 30).

Henty represented the incursion into China as an adventure in *With the Allies to Pekin* while Gilson articulated the stark hardships of the military campaign in *The Lost Column*. In terms of representations of the Boxer conflict, both attempted to explain the possible reasons for anti-foreign sentiment and comment on the 'scramble for China' during this period of instability. However, Gilson's treatment of war is not as formulaic as Henty's. Whereas Henty glorified the British army, and to a certain extent war, Gilson's depiction of conflict in China anticipated the suffering and disillusionment of the Great War. Considering that both authors witnessed war first-hand, it is curious that Henty, who served as a war correspondent in places such as Crimea, Turkey, Italy, and Abyssinia, does not provide realistic descriptions of warfare in *With the Allies to Pekin*. This may be because Henty, a proponent of empire known for being 'the most Imperialist of all Imperialists', addressed this book to potential future combatants, and did not want to include the harsh realities of war in his story.[104] While Henty, who informed his readers that the qualities of 'energy' and 'pluck' 'have made the British empire the greatest the world has ever seen', was still writing in the tradition of inculcating patriotism through optimistic wartime adventure stories, Gilson, having been invalided out of the army, used the same genre to reflect on the negative implications of war, the bleakness of its aftermath, and the questionable enterprise of imperialism.[105] Although both authors dealt with war, Henty's *With the Allies to Pekin* conformed more to the adventure story genre while Gilson's *The Lost Column* anticipated the genre of war stories that would rise out of the First World War.

---

[104] Edmund Downey, *Twenty Years Ago: A Book of Anecdote* (London, 1905), pp. 115–16.

[105] G.A. Henty, *The Lion of Saint Mark: A Story of Venice in the Fourteenth Century* (London, [1889?]), n. pag.

Conclusion
Quilts and Kaleidoscopes:
Visions of China in the Literary Imagination

> The impressions of childhood [reading] are those that last longest and
> cut deepest.
>
> —Virginia Woolf[1]

As Howard Pyle (1853–1911), American author and illustrator, observed: 'In one's mature years one forgets the books that one reads, but the stories of childhood leave an indelible impression, and the author always has a niche in the temple of memory from which the image is never cast out to be thrown into the rubbish-heap of things that are outgrown and outlived.'[2] Pyle's reference to the 'indelible' impressions of childhood reading is echoed in Virginia Woolf's assertion that these reading experiences 'cut deepest'. Both point to the importance of childhood reading and its long-lasting effects. Many critics have discussed the influence of reading in shaping children's sense of self and their perceptions of others.[3] Some have argued that Victorian and Edwardian children read stories that fostered a negative image of the Chinese as racially inferior. For example, Kathryn Castle claims that by 'examining the image of the "other" in materials [children's books and magazines] … one discovers how pervasive and controlling was the logic of racial and national superiority'.[4] Further, she states that '[i]f the young were being ill-served by a denial of balanced history and the distortions of race in their leisure reading, it is unlikely that they recognised it'.[5] However, one Victorian child who grew up in the late nineteenth century reveals that although he enjoyed a book on China 'specially designed for young children',

> one thing in it, apart from the remembered joy of the pictures, was a statement
> which I didn't credit then, and do not credit now, that so sympathetic were

---

1   Virginia Woolf, 'Defoe,' in *The Common Reader: First Series* (1925), The University of Adelaide Ebooks, 2012 <http://ebooks.adelaide.edu.au/w/woolf/virginia/w91c/chapter9.html> [accessed 21 June 2012].

2   Quoted in Charles D. Abbott, *Howard Pyle: A Chronicle* (New York, 1925), p. 131.

3   See, for example, David Milner, *Children and Race: Ten Years On* (London, 1983); Gillian Klein, *Reading into Racism* (London, 1985); Wallace E. Lambert and Otto Klineberg, *Children's Views of Foreign Peoples: A Cross-National Study* (New York, 1967).

4   Kathryn Castle, *Britannia's Children: Reading Colonialism through Children's Books and Magazines* (Manchester, 1996), p. 9.

5   Ibid., pp. 180–81.

the relations between Chinese parents and their children that even when miles apart a boy would tell if his mother had a pain in her elbow because he had just felt a pain in his.[6]

The above statement from J.A. Hammerton's memoir reveals that at least this particular child did not passively accept 'the distortions of race' without recognizing it. Furthermore, as this study has demonstrated, it is unhelpful to make broad generalizations about Victorian and Edwardian children's reading. For example, a child who grew up reading *The Wolf Boy of China* (1857) would have had a very different childhood memory of China compared with one fed on stories written during the Boxer Uprising, though both would fall under the rubric of 'Victorian children'.

In 1857, William Milne objected to authors such as Bayard Taylor who, after 'a flying visit to Shanghai ... and perhaps to one or two other ports in China', concluded that '[i]t is my deliberate opinion that the Chinese are morally the most debased people on the face of the earth'.[7] Just as Taylor did not hesitate in making such bold remarks about the Chinese after a brief visit to China, some twentieth-century critics have only skimmed through the large corpus of children's texts on China before concluding that they overwhelmingly reflect imperialist tendencies and racial essentialism of the age. To prove their argument, these critics highlighted some parts of the texts and ignored others or selected only texts that support their views. This has led to an obscuring of the nuances of British writing on China for children. Throughout this study, I have attempted to point out some of the neglected areas of the writings, presenting both the virtues and vices of the Chinese and noting how the change in perceptions of China hinged upon the nature of Sino-British relations at the time of the texts' production.

By tracing the development of how knowledge of China was transmitted to Victorian and Edwardian children via different genres of children's fiction, I have aimed to complicate the notion that this body of work predominantly presented the Chinese as opium-smoking, cowardly, xenophobic, and 'inscrutable' cheats. It is important to examine in detail how differences in perceptions of the Chinese existed over the 60-year period between 1851 and 1911. As my discussion of Bowman and Dalton's travelogue stories in Chapter 2 has shown, these differences are evident even among single authors' works published within the space of a few years. Considering that a mixture of attitudes towards the Chinese has been disclosed throughout this book, we need to reorient how we think about representations of China during this period.

If we imagine the children's texts about China written during the Victorian and Edwardian period as a large quilt and examined it from an aerial view, the brightly coloured fabrics (negative stereotypes) would be very obvious. However, it is important not to treat these texts as a homogeneous whole, for it increases the

---

[6]   J.A. Hammerton, *Books and Myself: Memoirs of an Editor* (London, 1944), p. 14.

[7]   William Milne, *Life in China* (London, 1857), p. 401.

possibility of overlooking the intricate stitching on the quilt which deserves to be explored more closely. From this vantage point, we can find disparate attitudes toward the Chinese instead of the uniform voicing of stereotypes.

Through the process of identifying the various sources that children's authors such as Dalton consulted, I have attempted to trace some of the strands that form the web of knowledge about China and how information about this country was transmitted to children in the Victorian and Edwardian era. Authors such as Dalton played a crucial role in making information about China, previously confined to a small section of the elite classes in the works of Du Halde, Staunton, Huc, and others, more accessible to the public by incorporating parts of their texts into stories for the young. Considering that many of the authors often replicated paragraphs from the works they consulted without making much effort to rephrase the content, their writing process is analogous to quilting because they selected and 'cut out' parts of the source texts ('fabrics') while creating their stories.

Many authors presented an image of themselves as being fastidious about the 'fabrics' they chose. For example, in *The Celestial Empire; or, Points and Pickings of Information about China and the Chinese* (1844), the narrator asserts that he aims to '*pick out*' the information most worthy of children's attention and 'will neither represent the tails of the Chinamen to be an inch longer, nor the feet of the Chinawomen to be a hair's breadth shorter, than they really are'.[8] The pieces of information borrowed from the China 'experts' can be viewed as patches of old cloth passed down from previous centuries that are stitched in with more contemporary concerns and images of China. Authors, some more skilled than others, used the pieces of old cloth in different ways. For example, reviewers of Mossman and Graydon's books complained that they learned nothing new from the novels, which suggests that the authors' technique of recycling old 'cloth' formed an unappealing pattern.

More 'patches' of cloth were handed down and became available to authors over time. With new pieces of information coming in, old 'patches' such as the popular term 'Celestial Empire', which Bowman and Mossman readily employed as a synonym for China, were discarded by some later authors. In 1876, a *Children's Friend* author informed his readers that 'The Chinese call their country the "Flowery Land" and the "Celestial Empire"'.[9] However, by 1903, the term was regarded as inaccurate, as Rex Bateman, the hero of G.A. Henty's *With the Allies to Pekin* points out:

> By a misunderstanding, when we first had diplomatic relations with them the word Celestial was applied to their empire, and people ever since have believed that that is what they call the country. The word Celestial is applied only to the emperor, who is viewed almost as a god, but they would never dream of

---

[8]   Old Humphrey, *The Celestial Empire; or, Points and Pickings of Information About China and the Chinese* (London, 1844), pp. 2; 4–5. (emphasis in the original).

[9]   'Travels to Other Countries: No.1– China', *The Children's Friend*, XVI (1876): pp. 4–6 (p. 4).

applying it to the country. Because the document said the Celestial Emperor, it was supposed that the kingdom over which he reigned was called the Celestial Kingdom. On the contrary, they call it the Terrestrial Kingdom ...[10]

Each text examined in this book has its own unique pattern and texture. While elements of adventure exist in all of the stories, the characters that experience these events are diverse: from the half-Miao, half-British Lyu Payo to the 'supposed' Peking native Ching-Ching to the American medical missionary Margaret Hayes. Even the minor characters resist easy categorization because not all of the Western characters are paragons of virtue – Mr Pannick in *The Lost Column* is a cowardly Englishman and Henry Burgevine in *Among Hostile Hordes* is a renegade American. While the earlier texts by Bowman and Dalton are more 'fact-driven', later stories such as those by Marchant, Henty, and Gilson are more 'action-driven'. Some authors demonstrated racial pride, while others tried to show racial understanding, eschewing monolithic representations of 'the Chinese'. Therefore, if only one single-coloured fabric was used to represent 'the Chinese' in some stories, in others such as *The Wolf Boy of China*, different coloured patches were used to represent the Han Chinese, the Miao, the Si-fan, and the Tartars.

The same fabric might be utilized in vastly different ways. For example, Burrage employed stereotypes of the Chinese as cunning and mysterious to create a vivid and light-hearted picture of Ching-Ching while authors of the Boxer and Taiping tales used the same images to portray the Chinese as cruel and unpredictable. While one could argue that all the authors employed stereotypes, Burrage did it for comic effect while Marchant, Henty, and Gilson had other motives. Furthermore, not all of the texts conform to the dictates of genre. For example, Burrage reformulated the conventions of the penny dreadful, transforming the comic foreigner into the detective hero, while Gilson used the adventure story to reflect on the traumas of war and criticize children's participation in it. These attitudes and representations, inextricably linked to the historical moment, reveal more about 'the history of the observer rather than the observed'.[11]

In the 1850s, it was assumed that China was little-known to the children of Britain, but as the century progressed, authors reflected a confidence in children's knowledge of China and the world. Although the didactic tendency to educate readers on the 'customs and manners' of the Chinese lessened as more information was being sent back from China, the historical novels in the latter part of the century reflected a strong pedagogical intent to teach lessons about the conflicts in China such as the Taiping Rebellion and the Boxer Uprising. As more knowledge of China became available towards the end of the nineteenth century, paradoxically, the idea of the Chinese as barbaric and unpredictable became more prevalent,

---

[10]   G.A. Henty, *With the Allies to Pekin: A Tale of the Relief of the Legations* (New York, 1903), p. 15.

[11]   Raymond Stanley Dawson, *The Chinese Chameleon: An Analysis of European Conceptions of Chinese Civilization* (London, 1967), p. 8.

particularly during the Boxer Uprising, when the image of China reached its nadir. Therefore, unlike some have argued, racism was not necessarily predicated on ignorance but much more related to the historical moment.

As the last chapter has demonstrated, the dynamics between China and Britain at the turn of the century had changed dramatically since Britain's victories in the Opium Wars. Britain realized that its position in East Asia was much more precarious than in the past due to its relationships between Russia, Japan, and other European countries which became increasingly complex after events such as the Sino-French War (1884–1885), the Sino-Japanese War (1894–1895), the Boxer Uprising (1899–1901), and the Russo-Japanese War (1904–1905). Many early twentieth-century children's texts commented on China's awakening from what was viewed as a deep slumber. According to a character in 'The Sway of the World: A Story of Mystery and Adventure', a story serialized in *Young England* (1895–1937), China's importance cannot be ignored because of its geographical location in Asia and its possible influence on India and Tibet:

> China – this great, unwieldy, amorphous empire we call China, whose might we but half suspect, even whose boundaries we do not exactly know – this ancient and weary empire that is the pivot of all the power of Asia, whose unguessed influence extends into unknown regions of India and Thibet – this great, blind, and dreaming monster is about to wake. The signs are everywhere; Europe, having had warning of the approaching cataclysm, is taking precautions. Already the Empire is breaking up, and the strong hands of the nations of the West are filching what they can, what their jealousy of each other allows them to take, from this helpless and drowsy beast.[12]

This 'New' China could no longer be portrayed as a sleeping giant on the peripheries of Empire because it had become a potentially dangerous power that needed to be carefully watched. Because of China's large population, the country's influence on global politics could not be ignored.

In *The New China: A Traveller's Impressions* (1912), Henri Borel recalls reading a very interesting essay by a ten-year-old student who attended 'a private Chinese school somewhere in Java' which stated that the Japanese defeated Russia in the Russo-Japanese War (1904–1905) 'by its knowledge, by its education'. The student was confident that when the 'more than four hundred millions of inhabitants' in China 'are instructed and know', 'China will be much more powerful than little Japan or the strongest peoples of Europe'.[13] As the student's essay reveals, even children were aware of the empowering qualities of knowledge and the importance of education. To varying degrees, the authors examined in this

---

[12] Lawrence Zeal, 'The Sway of the World: A Story of Mystery and Adventure', *Young England*, 25 (1903–1904): pp. 1–8, 66–73, 102–9, 157–62, 185–91, 237–44, 282–9, 317–22, 346–52, 388–94, 438–44, 464–9 (p. 188).

[13] Henri Borel, *The New China: A Traveller's Impressions*, trans. Carel Thieme (London, 1912), pp. 16–17.

book wrote with a desire for their child readers to put on the mantle of power with the knowledge about China they acquired from the stories.

As the inventor of the kaleidoscope Sir David Brewster (1781–1868) explained in 1858, although the coloured pieces inside the kaleidoscope are the same, 'variations in form and colour' differ depending on the person twisting it.[14] Sometimes 'dull and gloomy masses, moving slowly before the eye excite feelings of sadness and distress', while at other times, 'the aerial tracery of light and evanescent forms, enriched with lively colours' inspire 'cheerfulness and gaiety'.[15] Similarly, knowledge of China took on different shapes and forms in the Victorian and Edwardian writers' literary creations. When arranged in a certain manner, such as in the Boxer narratives, they produce feelings of 'distress'. When twirled in other ways, such as in the Ching-Ching series, they inspire 'cheerfulness'. Regardless of the feelings that are produced, one thing is certain: images of China are never static in the 'ever-shifting kaleidoscope of imagination'.[16]

---

[14] David Brewster, *The Kaleidoscope, Its History, Theory and Construction with Its Application to the Fine and Useful Arts*, 2nd edn (London, 1858), p. 161.

[15] Ibid., p. 160.

[16] Charlotte Brontë, *Jane Eyre* (New York, [1847] 1864), p. 246. Sir David Brewster guided Charlotte Brontë around the Crystal Palace during the Great Exhibition of 1851. Heather Glen, *Charlotte Brontë: The Imagination in History* (Oxford, 2002), p. 218.

Appendix: Timeline

1839–1842	First Opium War
1842	'Ten Thousand Chinese Things' exhibition opens in Hyde Park. Treaty of Nanjing signed on 29 August 1842. Articles in the treaty stipulated that Hong Kong be ceded to Britain; Shanghai, Canton, Amoy, Fuzhou, and Ningbo be opened as treaty ports, and over 20 million dollars in silver be paid to the British.
1843	Hong Kong proclaimed a crown colony.
1851	The Great Exhibition of the Works of Industry of All Nations held in London.
1853	The Taipings capture Nanjing.
1853	Anne Bowman's *The Travels of Rolando* published.
1856	Chinese soldiers and officers board the *Arrow* and arrest 12 of the crew for suspected piracy. This incident marks the beginning of the Second Opium War (1856–1860).
1857	William Dalton's *The Wolf Boy of China* published.
1858	Treaties of Tianjin signed, granting foreigners the right to travel in the interior of China, opening treaty ports along the Yangzi River, and allowing Christian missionaries to do mission work inside China.
1859	Anne Bowman's *The Boy Voyagers* published.
1860	British and French troops sent to enforce the Treaties of Tianjin. Lord Elgin orders troops to burn down the Chinese Emperor's Summer Palace (*Yuanmingyuan*). British and French forces bring treasures looted from the Palace back home.
	Convention of Peking signed.
	Charles Gordon arrives in China to help the Imperialist troops against the Taipings.
1862	Bessie Marchant born in Kent.
1864	Taiping Rebellion ends.
	William Dalton's *The Wasps of the Ocean* published.
1870	Forster's Elementary Education Act passed.
	The Tianjin Massacre
1873	The Chinese Emperor receives representatives from Japan, Russia, the United States, Britain, France, and Holland for the first time without demanding the kow-tow.
1875	The Guangxu Emperor ascends the throne.
	British diplomat Raymond Augustus Margary murdered in Yunnan.

	Samuel Mossman's *The Mandarin's Daughter* published.
1876	China's first railway opened, sparking the Wusong Railway dispute.
	Ching-Ching first appears in E. Harcourt Burrage's 'Handsome Harry of the Fighting Belvedere'.
	China agrees to open five new trading ports after signing the Chefoo [Yantai] Convention.
1878	Charles Gilson born.
1879	*Boy's Own Paper* issued by the Religious Tract Society.
1884–1885	Sino-French War
1888	The first issue of *Ching Ching's Own* published.
1889	The Guangxu Emperor assumes the reins of government. The Empress Dowager's regency officially ends.
1890	Ministers of foreign countries are granted an audience with the Emperor in the first month of every year beginning in 1891.
1892	*Chums* issued.
1893	The Qing government lifts the ban on Chinese emigration.
1894–1895	Sino-Japanese War
1896	Li Hongzhang is made Imperial Commissioner to Russia, Britain, France, Germany, and the United States.
1898	The Hundred Days Reform under the Guangxu Emperor begins in mid-June and ends in late September.
	Anti-Christian uprisings in Northern China erupt.
1899	Boxer forces defeat Qing troops near Pingyuan (Shandong).
	The Captain issued.
1900	The Zongli Yamen (foreign office) receives a notice from the ministers of Britain, France, America, Germany, and Italy demanding suppression of the Boxers and the Big Sword Society.
	10 June: Edward Seymour's troops dispatched to Peking.
	20 June to 14 August: British, Japanese, German, Italian, French, American, Russian, Belgian, Austrian, and other residents trapped inside the walls of the beleaguered Peking Legations for 55 days until relieved by the Allies on 14 August.
	9 July: 45 European and Americans (mostly missionaries) killed at Taiyuan, the capital of Shanxi. Many more Chinese Christians were also killed in what became known as the Taiyuan Massacre.
1901	The Boxer Protocol is signed with 11 nations. The conditions include an indemnity of 450 million taels of silver and permission for foreign occupation in places such as Tangshan, Qinhuangdao, Shanhaiguan, and Langfang.
	Bessie Marchant's *Among Hostile Hordes* published.

1903	G.A. Henty's *With the Allies to Pekin* published.
1904–1905	Russo-Japanese War
1905	The Chinese Revolutionary League (Zhongguo Tongmenghui) is established in Tokyo with Sun Yatsen as its Secretary General.
1908	The Guangxu Emperor dies.
1909	Charles Gilson's *The Lost Column* published.
1911	The Wuchang Uprising begins. On 29 December Sun Yatsen is elected Provisional President of the Republic of China.[1]

[1] The following work was consulted in the preparation of the timeline: Frederic Alan Sharf and Peter Harrington, *China, 1900: The Eyewitnesses Speak: The Experience of Westerners in China during the Boxer Rebellion, as Described by Participants in Letters, Diaries and Photographs* (London, 2000).

Works Cited

Primary Sources: Children's Texts

'100 Handsome Prize Cups', *Ching Ching's Own*, I.11 (1888), 83.

'Advertisement', *The Best for Boys: Ching Ching's Own*, VII (New Series).83 (1892), 80.

'Advertisement', *Ching Ching's Own*, VII (New Series).81 (1892), 48.

'Anecdote of Gordon', *Chatterbox*, III (1907), 22.

'Announcement', *Ching Ching's Own*, VI.73 (1889), 127.

'Babes in China', *Juvenile Missionary Magazine*, XXI.239 (1864), 91–2.

Barber, W.T.A., *The Lands of the Rising Sun: A Talk with English Boys and Girls about China, Corea and Japan* (London: Charles H. Kelly, 1895).

'"The Best for Boys" Library', *The Best for Boys: Ching Ching's Own*, II (New Series).15 (1891), 30.

Binyon, Cicely Margaret, *Heroes in History* (London: Hodder & Stoughton, [n.d.]).

Bott, Jerry, 'Correspondence', *Ching Ching's Own*, I.8 (1888), 63.

Bowman, Anne, *The Travels of Rolando; or, a Tour Round the World. Second Series, Containing a Journey through Mesopotamia, Persia, Kamschatka, China, and Thibet*, 2nd edn (London: G. Routledge, [1853] 1854).

———, *Esperanza; or, the Home of the Wanderers* (London: G. Routledge, 1855).

———, *The Castaways; or, the Adventures of a Family in the Wilds of Africa* (London: G. Routledge, 1857).

———, *The Boy Voyagers; or, the Pirates of the East* (London: G. Routledge, 1859).

———, *The Boy Pilgrims* (London: G. Routledge, 1866).

'Boys and Girls in the Flowery Land', *The Best for Merry Boys: Ching Ching's Own*, X (New Series).127 (1893), 159.

Brereton, F.S., *The Dragon of Pekin: A Tale of the Boxer Revolt* (London: Blackie and Son, 1902).

Bridges, Adam, 'Correspondence', *Ching Ching's Own*, I.5 (1888), 39.

Bryson, Mary Isabella, *Child Life in China* (London: Religious Tract Society, 1900).

Burrage, E. Harcourt, *Cheerful-Daring-Wonderful Ching-Ching* (London: W. Lucas, [n.d.]).

———, *Ching Ching on the Trail: A New Style of Detective Story* (London: Best for Boys' Library, [n.d.]).

———, 'Cheerful Ching-Ching', in *Handsome Harry of the Fighting Belvedere. Vols. 1–3; &, Its Sequel Cheerful Ching-Ching* (London: Hogarth House, [1876?]), 1–180.

————, *Handsome Harry of the Fighting Belvedere. Vols. 1–3; &, Its Sequel Cheerful Ching-Ching* (London: Hogarth House, [1876?]).

————, 'Royal Feasting: A Ching-Ching Paper', *The Boys' Standard*, 305 (1881), 268–70.

————, *Daring Ching-Ching: Sequel to Handsome Harry and Cheerful Ching-Ching* (London: C. Fox, 1886).

————, *Young Ching-Ching* (London: C. Fox, 1886).

————, 'Ching Ching and His Chums Chapter I to Chapter II', *Ching Ching's Own*, I.1 (1888), 1–3.

————, 'Ching Ching and His Chums Chapter XI to Chapter XII', *Ching Ching's Own*, I.6 (1888), 41–3.

————, 'Ching Ching and His Chums: A Most Mirthful, Moving and Mysterious Story', *Ching Ching's Own*, I–II (1888), 1–3, 9–11, 17–19, 25–7, 33–5, 41–3, 49–51, 57–9, 65–7, 73–5, 81–3, 89–91, 97–9 (Vol. I); 5–6, 13–14, 21–2, 29–30, 38–9, 46–7, 54–5, 62–3, 70–71, 78–9, 86–7 (Vol. II).

————, 'Ching Ching's Christmas Number', *Ching Ching's Own*, III.27 (1888), n. pag.

————, 'Ching Ching's Natural History', *Ching Ching's Own*, I.3 (1888), 23.

————, 'Ching Ching's Natural History', *Ching Ching's Own*, I.7 (1888), 55.

————, 'Correspondence', *Ching Ching's Own*, I.12 (1888), 95.

————, 'Correspondence', *Ching Ching's Own*, II. Novelette No.17 (1888), 4.

————, 'Correspondence', *Ching Ching's Own*, II. Novelette No.21 (1888), 4.

————, 'Young Ching at School, or Grand Times for the Slapcrashers (Chapter XXVI–Chapter XXVIII)', *Ching Ching's Own*, II.26 (1888), 101–3.

————, 'Announcement', *Ching Ching's Own*, IV.51 (1889), 191.

————, 'Important Notice', *Ching Ching's Own*, IV.43 (1889), 63.

————, 'In the Editorial Room: Confidential Chats with Our Boys No. 19', *Ching Ching's Own*, V.59 (1889), 112.

————, 'In the Editorial Room: Confidential Chats with Our Boys No. 31', *Ching Ching's Own*, VI.71 (1889), 96.

————, 'A Jolly Christmas Eve: Ching Ching's Own Double Christmas Number', *Ching Ching's Own*, VI.75 (1889), n. pag.

————, 'The Ching Ching Mystery', *Ching Ching's Own*, I–II (New Series) (1890), 9–10 (1), 25–6 (2), 41–2 (3), 57–8 (4), 73–4 (5), 87–8 (6), 103–4 (7), 19–20 (8), 35–6 (9), 55 (10), 65 (11), 88 (12), 204 (13), 11–13 (14).

————, *Ching Ching's Own*, IX.113 (1890), 127.

————, 'Confidential Chats with Our Boys No. 48', *Ching Ching's Own*, VII.88 (1890), 160.

————, 'In the Editorial Room: Confidential Chats with Our Boys – New Series – IX', *The Best for Boys: Ching Ching's Own*, I (New Series).9 (1890), 134.

————, 'Correspondence', *The Best for Boys: Ching Ching's Own*, II (New Series).17 (1891), 62.

————, 'In the Editorial Room', *The Best for Boys: Ching Ching's Own*, X (New Series).119 (1892), 30.

————, 'One Word More', *The Best for Merry Boys: Ching Ching's Own*, VII (New Series).101 (1892), 368.

————, 'Please Read Carefully', *The Best for Merry Boys: Ching Ching's Own*, VII (New Series).100 (1892), 351.

————, 'Correspondence Column', *The Best for Merry Boys: Ching Ching's Own*, X (New Series).137 (1893), 111.

————, 'In the Editorial Room: New Series–LXXXV', *The Best for Merry Boys: Ching Ching's Own*, X (New Series).120 (1893), 47.

'The Chinese "Cangue"', *The Best for Boys: Ching Ching's Own*, I (New Series).10 (1890), 148.

'Chinese Gordon', *Boy's Own Paper*, 6 (1884), 487–8.

'"Chinese Gordon": A Brief Sketch of a Wonderful Career', *The Boy's Journal*, 7 (1913), 207.

'Ching Ching Debating Society', *The Best for Boys: Ching Ching's Own*, V (New Series).59 (1891), 103.

'Ching-Ching's Christmas Party', *The Boy's Leisure Hour*, V (1886), n. pag.

'Ching Ching's Order of Merit', *Ching Ching's Own*, II.Novelette No.18 (1888), 4.

'Chingy's Own Yarns', *Ching Ching's Own*, II. Novelette No.17 (1888), 4.

Colbeck, Alfred, 'Wang T'ien Pin: The Story of the Boxer Rising', *Boy's Own Paper*, 24 (1901–1902), 631–2, 43–5, 61–3, 76–9.

————, 'Dodging the Boxers. A True Story of Desperate Days', *Boy's Own Paper*, 34 (1911–1912), 342–4, 59–62, 73–5, 90–92, 404–6.

Collins, Helen [Aunt Helen], *China and Its People: A Book for Young Readers* (London: James Nisbet, 1862).

'Correspondence', *The Best for Boys: Ching Ching's Own*, II.26 (1891), 206.

'Correspondence', *The Best for Boys: Ching Ching's Own*, III.30 (1891), 110.

'Correspondence', *Ching Ching's Own*, II. Novelette No.15 (1888), 4.

'Correspondence', *Ching Ching's Own*, III.29 (1889), 47.

'Correspondence', *Ching Ching's Own*, V.56 (1889), 63.

'Correspondence', *Ching Ching's Own*, V.57 (1889), 78.

'Correspondence Column', *Boy's Own Paper*, 40 (1917–1918), 391.

Cox, Lilian Edith, *If I Lived in China* (London: Edinburgh House, 1933).

Dalton, William, *The English Boy in Japan: or, The Perils and Adventures of Mark Raffles Among Princes, Priests, and People, of that Singular Empire* (London: T. Nelson and Sons, 1858).

————, *John Chinaman: or, Adventures in Flowery Land* (Boston: Crosby and Nichols, 1858).

————, *Lyu-Payo, Der Wolfssohn: Abenteuer, Natur- U. Sittenschilderungen, Kriegs- Und Friedensbilder Aus Dem Reiche Der Mitte*, trans. Johannes Ziethen (Leipzig: Spamer, 1859).

————, *The White Elephant; or, the Hunters of Ava and the King of the Golden Foot* (New York: W.A. Townsend, 1860).

————, *Lost in Ceylon: in the Woods and the Wilds of the Lion King of Kandy* (London: Griffith and Farran, 1861).

————, *The Wasps of the Ocean: or, Little Waif and the Pirate of the Eastern Seas. A Romance of Travel and Adventure in China and Siam* (London: E. Marlborough, [1864] 1869).

————, *The Wolf Boy of China; or, Incidents and Adventures in the Life of Lyu-Payo* (New York: The World Publishing House, [1857] 1875).

————, *The Wolf Boy of China; or, Incidents and Adventures of Lyu-Payo* (Philadelphia: Lippincott, [1857] 1884).

Dufresnoy, Nicolas Lenglet, *Geography for Children, or, a Short and Easy Method of Teaching and Learning Geography: Designed Principally for the Use of Schools*, 22nd edn (London: J. Johnson, 1806).

'Faced by Chinese Rebels: And the Ruse that Outwitted Them', *Chums*, VIII (1900), 814–15.

'First List of One Hundred Winners of Ching Ching's Medal', *Ching Ching's Own*, I.9 (1888), 71.

F.R.R., 'How to Become a Student Interpreter in China, Japan, and Siam', *Boy's Own Paper*, 16 (1893–1894), 207.

General Gordon and Lord Dundonald: The Story of Two Heroic Lives (London: W. & R. Chambers, [n.d.]).

Geography, by a Lady; for the Use of Children (London: Houlston and Stoneman, 1849).

Gilson, Barbara, *Beyond the Dragon Door: A Story of Adventure for Girls* (London: F. Warne, 1934).

Gilson, Charles, 'The Lost Island: A Strange Tale of Adventure in the Far East', *The Captain*, XVIII (1907–1908), 3–17, 99–112, 96–205, 303–15, 99, 409, 93, 506.

————, *The Lost Column: A Story of the Boxer Rebellion in China* (London: Henry Frowde, 1909).

————, 'The Scarlet Hand: A Thrilling Tale of Adventure in China', *The Captain*, XXVI (1911–1912), 386–94.

————, *The Mystery of Ah Jim: A Story of the Chinese Under-World, and of Piracy and Adventures in Eastern Seas* (London: 'The Boy's Own Paper' Office, [1919]).

————, *The Scarlet Hand: Being the Adventures of Travers Humphreys and His Friend, Jack Haliday, Together with Authenticated Facts in Connection with the Secret Society of the Scarlet Hand, and Some Mention of Jugatai, the Tartar* (London: 'The Boy's Own Paper' Office, [1920]).

————, 'About My Own Stories', *Boy's Own Paper*, 44 (1921), 21–2.

————, 'Through the Boxer Lines', *Chums*, XXXXII (1934), 663–75, 704.

Goodrich, Samuel Griswold, *Manners and Customs of the Principal Nations of the Globe* (Boston: Rand and Mann, 1849).

'Gordon's Generosity', *Chatterbox*, XLIX (1901), 390.

Graydon, William Murray, *The Perils of Pekin* (London: John F. Shaw, 1904).

Groser, Horace G., 'General Gordon', *Young England*, 6 (1885), 176–8.

Guy, John, *Geography for Children*, 21st edn (London: T. Allman, 1848).

Hartley, Cecil (ed.), *The Travels of Rolando; or, a Tour Round the World*, trans. Lucy Aikin, rev. edn (New York: C.S. Francis, 1852).

Hemyng, Bracebridge, *Jack Harkaway and His Son's Adventures Round the World* (London: 'Boys of England' Office, [1875] 1880).

Henty, G.A., *With Lee in Virginia; a Story of the American Civil War* (London: W. Foulsham, [n.d.]).

———, *With Clive in India, or, the Beginnings of an Empire* (London: Blackie, 1880).

———, *The Lion of Saint Mark: A Story of Venice in the Fourteenth Century* (London: Blackie, [1889?]).

———, 'Interview', *Chums*, 2 (1894), 159.

———, *With Kitchener in the Soudan: A Story of Atbara and Omdurman* (London: Blackie, 1900).

———, 'Writing Books for Boys', *Answers* (1902), 105.

———, 'How Boys Books Are Written', *Great Thoughts from Master Minds*, 2 (1902–1903), 8–10.

———, *With the Allies to Pekin: A Tale of the Relief of the Legations* (New York: Charles Scribner's Sons, 1903).

J.L., 'General Gordon', *The Children's Friend*, LIII (1913), 2–3.

J.M.B, *He and She from O'er the Sea: Missionary Recitations and Hymns for Twelve Boys and Girls* (London: London Missionary Society, [1900]).

Kenyon, Arthur, *Letters from Spain, to His Nephews at Home* (London: Richard Bentlby, 1853).

Kingston, W.H.G., *The Three Midshipmen* (London: Ward, Lock & Co., 1862).

Knight, E.F., *The Cruise of the "Falcon": A Voyage to South America in a 30-ton Yacht* (London: Sampson Low, Marston, Searle, & Rivington, [1884] 1886).

Lang, Jeanie, *The Story of General Gordon* (London: T.C. & E.C. Jack, 1900).

Lang, Mrs, 'Gordon', in Andrew Lang (ed.), *The Red Book of Heroes* (London: Longmans, Green, and Co., 1925), 281–333.

Macdonald, Alexander, *The Invisible Island* (London: Blackie and Sons, [1910]).

Marcet, Jane, *Conversations on Natural Philosophy: In which the Elements of that Science are Familiarly Explained and Adapted to the Comprehension of Young Pupils* (Hartford: G. Goodwin & Sons, 1821).

Marchant, Bessie, *Among Hostile Hordes: A Story of the Tai-ping Rebellion* (London: Gall and Inglis, 1901).

Marryat, Frederick, *Mr. Midshipman Easy* (London: Saunders and Otley, 1836).

Miller, W.L., 'Correspondence', *Ching Ching's Own*, I.5 (1888), 39.

Morrison, John, 'A Trip up the Yang-tze Kiang', *Boy's Own Paper*, 20 (1897–1898), 27.

[Morrison, Robert], *China: A Dialogue, for the Use of School: Being Ten Conversations, between a Father and His Two Children, Concerning the History and Present State of that Country* (London: James Nisbet, 1824).

Mossman, Samuel, *The Mandarin's Daughter: A Story of the Great Taiping Rebellion, and Gordon's "Ever-Victorious Army"* (London: Griffith and Farran, 1876).

'Not to be Flooded Out', *Ching Ching's Own*, I.9 (1888), 71.

'Notice', *Ching Ching's Own*, III.34 (1889), 126.

'Notice to Subscribers', *Ching Ching's Own*, V.57 (1889), 78.

'Notices', *Ching Ching's Own*, I.6 (1888), 47.

'Notices', *Ching Ching's Own*, I.7 (1888), 55.

The Old Fag, 'Editorial (Captain Charles Gilson)', *The Captain*, XVII (1907), 568–9.

Old Humphrey, *The Celestial Empire; or, Points and Pickings of Information About China and the Chinese* (London: Grant and Griffith, 1844).

'Our Friends', *The Best for Boys: Ching Ching's Own*, IV (New Series).50 (1891), 172.

'Our New Heading', *Ching Ching's Own*, VII.91 (1890), 208.

Parsons, Nell, *The Little Chinese Girl* (London: Robert Culley, 1909).

Paterson, Katherine, *Rebels of the Heavenly Kingdom* (New York: Dutton, 1983).

'A Peep at a Chinese Family', *Juvenile Missionary Magazine*, XXII.254 (1865), 313–20.

'The Perils of Pekin', *The Captain*, XII.70 (1905), 339–40.

'The Place for Boys', *The Best for Boys: Ching Ching's Own*, II (New Series).15 (1891), 20.

Preston, Ernest J., 'Correspondence', *Ching Ching's Own,* III.27 (1888), 15.

Quiller-Couch, Arthur Thomas, *The Roll-Call of Honour: A New Book of Golden Deeds* (London: Nelson, [n.d.]).

'The Rebellion in China', *Juvenile Missionary Magazine*, 113 (1853), 220–24.

The Royal Game of the Assembling of the Nations: Exhibition of the Industry of All Nations (London: John Betts, [1851]).

Sayers, Alfred G., 'The Story of General Gordon', in Alfred H. Miles (ed.), *Fifty-Two Stories of the British Army: Stories of Battles, Histories of Regiments, Lives of Great Soldiers, and Reminiscences of Military Campaigns Chronologically Arranged* (London: Hutchinson, 1897), 441–57.

Serjeant, Constancia, *A Tale of Red Pekin* (London: Marshall Bros, 1902).

Simple Stories from English History for Young Readers (New York: Longmans, Green, and Co., 1898).

Smith, George Barnett, *General Gordon: The Christian Soldier and Hero* (London: S.W. Partridge & Co., 1898).

Stables, Gordon, *For Honour, Not Honours: Being the Story of Gordon of Khartoum* (London: John F. Shaw, 1896).

'Stories from the Lives of Famous Men No.4 (Charles Gordon)', *Chatterbox*, XXIII (1892), 179–81.

'A Ticklish Trip in a Chinese House-Boat', *Boy's Own Paper*, 19 (1896–1897), 488.

'To All Boys who Speak the English Tongue at Home and Abroad', *Ching Ching's Own*, I.1 (1888), 3.

'A Tour around the World: 16. China', *Chatterbox*, XXII (1881), 173–5.

'Travels to Other Countries: No.1– China', *The Children's Friend*, XVI (1876), 4–6.

Verne, Jules, *The Tribulations of a Chinaman in China* (New York: C.T. Dillingham, 1879).

Ward, Annie, *My Mother, or Home Scenes in Yorkshire* (London: Marlborough, 1866).

'Weekly Chat New Series XLIV', *The Best for Boys: Ching Ching's Own*, VI (New Series).72 (1892), 102.

Westerman, Percy Francis, *When East Meets West. A Story of the Yellow Peril* (London: Blackie & Son, 1913).

Yep, Laurence, *The Serpent's Children* (New York: Harper & Row, 1984).

Yonge, Charlotte Mary, *The Making of a Missionary, or, Daydreams in Earnest* (New York: Thomas Whittaker, 1900).

Zeal, Lawrence, 'The Sway of the World: A Story of Mystery and Adventure', *Young England*, 25 (1903–1904), 1–8, 66–73, 102–9, 57–62, 85–91, 237–44, 82–9, 317–22, 46–52, 88–94, 438–44, 64–9.

Primary Sources: Other

'Agassiz and the Edinburgh Chair of Natural History', *The Monthly Journal of Medicine*, XX (1855), 363–73.

Alexander, William, *The History of Women: From Their Earliest Antiquity, to the Present Time; Giving an Account of Almost Every Interesting Particular Concerning That Sex, Among All Nations, Ancient and Modern*, 3rd edn (2 vols, London: C. Dilly, 1782).

Allen, Roland, *The Siege of the Legations, Being the Diary of Rev. Roland Allen* (London: Smith, Elder and Co., 1901).

'Allen's (Rev. Roland) the Siege of the Pekin Legations (Book Review)', *Academy*, 60 (1901), 441.

Anderson, Aeneas, *A Narrative of the British Embassy to China, in the Years 1792, 1793, and 1794: Containing the Various Circumstances of the Embassy, with Accounts of Customs and Manners of the Chinese; and a Description of the Country, Towns, Cities, Etc.* (London: J. Debrett, 1795).

Austen, Jane, *Mansfield Park: A Novel*, ed. James Kinsley (Oxford: Oxford University Press, [1814] 1990).

Barrow, John, *Travels in China: Containing Descriptions, Observations, and Comparisons, Made and Collected in the Course of a Short Residence at the Imperial Palace of Yuen-Min-Yuen, and on a Subsequent Journey through the Country from Pekin to Canton*, 2nd edn (London: T. Cadell and W. Davies, 1806).

Beals, Zephaniah Charles, *China and the Boxers: A Short History on the Boxer Outbreak, with Two Chapters on the Sufferings of Missionaries and a Closing One on the Outlook* (Toronto: W. Briggs, 1901).

The Best Authority in the World, 'What Should be Done in China', *The Review of Reviews*, XXII (1900), 447–9.

Blackie, John Stuart, 'Chinese Gordon', 1886, *Literature Online* <http://lion.chadwyck.com> [accessed 24 November 2012].

Blakiston, Thomas W., *Five Months on the Yang-tsze; with a Narrative of the Exploration of Its Upper Waters, and Notices of the Present Rebellions in China* (London: John Murray, 1862).

'Book Review', *Atheneaum*, 2515 (1876), 52–3.

'The Bookman Christmas: The Lost Column', *Bookman*, 35 (1908), 56–7.

'Books for Boys and Girls', *Academy Christmas Supplement*, 61 (1901), 555–9.

'Books for the Young', *Atheneaum*, 3872 (1902), 47.

Borel, Henri, *The New China: A Traveller's Impressions*, trans. Carel Thieme (London: T.F. Unwin, 1912).

Bowman, Anne, and Thomas Bowman, *Bowman's Guide to Richmond and the Neighbourhood Including Rokeby; with Four Lithographic Views of Richmond, a Plan of St. Agatha's Abbey and a Complete and Accurate List of the Rare Plants of the District* (Richmond: Bowman, 1836).

Brewster, David, *The Kaleidoscope, Its History, Theory and Construction with Its Application to the Fine and Useful Arts*, 2nd edn (London: John Murray, 1858).

Brontë, Charlotte, *Jane Eyre* (New York: Carleton, [1847] 1864).

Brough, William, 'Letter to the General Committee of the Royal Literary Fund', in *Archives of the Royal Literary Fund, 1790–1918* (London: World Microfilm Publications, 1982).

Brown, F., *From Tientsin to Peking with the Allied Forces* (London: C.H. Kelly, 1902).

Burrage, E. Harcourt, *The Ruin of Fleet Street* (London: E.W. Allen, 1885).

Callery, J.M., and Melchior Yvan, *History of the Insurrection in China, with Notices of the Christianity, Creed and Proclamations of the Insurgents*, trans. John Oxenford (New York: Harper & Brothers 1853).

'Career of General Gordon', *Aberdeen Weekly Journal*, 14 February 1885, 8.

'Children's Books for Christmas', *Pall Mall Gazette*, 22 December 1875, 12.

'China', *Saturday Review*, 6 August 1864, 182–3.

'The Chinese', *Saturday Review*, 25 July 1857, 87.

'The Chinese Collection', *The Times*, 5 November 1844, 1.

'The Chinese Collection, Hyde Park Corner', *Illustrated London News*, 6 August 1842, 204–5.

'Christmas Books', *The Times*, 28 December 1875, 10.

'Christmas Books for Girls at School and on Holiday', *The Times*, 8 December 1939, 4.

Colles, Hester Janet, 'Books for Girls: Australian Stories', *The Times Literary Supplement*, 8 December 1921, 127.

Conrad, Joseph, *Lord Jim: A Tale* (London: Blackwood, 1900).

Cooper, Thompson, *Men of the Time: A Dictionary of Contemporaries, Containing Biographical Notices of Eminent Characters of Both Sexes*, 8th edn (London: Routledge, 1872).

Cordier, Henri, *Half a Decade of Chinese Studies (1886–1891)* (Leyden: E.J. Brill, 1892).

Dalton, William, 'Letter to the General Committee of the Royal Literary Fund', in *Archives of the Royal Literary Fund, 1790–1918* (London: World Microfilm Publications, 1982).

Davis, John Francis, *The Chinese: A General Description of the Empire of China and Its Inhabitants* (2 vols, London: C. Knight, 1836).

———, *Sketches of China: Partly during an Inland Journey of Four Months, between Peking, Nanking, and Canton; with Notices and Observations Relative to the Present War* (2 vols, London: C. Knight, 1841).

'The Death of Mr. E.H. Burrage', *Surrey Mirror and County Post*, 10 March 1916, 5.

Dickens, Charles, and R.H. Horne, 'The Great Exhibition and the Little One', *Household Words*, 3 (1851), 356–60.

'Disturbances in Kwangsi', *Chinese Repository*, XIX (1851), 462.

Dix, Charles Cabry, *The World's Navies in the Boxer Rebellion (China 1900)* (London: Digby, Long & Co., 1905).

Douglas, Robert K., 'Colonel Gordon – Letter to the Editor', *The Times*, 1 January 1877, 8.

Downey, Edmund, *Twenty Years Ago: A Book of Anecdote* (London: Hurst & Blackett, 1905).

Doyle, Arthur Conan, *The Adventures of Sherlock Holmes* ([London]: John Murray, [1930]).

'Dr. G.E. Morrison', *The Times*, 17 July 1900, 4.

Du Halde, Jean Baptiste, *The General History of China: Containing a Geographical, Historical, Chronological, Political and Physical Description of the Empire of China, Chinese-Tartary, Corea and Thibet*, trans. Richard Brookes, 3rd edn (4 vols, London: J. Watts, [1736] 1741).

———, *A Description of the Empire of China and Chinese-Tartary, Together with the Kingdoms of Korea and Tibet: Containing the Geography and History (Natural as well as Civil) of those Countries*, trans. Green and Guthrie (2 vols, London: E. Cave, 1741).

Edgeworth, Maria, and Richard Lovell Edgeworth, *Practical Education* (New York: Harper & Brothers, 1855).

Edwards, E.H., *Fire and Sword in Shansi: The Story of the Martyrdom of Foreigners and Chinese Christians* (Edinburgh: Oliphant, 1903).

'English Policy in China', *Saturday Review*, 5 December 1863, 714–15.

'Execution of the Fenian Barrett', *Leeds Mercury*, 30 May 1868, 12.

'The Execution of the Fenian Convict, Barrett', *Reynolds's Newspaper*, 31 May 1868, 7.

'Execution of the Fenian Michael Barrett', *Illustrated Police News*, 30 May 1868, 2.

'Exeter Hall on the Chinese War', *Saturday Review*, 9 May 1857, 422–3.

Farrell, John, 'Charles Gordon', 1905, *Literature Online* <http://lion.chadwyck.com> [accessed 4 August 2010].

Fenn, George Manville, *George Alfred Henty; the Story of an Active Life* (London: Blackie, 1907).

'The Flood of Books about China', *North China Herald and Supreme Court and Consular Gazette*, 29 July 1904, 234–5.

'Foolah', in George Ripley and Charles Anderson Dana (eds), *The New American Cyclopaedia: A Popular Dictionary of General Knowledge* (New York: D. Appleton, 1860), 592–3.

'For Girls', *The Times*, 4 December 1935, 20.

'For Girls: Adventurous Heroines', *The Times*, 25 November 1941, 9.

Forsyth, Robert Coventry (ed.), *The China Martyrs of 1900. A Complete Roll of the Christian Heroes Martyred in China in 1900 with Narratives of Survivors* (London: Religious Tract Society, 1904).

Fortune, Robert, *Three Years' Wanderings in the Northern Provinces of China, Including a Visit to the Tea, Silk, and Cotton Countries: With an Account of the Agriculture and Horticulture of the Chinese, New Plants, etc.*, 2nd edn (London: John Murray, 1847).

———, *A Journey to the Tea-Countries of China, Including Sung-Lo and the Bohea Hills: With a Short Notice of the East India Company's Tea Plantations in the Himalaya Mountains* (London: John Murray, 1852).

———, *A Residence among the Chinese: Inland, on the Coast, and at Sea* (London: John Murray, 1857).

Fraser, George MacDonald, *Flashman and the Dragon* (Glasgow: William Collins Sons, 1985).

'General Gordon', *The Times*, 12 February 1885, 5.

Gilson, Charles, *Chances and Mischances: The Memories of a Writer, a Sportsman, a Soldier and a Wanderer in Five Continents, in War and Peace* (London: Jarrolds, 1932).

Glover, Archibald Edward, *A Thousand Miles of Miracle in China: A Personal Record of God's Delivering Power from the Hands of the Imperial Boxers at Shan-si* (London: Pickering & Inglis, 1904).

Goldsmith, Oliver, *The Citizen of the World; and, The Bee* (London: J.M. Dent, [1934]).

Greene, Graham, *A Sort of Life* (London: The Bodley Head, 1971).

Gutzlaff, Charles, *Journal of Three Voyages Along the Coast of China, in 1831, 1832, & 1833, with Notices of Siam, Corea, and the Loo-Choo Islands* (London: Frederick Westley and A.H. Davis, 1834).

———, *A Sketch of Chinese History, Ancient and Modern: Comprising a Retrospect of the Foreign Intercourse and Trade with China* (2 vols, London: Smith, Elder and Co., 1834).

————, *China Opened: or, a Display of the Topography, History, Customs, Manners, Arts, Manufactures, Commerce, Literature, Religion, Jurisprudence, etc. of the Chinese Empire* (2 vols, London: Smith, Elder and Co., 1838).

Guy, Joseph, *Guy's Pocket Cyclopaedia: Or Miscellany of Useful Knowledge* (London: Cradock, 1810).

Hake, Alfred Egmont, *The Story of Chinese Gordon* (London: Remington, 1884).

Halcombe, Charles J.H., *Children of Far Cathay: A Social and Political Novel* (London: Hongkong Daily Press Office, 1906).

Hamberg, Theodore, *The Visions of Hung-siu-tshuen, and Origin of the Kwang-si Insurrection* (Hong Kong: China Mail, 1854).

Hammerton, J.A., *Books and Myself: Memoirs of an Editor* (London: Macdonald, 1944).

Hart, Robert, *"These from the Land of Sinim": Essays on the Chinese Question* (London: Chapman & Hall, 1903).

————, *Entering China's Service: Robert Hart's Journals, 1854–1863* (Cambridge, MA: Harvard University Asia Center, 1986).

Herschel, John F.W., *A Preliminary Discourse on the Study of Natural Philosophy*, new edn (London: Longman, 1840).

Hewlett, W.M., *Diary of the Siege of the Peking Legations, June to August, 1900* (London: Pewtress, 1900).

Hitchman, Francis, 'The Penny Press', *Macmillan's Magazine*, 43 (1881), 385–98.

————, 'Penny Fiction', *Quarterly Review*, 171 (1890), 150–71.

Hooker, Mary, *Behind the Scenes in Peking: Being Experiences during the Siege of the Legations* (London: John Murray, 1910).

Huc, Evariste Régis, *Travels in Tartary, Thibet and China, During the Years 1844–1846*, trans. William Carew Hazlitt (2 vols, London: Office of the National Illustrated Library, 1851).

————, *Travels in Tartary, Thibet and China, During the Years 1844–1846*, trans. William Carew Hazlitt, 2nd repr. edn (2 vols, Chicago: Open Court, 1900).

'Imperialist Expedition to Fungwha', *Illustrated London News*, 7 February 1863, 150.

Knox, Robert, *The Races of Men: A Fragment* (Philadelphia: Lea & Blanchard, 1850).

Langdon, William B., *Ten Thousand Chinese Things: A Descriptive Catalogue of the Chinese Collection, Now Exhibiting at St. George's Place, Hyde Park Corner, with Condensed Accounts of the Genius, Government, History, Literature, Agriculture Arts, Trade, Manners, Customs, and Social Life of the People of the Celestial Empire*, 19th English edn (London: Printed for the Proprietor, 1842).

Leland, Charles G., *Pidgin-English Sing-Song; or, Songs and Stories in the China-English Dialect, with a Vocabulary*, 2nd edn (London: Trübner, [1876] 1887).

Lemoine, Henry, and James Caulfield (eds), *The Eccentric Magazine, or, Lives and Portraits of Remarkable Characters* (London: Smeeton, 1812).

Lindley, Augustus F., *Ti-Ping Tien-Kwoh: The History of the Ti-Ping Revolution, Including a Narrative of the Author's Personal Adventures* (2 vols, London: Day, 1866).

'List of Works upon China', *Chinese Repository*, XVIII.VIII (1849), 416–44.

'The Literature of the Streets', *Edinburgh Review*, 165.337 (1887), 40–64.

'London Music Halls', *The Era*, 8 March 1863, 11.

'The London Music Halls', *The Era*, 18 January 1890, 16.

Lynch, George, *The War of the Civilisations: Being the Record of a Foreign Devil's Experiences with the Allies in China* (London: Longmans, 1901).

Martin, William Alexander Parsons, *The Siege in Peking: China against the World* (Edinburgh: Oliphant Anderson & Ferrier, 1900).

Mason, George Henry, *The Punishments of China: Illustrated by Twenty-two Engravings with Explanations in English and French* (London: W. Bulmer, 1801).

McBey, James, *The Early Life of James McBey: An Autobiography, 1883–1911* (Oxford: Oxford University Press, 1977).

McDonough, John E., *Idyls of the Old South Ward* (Chester: Chester Times, [1932]).

Meadows, Thomas Taylor, *The Chinese and Their Rebellions* (Stanford, CA: Academic Reprints, [1953]).

'Memorials of General Gordon', *Birmingham Daily Post*, 26 April 1886, 7.

Milne, William, *Life in China* (London: G. Routledge, 1857).

Mossman, Samuel, *China: A Brief Account of the Country, Its Inhabitants and Their Institutions* (London: Society for Promoting Christian Knowledge, 1867).

——— (ed.), *General Gordon's Private Diary of His Exploits in China* (London: Sampson Low, 1885).

Murray, D.L., 'Bessie Marchant', *Times Literary Supplement*, 15 November 1941, 569.

Paley, William, *Natural Theology: or, Evidence of the Existence and Attributes of the Deity*, 14th edn (London: J. Faulder, [1802] 1813).

'P.I.P. Playgoer', *P.I.P.: Penny Illustrated Paper and Illustrated Times*, 17 April 1909, 249.

Polo, Marco, *The Travels of Marco Polo, a Venetian in the Thirteenth Century: Being a Description, by That Early Traveller, of Remarkable Places and Things in the Eastern Parts of the World*, trans. William Marsden (London: Baylis, 1818).

'Publications Received', *Literary Gazette*, 24 October 1857, 1021–2.

Puleston, F.W., 'Correspondence', *Collector's Miscellany*, 1.1 (1928), 5.

'The Rebellion of China', *Saturday Review*, 1 October 1864, 418–19.

'The Relief of Peking', *The Times*, 2 October 1900, 10.

'The Rev. W. Binns on the Death Roll of 1885', *Liverpool Mercury*, 5 January 1886, 7.

'Reviews: Christmas Books for Children', *Baptist Magazine*, L (1858), 31–4.

'Reviews of Books', *The Times*, 20 August 1901, 5.

Rohmer, Sax, *The Insidious Dr. Fu-Manchu: Being a Somewhat Detailed Account of the Amazing Adventures of Nayland Smith in His Trailing of the Sinister Chinaman* ([n.p.]: McBride, Nast, 1913).

———, *The Return of Dr. Fu-Manchu* (New York, 1916).

'Royal Aquarium. Chang the Great Chinese Giant', British Library <http://www.bl.uk/catalogues/evanion/Record.aspx?EvanID=024-000001743&ImageIndex=0> [accessed 19 September 2011].

Russell, S.M., *The Story of the Siege in Peking* (London: Eliot Stock, 1901).

Salmon, Edward, 'Books for Boys [1888]', in *A Peculiar Gift: Nineteenth Century Writings on Books for Children*, 371–86.

———, *Juvenile Literature as It Is* (London: Henry J. Drane, 1888).

———, 'Should Children Have a Special Literature?' [1890] in *A Peculiar Gift: Nineteenth Century Writings on Books for Children*. Ed. Lance Salway (Harmondsworth, 1976), 332–9.

Shiel, Matthew Phipps, *The Yellow Danger* (London: Grant Richards, 1898).

St. John, Horace Stebbing Roscoe, 'Our Library Table: The Kangaroo Hunters; or, Adventures in the Bush', *Athenaeum*, 1628 (1859), 48.

Staunton, George Leonard, *An Authentic Account of an Embassy from the King of Great Britain to the Emperor of China: Including Cursory Observations Made, and Information Obtained, in Travelling through that Ancient Empire, and a Small Part of Chinese Tartary; Together with a Relation of the Voyage Undertaken on the Occasion by H.M.S. Lion and the Ship Hindostan, in the East India Company's Service, to the Yellow Sea, and Gulf of Pekin, as Well as of Their Return to Europe* (3 vols, London: W. Bulmer, 1797).

Staunton, George Thomas, *Memoirs of the Chief Incidents of the Public Life of Sir George Thomas Staunton, Bart* (London: L. Booth, 1856).

———, 'Staunton Diary 1792–1793: Journey to China, 1792–1793', China: Trade, Politics & Culture, 1793–1980, 2007 <http://www.china.amdigital.co.uk/collections/doc-search-results.aspx?documentid=188041&searchmode=true&previous=0> [accessed 19 May 2012].

Swinhoe, Robert, *Narrative of the North China Campaign of 1860* (London: Smith, Elder and Co., 1861).

'Taeping Rebellion in China', *Illustrated London News*, 12 March 1864, 261–6.

'The Taepings and Their Remedy', *Blackwood's Edinburgh Magazine*, XCIII. DLXVIII (1863), 135–42.

'Ten Thousand Chinese Things Relating to China and the Chinese', *Chinese Repository*, XII.11 (1843), 561–82.

'The Theatres', *Illustrated London* News, 30 December 1865, 655.

Thomson, H.C., *China and the Powers: A Narrative of the Outbreak of 1900* (London: Longmans, Green, 1902).

Thornton, Edward, *Illustrations of the History and Practices of the Thugs* (London: William H. Allen, 1837).

'Twins in Edinburgh', *Hull Packet and East Riding Times*, 1 January 1869, 2.

Williams, Henry Smith (ed.), *The Historians History of the World: Volume XXIV: Poland, the Balkans, Turkey, Minor Eastern States, China, Japan* (London: The History Association, 1904).

Wilson, Andrew, *The 'Ever-Victorious Army': A History of the Chinese Campaign under Lt.Col. C.G. Gordon, C.B. R.E. and of the Suppression of the Tai-ping Rebellion* (London: William Blackwood & Sons, 1868).

'The Wolf-Boy of China', *Bentley's Miscellany Review*, 42 (1857), 424.

'The Wolf Boy of China', *Morning Advertiser*, 8 October 1857, 7.

'The Wolf Boy of China', *Morning Post*, 10 December 1857, 3.

'A "Wonder Book" on China', *The Times*, 11 September 1858, 9.

Wood, W.W., *Sketches of China, with Illustrations from Original Drawings* (Philadelphia: Carey & Lea, 1830).

Wright, Charles Henry Hamilton, and Charles Neil, *A Protestant Dictionary: Containing Articles on the History, Doctrines, and Practices of the Christian Church* (London: Hodder and Stoughton, 1904).

Wright, Thomas, 'On a Possible Popular Culture', *Contemporary Review*, 40 (1881), 25–44.

Yonge, Charlotte, *What Books to Lend and What to Give* (London: National Society's Depository, 1887).

Secondary Sources

Abbott, Charles D., *Howard Pyle: A Chronicle* (New York: Harper, 1925).

Adkins, Kaye, '"Foundation-Stones": Natural History for Children in *St. Nicholas Magazine*', in Sidney I. Dobrin and Kenneth B. Kidd (eds), *Wild Things: Children's Culture and Ecocriticism* (Detroit: Wayne State University Press, 2004), 31–47.

Altick, Richard Daniel, *The Shows of London* (Cambridge, MA: Belknap, 1978).

Anglo, Michael, *Penny Dreadfuls and Other Victorian Horrors* (London: Jupiter, 1977).

Arnold, Guy, *Held Fast for England: G.A. Henty, Imperialist Boys' Writer* (London: Hamilton, 1980).

Auerbach, Sascha, *Race, Law and 'The Chinese Puzzle' in Imperial Britain* (Basingstoke: Palgrave Macmillan, 2009).

Beaumont, Matthew, '"A Little Political World of My Own": The New Woman, the New Life, and *New Amazonia*', *Victorian Literature and Culture*, 35.1 (2007), 215–32.

Bellanca, Mary Ellen, *Daybooks of Discovery: Nature Diaries in Britain, 1770–1870* (Charlottesville: University of Virginia Press, 2007).

Bentley, Michael, 'The Evolution and Dissemination of Historical Knowledge', in Martin Daunton (ed.), *The Organisation of Knowledge in Victorian Britain* (Oxford: Oxford University Press, 2005), 173–98.

Benton, Gregor, and Edmund Terence Gomez, *The Chinese in Britain, 1800–Present: Economy, Transnationalism and Identity* (Basingstoke: Palgrave Macmillan, 2008).

Benzaquen, Adriana S., 'Childhood, Identity and Human Science in the Enlightenment', *History Workshop Journal*, 57 (2004), 35–57.

Bickers, Robert A., *Britain in China: Community Culture and Colonialism, 1900–1949* (Manchester: Manchester University Press, 1999).

Boone, Troy, *Youth of Darkest England: Working-Class Children at the Heart of Victorian Empire* (New York: Routledge, 2005).

Bourdieu, Pierre, 'The Market of Symbolic Goods', *Poetics*, 14.1–2 (1985), 13–44.

———, and Jean Claude Passeron, *Reproduction in Education, Society and Culture*, trans. Richard Nice, 2nd edn (London: Sage, 1990).

Boyd, Kelly, *Manliness and the Boys' Story Paper in Britain: A Cultural History, 1855–1940* (New York: Palgrave MacMillan, 2003).

Brennan, Jonathan (ed.), *Mixed Race Literature* (Stanford: Stanford University Press, 2002).

Bristow, Joseph, *Empire Boys: Adventures in a Man's World* (London: Unwin Hyman, 1991).

Brook, Timothy, Jerome Bourgon, and Gregory Blue, *Death by a Thousand Cuts* (Cambridge, MA: Harvard University Press, 2008).

Bruns, John, 'Get out of Gaol Free, or: How to Read a Comic Plot', *Journal of Narrative Theory*, 35.1 (2005), 25–59.

Bryce, William A., *Half-Hours with Famous Writers for Boys* (London: Wells Gardner, Darton & Co., [1935]).

Buckley, Matthew, 'Sensations of Celebrity: Jack Sheppard and the Mass Audience', *Victorian Studies*, 44.3 (2002), 423–63.

Burrage, A. Harcourt, 'Ching-Ching Memoirs', *Vanity Fair: An Illustrated Amateur Magazine Published in the Interests of Amateur Journalism*, II.22–4 (1926), 135–6, 49–50, 65–6.

Cadogan, Mary and Patricia Craig, *You're a Brick, Angela: A New Look at Girls' Fiction from 1839 to 1975* (London: V. Gollancz, 1976).

Campbell, Joseph, *The Hero with a Thousand Faces* (Princeton: Princeton University Press, 1968).

Caplan, Lionel, '"Bravest of the Brave": Representations of "The Gurkha" in British Military Writings', *Modern Asian Studies*, 25.3 (1991), 571–97.

Carpenter, Kevin, *Penny Dreadfuls and Comics: English Periodicals for Children from Victorian Times to the Present Day: A Loan Exhibition from the Library of Oldenburg University, West Germany at the Bethnal Green Museum of Childhood, 2 June–20 October 1983* (London: Victoria and Albert Museum, 1983).

Castle, Kathryn, *Britannia's Children: Reading Colonialism through Children's Books and Magazines* (Manchester: Manchester University Press, 1996).

Cech, John, 'The Violent Shadows of Children's Culture', in Nancy E. Dowd, Dorothy G. Singer and Robin Wilson (eds), *Handbook of Children, Culture, and Violence* (London: Sage, 2006), 135–48.

Chang, Elizabeth Hope, *Britain's Chinese Eye: Literature, Empire and Aesthetics in the Nineteenth Century* (Stanford: Stanford University Press, 2010).

Cheang, Sarah, 'The Ownership and Collection of Chinese Material Culture by Women in Britain, ca. 1890–1935' (unpublished doctoral thesis, University of Sussex, 2003).

——, '"Our Missionary Wembley": China, Local Community and the British Missionary Empire, 1901–1924', *East Asian History*, 32/33 (2006/2007), 177–98.

Ch'en, Jerome, *China and the West: Society and Culture, 1815–1937* (London: Hutchinson, 1979).

Chen, Jeng-Guo S., 'The British View of Chinese Civilization and the Emergence of Class Consciousness', *Eighteenth Century: Theory and Interpretation*, 45.2 (2004), 193–216.

Ching, Julia, and Willard Gurdon Oxtoby (eds), *Discovering China: European Interpretations in the Enlightenment* (Rochester: University of Rochester Press, 1992).

Clark, Gail S., 'Imperial Stereotypes: G.A. Henty and the Boys' Own Empire', *Journal of Popular Culture*, 18.4 (1985), 43–51.

Clarke, Prescott, and J.S. Gregory (eds), *Western Reports on the Taiping: A Selection of Documents* (Canberra: Australian National University Press, 1982).

Cohen, Paul A., *History in Three Keys: The Boxers as Event, Experience, and Myth* (New York: Columbia University Press, 1997).

Commire, Anne (ed.), *Yesterday's Authors of Books for Children: Facts and Pictures About Authors and Illustrators of Books for Young People, from Early Times to 1960* (2 vols, Detroit: Gale, 1978).

Corbey, Raymond, 'Ethnographic Showcases, 1870–1930', *Cultural Anthropology*, 8.3 (1993), 338–69.

Cox, Alan, 'Pagoda and Celestial Palace: The Chinese Collection in Knightsbridge', *Westminster History Review*, 3 (1999), 19–24.

Crossley, Pamela Kyle, *The Manchus* (Oxford: Wiley-Blackwell, 2002).

Cullingford, Cedric, *Children's Literature and Its Effects: The Formative Years* (London: Cassell, 1998).

Daunton, Martin (ed.), *The Organisation of Knowledge in Victorian Britain* (Oxford: Oxford University Press, 2005).

Davidis, Maria, '"Unarm, Eros!": Adventure, Homoeroticism, and Divine Order in *Prester John*', in Philip Holden and Richard R. Ruppel (eds), *Imperial Desire: Dissident Sexualities and Colonial Literature* (Minneapolis: University of Minnesota Press, 2003), 223–40.

Dawson, Raymond Stanley, *The Chinese Chameleon: An Analysis of European Conceptions of Chinese Civilization* (London: Oxford University Press, 1967).

de Certeau, Michel. 'Reading as Poaching', in *The Practice of Everyday Life*, trans. Steven Rendall (Berkeley: University of California Press, 2002), 165–76.

Denisoff, Dennis, 'Small Change: The Consumerist Designs of the Nineteenth-Century Child', in Dennis Denisoff (ed.), *The Nineteenth-Century Child and Consumer Culture* (Aldershot: Ashgate, 2008), 1–26.

Doyle, Brian, *The Who's Who of Children's Literature* (London: Evelyn, 1968).

Drotner, Kirsten, *English Children and Their Magazines, 1751–1945* (New Haven: Yale University Press, 1988).

Drucker, Alison R., 'The Influence of Western Women on the Anti-Footbinding Movement 1840–1911', *Historical Reflections*, 8.3 (1981), 179–99.

Dunae, Patrick A., 'Penny Dreadfuls: Late Nineteenth-Century Boys' Literature and Crime', *Victorian Studies*, 22.2 (1979), 133–50.

Egoff, Sheila A., *Children's Periodicals of the Nineteenth Century: A Survey and Bibliography* (London: Library Association, 1951).

Esherick, Joseph W., *The Origins of the Boxer Uprising* (Berkeley: University of California Press, 1987).

Evans, Eric, 'The Victorians at School: The Victorian Era in the Twentieth-Century Curriculum', in Miles Taylor and Michael Wolff (eds), *The Victorians since 1901: Histories, Representations and Revisions* (Manchester: Manchester University Press, 2004), 181–97.

Fan, Hong, *Footbinding, Feminism, and Freedom: The Liberation of Women's Bodies in Modern China* (Portland, OR: F. Cass, 1997).

'Fanatic', *Oxford English Dictionary*, Oxford University Press, 2nd edn, 1989; online edn <http://dictionary.oed.com> [accessed 19 August 2010].

Fergus, Jan, 'Solace in Books: Reading Trifling Adventures at Rugby School', in Andrea Immel (ed.), *Childhood and Children's Books in Early Modern Europe, 1550–1800* (New York: Routledge, 2006), 243–59.

Festa, Lynn, and Daniel Carey, 'Introduction: Some Answers to the Question: "What Is the Postcolonial Enlightenment?"', in Daniel Carey and Lynn Festa (eds), *The Postcolonial Enlightenment: Eighteenth-Century Colonialism and Postcolonial Theory* (Oxford: Oxford University Press, 2009), 1–33.

Flothow, Dorothea, '"Train Yourself to Defend Your Country": British Children's Novels in the First World War', in Andrew R. Wilson and Mark L. Perry (eds), *War, Virtual War and Society: The Challenge to Communities* (Amsterdam: Rodopi, 2008), 3–20.

Forman, Ross G., 'Peking Plots: Fictionalizing the Boxer Rebellion of 1900', *Victorian Literature and Culture*, 27.1 (1999), 19–48.

Frost, Linda, *Never One Nation: Freaks, Savages and Whiteness in U.S. Popular Culture, 1850–1877* (Minneapolis: University of Minnesota Press, 2005).

Gallagher, Catherine, 'Floating Signifiers of Britishness in the Novels of the Anti-Slave-Trade Squadron', in Wendy S. Jacobson (ed.), *Dickens and the Children of Empire* (New York: Palgrave, 2000), 78–93.

Gates, Barbara T., *Kindred Nature: Victorian and Edwardian Women Embrace the Living World* (Chicago: University of Chicago Press, 1998).

Gatrell, V.A.C., *The Hanging Tree: Execution and the English People 1770–1868* (Oxford: Oxford University Press, 1994).

Glen, Heather, *Charlotte Brontë: The Imagination in History* (Oxford: Oxford University Press, 2002).

Goble, Alan, 'Ching-Ching's Revenge', *The Complete Index to World Film since 1895* (2009) <http://www.citwf.com/film61907.htm> [accessed 19 August 2010].

Goodyear, R.A.H., 'Stories I Liked the Most – and Least', *Collector's Miscellany*, 3 (1933), 44–6.

Gray, Frank, 'James Williamson's "Composed Picture": Attack on a China Mission – Bluejackets to the Rescue (1900)', in John Fullerton (ed.), *Celebrating 1895: The Centenary of Cinema* (London: J. Libbey, 1998), 203–11.

Gray, Jack, *Rebellions and Revolutions: China from the 1800s to 2000*, 2nd edn (Oxford: Oxford University Press, 2002).

Green, Martin Burgess, *Dreams of Adventure, Deeds of Empire* (New York: Basic Books, 1979).

Gregory, James, 'Eccentric Biography and the Victorians', *Biography: An Interdisciplinary Quarterly*, 30.3 (2007), 342–76.

Gregory, J.S., *Great Britain and the Taipings* (Canberra: Australian National University Press, 1969).

Gribbin, Mary, and John Gribbin, *Flower Hunters* (Oxford: Oxford University Press, 2008).

Gubar, Marah, *Artful Dodgers: Reconceiving the Golden Age of Children's Literature* (Oxford: Oxford University Press, 2009).

Gunby, David, 'Henty and the Boxers: Sources and Attitudes', *Henty Society Bulletin* XI.88 (1999), 2–17.

Hade, Daniel, 'Curious George Gets Branded: Reading as Consuming', *Theory into Practice*, 40.3 (2001), 158–65.

Hannabuss, Stuart, 'The Henty Phenomenon', *Children's Literature in Education*, 24.2 (1983), 80–93.

Haviland, Virginia, *The Travelogue Storybook of the Nineteenth Century* (Boston: Horn Book, 1950).

Hazard, Paul, *Books, Children & Men*, trans. Marguerite Mitchell (Boston: Horn Book, 1944).

Headrick, Daniel R., *When Information Came of Age: Technologies of Knowledge in the Age of Reason and Revolution, 1700–1850* (New York: Oxford University Press, 2000).

Herbert, Christopher, *War of No Pity: The Indian Mutiny and Victorian Trauma* (Princeton: Princeton University Press, 2008).

Hettinga, Donald R., 'Bessie Marchant', in Donald R. Hettinga and Gary D. Schmidt (eds), *Dictionary of Literary Biography: British Children's Writers, 1914–1960* (Detroit: Gale Research, 1996), 166–9.

Hevia, James Louis, *Cherishing Men from Afar: Qing Guest Ritual and the Macartney Embassy of 1793* (Durham: Duke University Press, 1995).

————, *English Lessons: The Pedagogy of Imperialism in Nineteenth-Century China* (Durham: Duke University Press, 2003).

Hollindale, Peter, 'Ideology and the Children's Book', in Peter Hunt (ed.), *Literature for Children: Contemporary Criticism* (London: Routledge, 1992), 19–40.

Holmes, Colin, *John Bull's Island: Immigration and British Society, 1871–1971* (Basingstoke: Macmillan, 1988).

Howarth, Patrick, *Play up and Play the Game: The Heroes of Popular Fiction* (London: Eyre Methuen, 1973).

Hsia, Adrian (ed.), *The Vision of China in the English Literature of the Seventeenth and Eighteenth Centuries* (Hong Kong: Chinese University Press, 1998).

Hsu, Immanuel C.Y., 'Late Ch'ing Foreign Relations, 1866-1975', in Denis Twitchett and John King Fairbank (eds), *The Cambridge History of China* (15 vols, Cambridge: Cambridge University Press, 1980), vol. II, 70–141.

Huenemann, Ralph William, *The Dragon and the Iron Horse: The Economics of Railroads in China, 1876–1937* (Cambridge, MA: Harvard University Press, 1984).

Hunt, Peter, 'Necessary Misreadings: Directions in Narrative Theory for Children's Literature', *Studies in the Literary Imagination*, 18.2 (1985), 107–21.

Huttenback, Robert A., 'G.A. Henty and the Imperial Stereotype', *Huntington Library Quarterly*, 29 (1965), 63–75.

Hyde, Lewis, *Trickster Makes This World: Mischief, Myth, and Art* (New York: Farrar, Straus and Giroux, 1998).

Isaacs, Harold Robert, *Scratches on Our Minds: American Images of China and India* (New York: J. Day, [1958]).

Jackson, H. J., *Marginalia: Readers Writing in Books* (New Haven: Yale University Press, 2001).

James, Elizabeth, and Helen R. Smith, *Penny Dreadfuls and Boys' Adventures: The Barry Ono Collection of Victorian Popular Literature in the British Library* (London: British Library, 1998).

Jenks, Robert D., *Insurgency and Social Disorder in Guizhou: The "Miao" Rebellion, 1854–1873* (Honolulu: University of Hawaii Press, 1994).

Jones, John Bush, 'From Melodrama to Tragedy: The Transformation of Sweeney Todd', *New England Theatre Journal*, 2.1 (1991), 85–97.

Judd, Dennis, 'Gordon of Khartoum: The Making of an Imperial Martyr', *History Today*, 35.1 (1985), 19–25.

Kearney, Anthony, 'The Missionary Hero in Children's Literature', *Children's Literature in Education*, 14.2 (1983), 104–12.

————, 'Savage and Barbaric Themes in Victorian Children's Writing', *Children's Literature in Education*, 17.4 (1986), 233–40.

King, Andrew, *The London Journal, 1845–83: Periodicals, Production, and Gender* (Aldershot: Ashgate, 2004).

Kitzan, Laurence, *Victorian Writers and the Image of Empire: The Rose-Colored Vision* (Westport, CT: Greenwood, 2001).

Klein, Gillian, *Reading into Racism* (London: Routledge, 1985).

Knüsel, Ariane, '"Western Civilization" against "Hordes of Yellow Savages". British Perceptions of the Boxer Rebellion', *Asiatische Studien/Etudes Asiatiques*, LXII.I (2008), 43–84.

Ko, Dorothy, *Cinderella's Sisters: A Revisionist History of Footbinding* (Berkeley: University of California Press, 2005).

Kriegel, Lara, 'Narrating the Subcontinent in 1851: India at the Crystal Palace', in Louise Purbrick (ed.), *The Great Exhibition of 1851: New Interdisciplinary Essays* (Manchester: Manchester University Press, 2001), 147–9.

———, *Grand Designs: Labor, Empire, and the Museum in Victorian Culture* (Durham: Duke University Press, 2008).

Lambert, Wallace E., and Otto Klineberg, *Children's Views of Foreign Peoples: A Cross-National Study* (New York: Appleton-Century-Crofts, 1967).

Lee, Robert H.G., 'Frontier Politics in the Southwestern Sino-Tibetan Borderlands during the Ch'ing Dynasty', in Joshua A. Fogel and William T. Rowe (eds), *Perspectives on a Changing China: Essays in Honor of Professor C. Martin Wilbur on the Occasion of His Retirement* (Boulder, CO: Westview, 1979), 35–68.

Lee, Thomas H.C. (ed.), *China and Europe: Images and Influences in Sixteenth to Eighteenth Centuries* (Hong Kong: The Chinese University Press, 1991).

Lin, Dong Ning, 'Power and Representation in Victorian Discourse on China', (unpublished doctoral dissertation, University of Maryland, 1994).

Lorimer, Douglas A., 'Reconstructing Victorian Racial Discourse: Images of Race, the Language of Race Relations, and the Context of Black Resistance', in Gretchen Holbrook Gerzina (ed.), *Black Victorians/Black Victoriana* (New Brunswick, NJ: Rutgers University Press, 2003), 187–207.

Lü, Yixu, 'Germany's War in China: Media Coverage and Political Myth', *German Life and Letters*, 61.2 (2008), 202–14.

MacDonald, Robert H., *The Language of Empire: Myths and Metaphors of Popular Imperialism, 1880–1918* (Manchester: Manchester University Press, 1994).

MacKenzie, John M. (ed.), *Imperialism and Popular Culture* (Manchester: Manchester University Press, 1986).

Mackerras, Colin, *Western Images of China* (Oxford: Oxford University Press, 1989).

———, *Sinophiles and Sinophobes: Western Views on China* (Oxford: Oxford University Press, 2000).

Maddy, Yulisa Amadu, and Donnarae MacCann, *African Images in Juvenile Literature: Commentaries on Neocolonialist Fiction* (Jefferson, NC: McFarland, 1996).

Major, Alan, 'Bessie Marchant: The Maid of Kent whose Exciting Stories Thrilled Thousands of English Children', *This England*, Winter (1991), 30–33.

Mander, Raymond, and Joe Mitchenson, *Pantomime: A Story in Pictures* (London: Peter Davies, 1973).

May, J.P., 'The Chinese in Britain, 1860–1914', in C. Holmes (ed.), *Immigrants and Minorities in British Society* (London: Allen & Unwin, 1978), 111–24.

Mayer, David, *Harlequin in His Element: The English Pantomime, 1806–1836* (Cambridge, MA: Harvard University Press, 1969).

McBratney, John, 'Racial and Criminal Types: Indian Ethnography and Sir Arthur Conan Doyle's *The Sign of Four*', *Victorian Literature and Culture*, 33.1 (2005), 149–67.

McClintock, Anne, *Imperial Leather: Race, Gender, and Sexuality in the Colonial Conquest* (New York: Routledge, 1995).

McCutcheon, James M., '"Tremblingly Obey": British and Other Western Responses to China and the Chinese Kotow', *The Historian*, XXXIII.4 (1970), 557–77.

McDonald, Peter D., *British Literary Culture and Publishing Practice, 1890–1914* (Cambridge: Cambridge University Press, 1997).

Methodist Times and Leader, *Who's Who in Methodism 1933: An Encyclopaedia of the Personnel and Departments, Ministerial and Lay in the United Church of Methodism* (London: Methodist Times and Leader, 1933).

Mickenberg, Julia L., *Learning from the Left: Children's Literature, the Cold War, and Radical Politics in the United States* (Oxford: Oxford University Press, 2006).

Mijares, Loretta M., 'Distancing the Proximate Other: Hybridity and Maud Diver's *Candles in the Wind*', *Twentieth Century Literature*, 50.2 (2004), 107–41.

Miller, Brook, 'Our Abdiel: The British Press and the Lionization of "Chinese" Gordon', *Nineteenth-Century Prose*, 32.2 (2005), 127–53.

Miller, Stuart Creighton, *The Unwelcome Immigrant: The American Image of the Chinese, 1785–1882* (Berkeley: University of California Press, 1969).

Mills, Sara, 'Knowledge, Gender, and Empire', in Gillian Rose and Alison Blunt (eds), *Writing Women and Space: Colonial and Postcolonial Geographies* (New York: Gulford, 1994), 29–50.

Milner, David, *Children and Race: Ten Years On* (London: Ward Lock Education, 1983).

Mitchell, Sally, *The New Girl: Girls' Culture in England, 1880–1915* (New York: Columbia University Press, 1995).

Moses, Montrose J., *Children's Books and Reading* (New York: M. Kennerley, 1907).

Muir, Percy H., *English Children's Books: 1600 to 1900*, 3rd rev. impression edn (London: Batsford, 1979).

Mungello, David E., *The Great Encounter of China and the West, 1500–1800* (Lanham, MD: Rowman & Littlefield, 1999).

Myers, Mitzi, 'Missed Opportunities and Critical Malpractice: New Historicism and Children's Literature', *Children's Literature Association Quarterly*, 13.1 (1988), 41–3.

———, 'Storying War: A Capsule Overview', *The Lion and the Unicorn*, 24.3 (2000), 327–36.

Naidis, Mark, 'G.A. Henty's Idea of India', *Victorian Studies*, VIII.1 (1964), 49–58.

Nelson, Claudia, *Boys Will Be Girls: The Feminine Ethic and British Children's Fiction, 1857–1917* (New Brunswick, NJ: Rutgers University Press, 1991).

Nevins, Jess, *The Encyclopedia of Fantastic Victoriana* (Austin, TX: MonkeyBrain, 2005).

Newsinger, J., 'Taiping Revolutionary: Augustus Lindley in China', *Race and Class*, 42.4 (2001), 57–72.

Oates, Joyce Carol, *The Faith of a Writer: Life, Craft, Art* (New York: Harper Collins, 2004).

O'Brien, John, 'Harlequin Britain: Eighteenth-Century Pantomime and the Cultural Location of Entertainment(s)', *Theatre Journal*, 50.4 (1998), 489–510.

———, *Harlequin Britain: Pantomime and Entertainment, 1690–1760* (Baltimore: Johns Hopkins University Press, 2004).

Ono, Barry, 'Camouflaged Blood Titles', *Collector's Miscellany*, 7 (1933–1934), 9–10.

Osterhammel, Jürgen, 'Britain and China, 1842–1914', in Andrew Porter (ed.), *The Oxford History of the British Empire III: The Nineteenth Century* (Oxford: Oxford University Press, 1998), 146–69.

Otis, Laura, 'The Empire Bites Back: Sherlock Holmes as an Imperial Immune System', *Studies in Twentieth Century Literature*, 22.1 (1998), 31–60.

Ouditt, Sharon, *Fighting Forces, Writing Women: Identity and Ideology in the First World War* (London: Routledge, 1994).

Pagani, Catherine, 'Chinese Material Culture and British Perceptions of China in the Mid-Nineteenth Century', in T.J. Barringer and Tom Flynn (eds), *Colonialism and the Object: Empire, Material Culture, and the Museum* (London: Routledge, 1998), 28–40.

———, 'Objects and the Press: Images of China in Nineteenth-Century Britain', in Julie F. Codell (ed.), *Imperial Co-Histories: National Identities and the British and Colonial Press* (Madison, NJ: Fairleigh Dickinson University Press, 2003), 147–66.

Pan, Lynn, *Sons of the Yellow Emperor: The Story of the Overseas Chinese* (London: Secker & Warburg, 1990).

Paris, Michael, *Warrior Nation: Images of War in British Popular Culture, 1850–2000* (London: Reaktion, 2000).

———, *Over the Top: The Great War and Juvenile Literature in Britain* (Westport, CT: Praeger, 2004).

Parrish, Câecile, *The Image of Asia in Children's Literature, 1814–1964* (Clayton, Vic.: Centre of Southeast Asian Studies Monash University, 1977).

Pelaud, Isabelle Thuy, '"Mettise Blanche": Kim Lefvre and Transnational Space', in Jonathan Brennan (ed.), *Mixed Race Literature* (Stanford: Stanford University Press, 2002), 122–36.

Phillips, Elizabeth, 'A Pagoda in Knightsbridge', *Journal of Pre-Raphaelite Studies*, IV.2 (1984), 37–42.

Phillips, Richard, *Mapping Men and Empire: A Geography of Adventure* (London: Routledge, 1997).

Pittard, Christopher, "'Cheap, Healthful Literature'": *The Strand Magazine*, Fictions of Crime, and Purified Reading Communities', *Victorian Periodicals Review*, 40.1 (2007), 1–23.

Pong, David, 'Confucian Patriotism and the Destruction of the Woosung Railway, 1877', *Modern Asian Studies*, 7.4 (1973), 647–76.

Popkin, Jeremy D., 'Periodical Publication and the Nature of Knowledge in Eighteenth-Century Europe', in Donald R. Kelley and Richard H. Popkin (eds), *The Shapes of Knowledge from the Renaissance to the Enlightenment* (Dordrecht: Kluwer Academic, 1991), 203–13.

Porter, David, 'A Peculiar but Uninteresting Nation: China and the Discourse of Commerce in Eighteenth-Century England', *Eighteenth-Century Studies*, 33.2 (2000), 181–99.

Pratt, Mary Louise, *Imperial Eyes: Travel Writing and Transculturation* (London: Routledge, 1992).

Qian, Zhongshu, 'China in the English Literature of the Eighteenth Century', in Adrian Hsia (ed.), *The Vision of China in the English Literature of the Seventeenth and Eighteenth Centuries* (Hong Kong: Chinese University Press, 1998), 117–213.

Rahn, B.J., 'Seeley Regester: America's First Detective Novelist', in Barbara A. Rader and Howard G. Zettler (eds), *The Sleuth and the Scholar: Origins, Evolution, and Current Trends in Detective Fiction* (Westport, CT: Greenwood, 1988), 47–61.

Ranson, Nicholas, 'G.A. Henty', in Laura M. Zaidman and Caroline C. Hunt (eds), *Dictionary of Literary Biography: British Children's Writers, 1880–1914* (Charleston: The Gale Group, 1994), 118–33.

Rauch, Alan, *Useful Knowledge: The Victorians, Morality, and the March of Intellect* (Durham: Duke University Press, 2001).

Reader, W.J., *At Duty's Call: A Study in Obsolete Patriotism* (Manchester: Manchester University Press, 1988).

Ready, Kathryn, 'The Enlightenment Feminist Project of Lucy Aikin's *Epistles on Women* (1810)', *History of European Ideas*, 31.4 (2005), 435–50.

Reinders, Eric Robert, *Borrowed Gods and Foreign Bodies: Christian Missionaries Imagine Chinese Religion* (Berkeley: University of California Press, 2004).

Reynolds, Kimberley, *Girls Only?: Gender and Popular Children's Fiction in Britain, 1880–1910* (London: Harvester Wheatsheaf, 1990).

———, *Radical Children's Literature: Future Visions and Aesthetic Transformations in Juvenile Fiction* (Basingstoke: Palgrave Macmillan, 2007).

———, 'Representations of Soldiers and Conflict in Writing for Children before World War I', *Children's Literature Association Quarterly*, 34.3 (2009), 255–71.

Richards, Thomas, *The Imperial Archive: Knowledge and the Fantasy of Empire* (London: Verso, 1993).

Romeo, Jacqueline, 'Irony Lost: Bret Harte's Heathen Chinee and the Popularization of the Comic Coolie as Trickster in Frontier Melodrama', *Theatre History Studies*, 26 (2006), 108–36.

Rose, Jonathan, 'Rereading the English Common Reader: A Preface to a History of Audiences', *Journal of the History of Ideas*, 53.1 (1992), 47–70.

Rothfield, Lawrence, *Vital Signs: Medical Realism in Nineteenth-Century Fiction* (Princeton: Princeton University Press, 1992).

Rowbotham, Judith, *Good Girls Make Good Wives: Guidance for Girls in Victorian Fiction* (Oxford: Blackwell, 1989).

————, '"Soldiers of Christ"? Images of Female Missionaries in Late Nineteenth-Century Britain: Issues of Heroism and Martyrdom', *Gender & History*, 12.1 (2000), 82–106.

Said, Edward W., *Orientalism* (New York: Vintage, 1978).

Salway, Lance (ed.), *A Peculiar Gift: Nineteenth Century Writings on Books for Children* (Harmondsworth, UK: Kestrel Books, 1976).

Schlesinger, Arthur Meier, *A Life in the Twentieth Century: Innocent Beginnings, 1917–1950* (Boston: Houghton Mifflin, 2000).

Searle, G.R., *A New England?: Peace and War 1886–1918* (Oxford: Oxford University Press, 2005).

Shacklock, David, 'The Henty Succession', *Henty Society Bulletin*, XI.88 (1999), 17–22.

Shang, Anthony, *The Chinese in Britain, Communities in Britain* (London: Batsford Academic and Educational, 1984).

Sharf, Frederic Alan and Peter Harrington, *China, 1900: The Eyewitnesses Speak: The Experience of Westerners in China During the Boxer Rebellion, as Described by Participants in Letters, Diaries and Photographs* (London: Greenhill Books, 2000).

Sharpe, James, *Dick Turpin: The Myth of the English Highway* (London: Highway, 2004).

Sharpe, Jenny, *Allegories of Empire: The Figure of Woman in the Colonial Context* (Minneapolis: University of Minnesota Press, 1993).

Shteir, Ann B., *Cultivating Women, Cultivating Science: Flora's Daughters and Botany in England, 1760 to 1860* (Baltimore: Johns Hopkins University Press, 1996).

Smith, Janet Adam, *The Royal Literary Fund, 1790–1990* (London: Royal Literary Fund, [1990]).

Smith, Michelle, 'Adventurous Girls of the British Empire: The Pre-War Novels of Bessie Marchant', *The Lion and the Unicorn*, 33.1 (2009), 1–25.

Spence, Jonathan D., *God's Chinese Son: The Taiping Heavenly Kingdom of Hong Xiuquan* (New York: Norton, 1996).

————, *The Chan's Great Continent: China in Western Minds* (New York: Norton, 1998).

Springhall, John, '"A Life Story for the People?": Edwin J. Brett and the London "Low Life" Penny Dreadfuls of the 1860s', *Victorian Studies*, 33.2 (1990), 223–46.

————, 'E.H. Burrage's 'Carbineer and Scout': Another Henty Clone?' *Henty Society Bulletin*, IX.77 (1995), 3–9.

————, '"Boys of Bircham School": The Penny Dreadful Origins of the Popular English School Story, 1867–1900', in Roy Lowe (ed.), *History of Education: Major Themes* (London: Falmer, 2000), 386–408.

————, 'Disreputable Adolescent Reading: Low-Life, Women-in-Peril and School Sport "Penny Dreadfuls" from the 1860s to the 1890s', in Mike Huggins and J.A. Mangan (eds), *Disreputable Pleasures: Less Virtuous Victorians at Play* (Abingdon, Oxon: Frank Cass, 2004), 103–23.

Starmer, Suzette, 'Well I Never, It is a Girl! Fiction and Empire', *The English Review*, 12.4 (2002), 30–33.

Steinmeyer, Jim, *The Glorious Deception: The Double Life of William Robinson, a.k.a. Chung Ling Soo, The "Marvelous Chinese Conjuror"* (New York: Carroll and Graf, 2005).

Stephens, John, *Language and Ideology in Children's Fiction* (Harlow, UK: Longman, 1992).

Sterrenburg, Lee, 'Significant Evidences and the Imperial Archive: Response', *Victorian Studies*, 46.2 (2004), 275–83.

Stetz, Margaret Diane, 'Life's "Half Portraits": Writers and Their Readers in Fiction of the 1890s', in Laurence S. Lockridge, John Maynard and Donald D. Stone (eds), *Nineteenth-Century Lives: Essays Presented to Jerome Hamilton Buckley* (Cambridge: Cambridge University Press, 1989), 169–87.

Stillman, E., and W. Pfaff, *The Politics of Hysteria: The Sources of Twentieth-Century Conflict* (London: V. Gollancz, 1965).

Stott, Andrew McConnell, *The Pantomime Life of Joseph Grimaldi: Laughter, Madness and the Story of Britain's Greatest Comedian* (Edinburgh: Canongate, 2009).

Sweet, Matthew, *Inventing the Victorians* (New York: St. Martin's Press, 2001).

Tao, Zhijian, *Drawing the Dragon: Western European Reinvention of China* (Bern: Peter Lang, 2009).

Teng, Ssu-yu, *The Taiping Rebellion and the Western Powers: A Comprehensive Survey* (Oxford: Clarendon Press, 1971).

Teng, Yuan Chung, 'Reverend Issachar Jacox Roberts and the Taiping Rebellion', *The Journal of Asian Studies*, 23.1 (1963), 55–67.

Thorington, J. Monroe, *Mont Blanc Sideshow: The Life and Times of Albert Smith* (Philadelphia: John C. Winston, 1934).

Thurin, Susan Schoenbauer, *Victorian Travelers and the Opening of China, 1842–1907* (Athens, OH: Ohio University Press, 1999).

————, 'Travel Writing and the Humanitarian Impulse: Alicia Little in China', in Douglas Kerr and Julia Kuehn (eds), *A Century of Travels in China: Critical Essays on Travel Writing from the 1840s to the 1940s* (Hong Kong: Hong Kong University Press, 2007), 91–103.

Trainor, Luke, *British Imperialism and Australian Nationalism: Manipulation, Conflict, and Compromise in the Late Nineteenth Century* (Cambridge: Cambridge University Press, 1994).

Trease, Geoffrey, *Tales out of School: A Survey of Children's Fiction* (London: Heinemann Educational Books, 1964).

Trodd, Anthea, 'Messages in Bottles and Collins's Seafaring Man', *Studies in English Literature 1500–1900*, 41.4 (2001), 751–64.

Turnbaugh, Roy, 'Images of Empire: George Alfred Henty and John Buchan', *Journal of Popular Culture*, 9.3 (1975), 734–40.

Turner, E.S., *Boys Will Be Boys: The Story of Sweeney Todd, Deadwood Dick, Sexton Blake, Billy Bunter, Dick Barton, Et Al* (London: Joseph, 1957).

Wagner, Kim A., *Thuggee: Banditry and the British in Early Nineteenth-Century India* (Basingstoke: Palgrave Macmillan, 2007).

Walker, David, *Anxious Nation: Australia and the Rise of Asia 1850–1939* (St. Lucia, Qld.: University of Queensland Press, 1999).

Waters, Hazel, *Racism on the Victorian Stage: Representation of Slavery and the Black Character* (Cambridge: Cambridge University Press, 2007).

Weedon, Alexis, *Victorian Publishing: The Economics of Book Production for a Mass Market, 1836–1916* (Aldershot: Ashgate, 2003).

White, Ann, 'Counting the Cost of Faith: America's Early Female Missionaries', *Church History*, 57.1 (1988), 19–30.

Wilson, Kim, '"Are They Telling Us the Truth?": Constructing National Character in the Scholastic Press Historical Journal Series', *Children's Literature Association Quarterly*, 32.2 (2007), 129–41.

Winskill, Ben, 'The Penny Dreadful Offices', *Vanity Fair: An Illustrated Amateur Magazine Published in the Interests of Amateur Journalism*, 17.2 (1925), 47–9.

Witchard, Anne Vernoica, *Thomas Burke's Dark Chinoiserie: Limehouse Nights and the Queer Spell of Chinatown* (Aldershot: Ashgate, 2009).

Witek, John W., 'Louis Le Comte', in Gerald H. Anderson (ed.), *Biographical Dictionary of Christian Missions* (Grand Rapids, MI: William B. Eerdmans, 1999), 390.

Woolf, Virginia, 'Defoe,' in *The Common Reader: First Series* (1925), The University of Adelaide Ebooks, 2012 <http://ebooks.adelaide.edu.au/w/woolf/virginia/w91c/chapter9.html> [accessed 21 June 2012].

Xiang, Lanxin, *The Origins of the Boxer War: A Multinational Study* (London: Routledge Curzon, 2003).

Young, Lola, 'Hybridity's Discontents: Rereading Science and "Race"', in Avtar Brah and Annie E. Coombes (eds), *Hybridity and Its Discontents: Politics, Science, Culture* (London: Routledge, 2000), 154–70.

Young, Robert, *Colonial Desire: Hybridity in Theory, Culture and Race* (London: Routledge, 1995).

Zhang, Longxi, *Mighty Opposites: From Dichotomies to Differences in the Comparative Study of China* (London: Macdonald and Jane's, 1976).

Zhonghua Dazidian (Xianggang: Zhonghua shu ju, 1977).

Index

For Product Safety Concerns and Information please contact our
EU representative GPSR@taylorandfrancis.com Taylor & Francis
Verlag GmbH, Kaufingerstraße 24, 80331 München, Germany